Lecture Notes in Computer Science

Lecture Notes in Computer Science

Edited by G. Goos and J. Hartmanis

331

M. Joseph (Ed.)

Formal Techniques in Real-Time and Fault-Tolerant Systems

Proceedings of a Symposium
Warwick, UK, September 22–23, 1988

Springer-Verlag

Editor

Mathai Joseph
Department of Computer Science, University of Warwick
Coventry CV4 7AL, U.K.

CR Subject Classification (1987): B.1.3, B.2.3, B.3.4, B.4.4, B.7.3, C.3, C.4,
D.2.4, D.4.5, F.3, J.7

ISBN 3-540-50302-1 Springer-Verlag Berlin Heidelberg New York
ISBN 0-387-50302-1 Springer-Verlag New York Berlin Heidelberg

PREFACE

There are many areas of computer science where the progress of practice has far outstripped the more tentative march of developments in theory, but few where this is more so than in real-time and fault-tolerant systems. We are surrounded, in the air and on and below the ground, by practical examples of safety-critical systems whose satisfactory functioning depends crucially on the correctness of the design and implementation of hardware and software systems. And yet, this correctness is often seen as arising from ingenuity and trust rather than from engineering certainty based on scientific fact. The papers in this volume suggest that this need not always be true but they do also point towards the work that is still to be done.

The Symposium on Formal Techniques in Real-time and Fault Tolerant Systems held at the University of Warwick on 22-23 September 1988 attracted a number of papers from all over the world. Seven of these were selected for full presentation. In addition, four papers representing ongoing work were selected for shorter presentation and thus appear in this volume as abstracts. The invited talks were chosen to broaden the discussions to include new views of theory and practice from universities, research institutions and industry.

The Symposium would not have been held but for the optimism and help provided by many people. Generous financial assistance from British Telecom, GEC Plessey Telecom, Racal Research and Sun Microsystems (UK) made it possible for the organisation to proceed without budgetary uncertainty. The administrative work has been cheerfully handled by Lesley Sims, and Liz Woolley and Josie Lloyd have been invaluable in helping with the mailing. Our thanks to all these people, to the reviewers whose comments were invaluable to the Programme Committee, and to everyone else who helped.

Department of Computer Science
University of Warwick

Mathai Joseph
Chairman, Programme Committee

Programme Committee

M. Joseph (U. of Warwick)   G.R. Martin (U. of Warwick)
A.K. Mok (U. of Texas, Austin)   R. Reed (GEC Plessey Telecom)
F.B. Schneider (Cornell U.)   S. Shrivastava (U. of Newcastle)
W.-P. de Roever (Tech. U. Eindhoven)

REVIEWERS

CONTENTS

HIGH INTEGRITY COMPUTING

W J Cullyer

Computing Division, RSRE, MOD, UK

SYNOPSIS

This paper reviews three areas of research which have a major bearing on the integrity of future digital monitoring and control systems. Work on formal methods of specification has reached a point where languages such as "VDM" and "Z" are realistic options. In the field of software verification the availability of static code analysis tools provides a fresh way of detecting deeply buried errors in computer programs. Hardware verification research has resulted in the production of a high integrity microprocessor, VIPER, which was invented and developed by the author's team at RSRE Malvern. By combining the advantages of these techniques it is believed that safer digital control systems can be produced in the 1990s.

1. INTRODUCTION

Computers are progressively invading every corner of our lives. For example, aircraft fly over the Earth's surface guided in three dimensions by on-board computers and in the chemical and nuclear industries microprocessors are used to monitor hazardous processes. These applications have one thing in common: design errors in the electronic hardware of the computers or mistakes in computer programs may affect the safety of the system. High integrity systems require the use of improved techniques if adequate margins of safety are to be preserved [1].

The UK Ministry of Defence (MOD) has a deep interest in the design of high integrity equipment and devotes considerable scientific and engineering resources to the development and certification of both weapon systems and the vehicles which carry such systems, including high performance aircraft. At Malvern, in the centre of England, the MOD has its central electronics research laboratory, the Royal Signals and Radar Establishment (RSRE). Basic research on high integrity software and the correct design of microchips is carried out by teams at RSRE and this paper gives some recent scientific conclusions.

Overall, the RSRE research programme has three main limbs. Chronologically the first area tackled was the verification of computer programs using automated tools based on representation of the program text as a directed graph. This has resulted in two separate sets of analysers for validation of programs, called MALPAS and SPADE, which are available commercially from UK companies [2, 3].

The second limb of the programme is the research on hardware verification, described in this paper, leading to the design of practical high integrity microchips which can be used in civil and military equipment. Currently the techniques in use employ Gordon's Higher Order Logic (HOL), invented at the University of Cambridge [4] and the ELLA logic description language, invented at RSRE [5]. The first chip produced by this means is the VIPER 32-bit microprocessor. This has been designed and verified using the most formal methods available to establish the functional correctness of the practical devices [6]. Three different realisations have been produced in widely differing VLSI technologies, based on specifications issued by RSRE. The Annex to this paper describes the development of VIPER and points out some of the practical problems encountered in the application of formal mathematical methods to the design of practical devices.

The final and most recent limb of the RSRE programme is the study of the techniques for designing a complete "black-box", which may control some vital actuator [7]. These studies embrace the whole area of n - channel systems, (n = 2, 3...) and are intended to demonstrate how high integrity processors can be combined with comparators and error detection on memories to produce high integrity systems.

The continuing programme of research on these and related topics at RSRE and in the UK generally shows early promise of being able to provide control and protection systems of higher integrity in the 1990s and beyond. This paper deals with some of the key issues in general terms. For those interested in a concrete example of the use of formal methods, Annex A describes the development of the VIPER microprocessor.

2. PROBLEMS ENCOUNTERED IN REAL-TIME CONTROL

2.1 Overview

Typically in control applications the role of the computer is to accept inputs from various sensor systems, perform some calculation or logic and then provide outputs to actuators. All designers of safety-critical systems should know the consequences of component failure in service. Random failures of microchips, sensors and actuators are coped with using redundancy, for example triplicated "autoland" systems in aircraft and quadruplicated shut-down systems in nuclear reactors.

Replication of identical hardware or software will not help if the underlying electronic components or programs have design flaws. Mistakes in computer programs have been known to stop the parallel computer channels in an equipment simultaneously, leaving no means of control. Equally serious, unsuspected design flaws in computer hardware and software may allow the system being monitored to carry on running, even though possibly crucial temperature and pressure limits have been exceeded. These technological problems require careful study whenever the plant or vehicle in question can imperil human life [1].

The threads of research in safety—critical computing tend to be concentrated in two directions. A great deal of work has been done on diverse systems, in which the parallel channels of a control or monitoring equipment use dissimilar hardware and software, each channel providing the same external functions. Then even if one channel exibits anomalous behaviour, due to a design error, there is a good chance that plant being controlled will survive, since the other 1, 2 or 3 channels are very unlikely to fail at the same instant. The second thread, with which the author has been very much concerned, is to design channels whose performance can be established in some limited sense to be "correct". These two concepts are not mutually exclusive. Even in a diverse implementation it is very helpful to show the correctness of individual channels with respect to the original specification.

2.2 Skills needed

To be proficient in the design and verification of high integrity computer systems needs a catholic knowledge of the disciplines outlined in this section. There is no suggestion that any individual designer must possess all of this technical knowledge. Rather the emphasis is on a small team, which may contain mathematicians, control theory specialists, design engineers with good mathematical abilities, software designers and electronic hardware specialists. Some of the disciplines which must be covered are:

1.   The writing and reading of formal specifications;

2.   Software engineering of an advanced nature;

3. Verification of computer programs using formal mathematics;

4. Implementation of multi-channel redundant protection systems;

5. Trusted computer architectures.

Such collective knowledge is not yet widespread in industry. Many companies work on critical real-time control problems with only a subset of these skills available.

It will be noted by those familiar with current work on control systems that nowhere in this paper is the topic of quantitative reliability addressed, ie the assignment of probabilities of failure on demand or the numerical probability of false alarms. The omission is deliberate. Although the probable frequency of random faults in hardware may be analysed by statistical means, the author, together with many other scientists, does not believe that any such numerical criteria can be applied to systematic errors in software or to the design errors in microchips. Therefore it follows that overall failure probabilities for a complete electronic control system cannot be assessed, once microprocessors and software are brought into play.

2.3 Causes of systematic errors

It is important to understand the causes of design errors. The first point at which confusion can arise is in the writing of the technical specification for a particular "black box". Suppose the equipment in question has to deal with 12 incoming Boolean alarm signals, each of which can take the values TRUE or FALSE. Then the specification must cover the actions to be taken in (2 raised to the power 12) = 4096 sets of circumstances. If the specification only tells the design team what to do in, say, 2000 of these cases, it is seriously deficient.

Most technical specifications for control boxes in reactors and aircraft are written in plain English, with a little mathematics in the form of equations, plus possibly some tables of numerical values. Experience has shown that this is not good enough and leaves the designer of the control system with too much latitude. The design team often have to "guess" the response required from their equipment when certain combinations of inputs are present. Of course, they are free at every stage to go back to the prime contractor or other author of the specification and seek clarification. Sometimes this advice is not sought and a piece of equipment is produced with undesired characteristics in some modes of operation.

When it comes to writing the computer programs which implement the desired algorithms, high integrity projects usually have two teams. One team writes the software and the second "verification" team follows the design in detail. The verification team checks, by eye and conventional testing, that each module of the computer program obeys its specification. This may seem to be a reasonable arrangement in human terms but it suffers from a serious flaw. Work by RSRE and other laboratories has shown that conventional testing of software may only explore a small fraction of the logical paths through a computer program. Far more powerful techniques are needed to scan a program thoroughly, as discussed in Section 3.

There is a third potential source of error. The microprocessor chips used in control systems are mass produced devices. Admittedly, the devices selected for use in aircraft and nuclear reactors are carefully screened samples, but they may still suffer from unexpected behaviour. It has been concluded from studies at RSRE and elsewhere that many of the types of microprocessor on the market have internal design errors. It is reasonable to conclude that low cost, mass produced microprocessors are a dubious basis for computation in systems which must be certified as safe by independent authorities. This realisation caused MOD to pursue the research which has led to the development of the VIPER microprocessor.

The final area which may be a source of error is the architecture used to combine 2 or more microprocessors, with their attendant software, in such a manner that a control system is created with some tolerance to both random and systematic faults. Known techniques provide reasonable protection against random hardware failures. The primary means of preventing accidents caused by systematic errors is to design the individual channels of the system in such a rigorous manner that the crucial safety properties are assured by the original work in the development laboratory plus the scrutiny provided by independent safety assessors. This philosophy is sound for systems using identical parallel channels and for those utilising some form of diversity.

Following this broad survey of the problems, the next section considers some improvements in technique which help to reduce the incidence of design errors.

3. TECHNIQUES TO REDUCE SYSTEMATIC ERRORS

3.1 Formal specifications

Taking the issue of specifications first, there is no general answer to the problem of writing unambiguous specifications for real-time systems which contain microprocessors and software. Some progress has been made on the definition of the requirements for systems in which asynchronous behaviour is very limited but the general problem of specifying the behaviour of totally unsynchronised processes has not been solved.

Certainly the use of plain English with a little associated mathematics has not proved to be adequate. What is needed is a formal method of writing top level specifications and then proceeding in a mathematically rigorous manner to an ultimate implementation which can be proved to be correct, at least with respect to some narrow group of safety properties. The need for hierarchic decomposition during the design process implies that the same language should be used in a number of layers of documentation which will be produced as the project proceeds. An example of this progression is given in Annex A, in relation to the design of the VIPER microprocessor.

The essence of a sound top level specification is that it should define with great precision what a piece of equipment should do, without saying how these functions are to be achieved. It is crucial that the team writing the specification should agree with those who wrote the preceeding informal operational requirement that the description is complete. This leads to the important issue of "animating" or "simulating" abstract specifications. By this means those skilled in forml mathematical techniques can communicate with the other members of the design team and with the customer who needs the completed product.

Looking at the specification languages available, it is noticeable that universities have played a major role in developing current capabilities. For example, the language "Z" came from the University of Oxford [8] and Manchester developed "VDM" from original work by IBM [9]. Both have been used on practical real-time projects. In the world of hardware verification, "HOL" from the Computer Laboratory in the University of Cambridge is dominant and has been used in the development of the VIPER microprocessor [6, 10].

All of the approaches listed above have a very sound mathematical basis. However, texts written in such languages inevitably contain constructs which are not familiar to the majority of development engineers. If the full power of these techniques is to be exploited, the key staff need a knowledge of first order logic, higher order logic, set theory and the theory of functions. Practical experience shows that all design teams working with formal specification languages need two or more senior members who have been trained in the writing and reading of formal specifications and the derivation of proofs of correctness of computer-based systems. If such expertise is not available within a company, skilled effort may have to be hired from specialised organisations.

3.2 Software analysis and verification

Until the early 1980s there was a widespread supposition that the major cause of accidents in high integrity computer applications would be the errors made by programmers. During the 1970s and 1980s considerable advances have been made in techniques for proving short computer programs to be correct with respect to a high level formal specification. As this knowledge was applied, the effects of errors in specifications and in the design of microchips became more apparent.

The improvements in mathematical methods of checking programs against specifications are being used in industry but as yet play a minor part in assuring the accuracy of software. In most centres dealing with real-time control problems the "verification" of software is done mainly by dynamic testing. For example, an airborne computer may be driven in the laboratory from a second computer which simulates the inputs which will be received from pitot tubes and other sensors. By simulating the atmosphere at various flight levels and injecting details of Mach number, the performance of the system can be checked against the technical specification. This process is essential, to give both designers and the customer confidence in the equipment.

In any reasonable amount of time only a small part of the multi-dimensional input data space (eg dynamic pressure vs. static presssure vs. ambient temperature vs. Mach number) can be explored. In older analogue equipments a limited exploration of this (four - dimensional) space gave reasonably confidence, since analogue amplifiers and filters exhibit continuous behaviour, within the limits imposed by power supplies and saturation of signals. This is not so in digital equipment. Sampled data filters do not behave in the same way as their analogue counterparts and effects such as overflow in arithmetic in processors can cause actuators to move in the wrong direction.

One of the techniques which has been developed to provide objective evidence of the correctness of software is called "static code analysis". This has been devised by RSRE and the University of Southampton during the last 12 years and has resulted in the development and industrial use of powerful tools for finding mistakes in computer programs. These analysers use algebraic methods which are totally independent of dynamic testing. The deliberately contrasting name, "static code analysis" has been chosen to describe the method, since at no time during the investigation is the program executed dynamically.

The technique works as follows. The source text of the original computer program, written in languages such as CORAL 66, Pascal or Ada, is converted into a standard form, known as "intermediate language". This transformation is done by a translator rather like a compiler and may require some human assistance. Once the text exists in intermediate language, the first part of the analyser turns it automatically into a labelled, directed graph, akin to a flow chart. This graph is then crushed and simplified by removal of nodes and arcs. Ideally, for a well-behaved program, the graph should reduce to a single start point and single end point, with a complex algebraic expression loabeeling the sole remaining arc.

Algebraic interpretation programs then print out listings for a human analyst, giving precise details of the behaviour of the program under investigation. Experience over the last 5 years has shown that these output listings enable deeply buried errors to be found. In addition, parts of the specification may be edited into the source text of the program, enabling the analyst to compare one against the other in a more automated way. When the original program is well structured, it may be possible to take the whole process to the stage of formal verification, ie to show by proof that the program has the safety properties described in the formal specification.

The vital point about static code analysis is that it explores every possible path through a program, using algebraic techniques. Dynamic testing, as used currently, may cover only a very small part of the input data space and hence probe less than 1% of the paths through the software. As described below, static code analysis has found many mistakes in real-time software which had already been subject to extensive dynamic testing.

Two sets of static code analysis tools aee available commercially [2,3]. Both derive from the original RSRE/University of Southampton research and both do broadly the same type of analysis, although their internal mathematical mechanisms are different. To date about 300 scientists and engineers have been trained in the use of static code analysis and some 30 industrial companies are now using these tools to vet critical software.

Application of static code analysis since 1985 has revealed some worrying results. Taking a broad average over the software checked by MOD or by contractors on behalf of MOD, up to 10% of the individual software modules analysed have been shown to deviate from the original specification. Such discrepancies have been found even in software which has been subject to extensive testing on multi-million pound test rigs. Many of the anomalies detected have been minor and did not threaten the integrity of the system being monitored.

However, about 1 in 20 of the defective functions which static code analysis had shown to be faulty, ie about 1 in every 200 of all new modules, proved to have errors which would have resulted in direct and observable effects on the vehicle or plant concerned. For example, potential overflows in integer arithmetic appears to be a common problem [11], involving a change in sign of the result of a calculation and hence the possibility of an actuator being driven in a dangerous direction. Note that in the context of this paragraph a software module which has undergone post-certification modifications must be regarded as "new".

Many lessons have been learned from the experiences recounted above. In order to provide a high degree of certainty in the safety-related properties of a piece of software, it is essential that the source text is written in an analysable and well defined high-order language so that the resulting software is amenable to static code analysis. In any high integrity application the critical computer programs must be capable of being analysed mathematically, down to and including the semantic behaviour.

3.3 Hardware analysis and verification

Difficulties can arise due to design errors or fabrication problems in many classes of microchips. The effects of some of these flaws can be minimised by the use of redundancy at the hardware level, for example by widening data busses to accommodate error detection bits. However, it not so easy to cope with potential design errors in very complex programmable devices, such as microprocessors.

In the course of the software analysis and verification described above, it became clear that there is a problem with the integrity of microprocessor chips. There was evidence that certain processors did not behave precisely as described in the handbook provided by the chip manufacturer. Subsequent investigations have revealed a number of causes for concern [11]. Overall, modern microprocessors are so complicated that even experienced equipment designers may misunderstand some aspects of their behaviour. As is well known, many of the devices on sale have anomalous behaviour in the presence of certain input signals. Once this is realised, the microprocessor manufacturer may issue a supplementary data sheet, as a warning to users. This process of notification is complicated by the frequent changes in the internal design of devices which are on sale, so that a processor from a recent batch may have different functionality when compared with a chip fabricated a year before.

Judging from discussions with commercial microprocessor manufacturers, few if any are interested in the special problems raised by high integrity applications. Such sales form a very small part of their market and there is little prospect of persuading the large manufacturers to adopt more rigorous techniques in the design of their future devices.

Analysis of a number of important MOD and civil procurements which are due to take place in the early 1990s showed that the perceived uncertainty about the precise behaviour of microprocessors could not be tolerated. To try and provide at least one "trusted" processing element, the author's team at RSRE has invented and developed the VIPER microprocessor, as described in Annex A. By combining work on hardware verification from the Computer Laboratory in the University of Cambridge with the ELLA logic description language, invented at RSRE, a method has been developed for producing synchronous chips whose functions are wholly predictable. Similar studies have been conducted by Hunt in the University of Texas but these have not resulted to date in commercially usable devices.

3.4 The design of multi-channel systems

Assuming for the moment that the problems of using formal specifications can be overcome, that static code analysis is employed to seek out errors in computer programs and that high integrity processor chips are in use, the designer still has many problems when creating a new "black box". In particular, the overall configuration of sensors, processors, software, hardware and actuators plays a major part in determining the safety of the final product. In a study by Cambridge Consultants Ltd, carried out for RSRE as part of the VIPER programme, the following criteria were proposed for the analysis of specific monitoring and control applications [7]:

1. Level of safety integrity required;

2. Nature of the state information about the system under control (none at all, short lived, convergent, indispensable);

3. Bandwidth of the inputs with respect to the sampling frequency of the digital control system;

4. Nature of outputs to actuators (single action, multiple action, discrete, continuous);

5. The maximum interruption time which can be tolerated during recovery from errors.

The inclusion of state information (item 2) is intended to draw attention to broad categories of systems which are described in various national and international standards eg the "HSE Guidelines" [12] and draft Defence Standard 00-55 [13]. It is essential to distinguish "shutdown systems" from those providing continuous control, since different computer configurations are needed in these two regimes.

The purpose of shutdown systems is to monitor the outputs of a number of sensors and decide if the point in the multi-dimensional input space at which the plant or vehicle is operating is within the safety envelope. Any excursion outside the specified regime must result in the controlled process coming to a halt. Examples of such programmable shutdown systems are found in the protection equipment in nuclear power stations and petrochemical plant. Broadly, shutdown systems are characterised by simple outputs to actuators and short lived state information, which often consists of nothing more than the last few values obtained by polling the sensors. In such systems the writing of formal specifications is usually straightforward, since the final output required from each cycle of digital computation consists often of a single Boolean value: "keep running" or "stop".

Turning to the class of systems which provide control as well as protection, these are characterised by having continuous outputs to a number of actuators. The demands on these actuators arise normally from the needs for efficient operation of the plant or vehicle and only exceptionally, in some crisis, will the computers cause the system to close down. An example is found in engine controllers in civil and military jet aircraft, where the normal computations are concerned with efficient running of the engine but the processors will exercise full authority and reduce the thrust if the tail pipe temperature or rotational speed become too high.

The instantaneous state of such systems will be represented by some vector which includes differential and integral terms and essentially "analogue" information. Indeed the initial specification of the system may well have been done in terms of the continuous Laplace transform ("s plane") before being mapped into the world of digital processing and sampled data ("z plane"). Great care is required when moving from the world of continuous transfer functions to a formal specification for digital controllers and when choosing the configuration inside the digital equipment. The criticality of these successive transformations depends on whether the system being controlled is inherently convergent or divergent.

If the plant being controlled is convergent, it will reach a safe state from current sensor inputs alone in an acceptably short time. The knowledge of the system state just before any malfunction of the digital controller can be thrown away. Examples are found in the autopilots of aerodynamically stable aircraft and the programmable logic controllers used in chemical production processes which are endothermic. In such regimes it may be possible to disconnect the automated means of control for a short while, without degrading the safety of the system. Computer control may be regained subsequently, possibly by human intervention.

In control systems where the system state must be preserved, since the vehicle or plant in question is divergent, the problems of specification, design and verification become severe. A good example is the "fly-by-wire" control systems needed to control aerodynamically unstable aircraft, as in the British Aerospace Experimental Aircraft Programme (EAP). Where the vehicle exhibits gross instability, the system state must be preserved throughout the disconnection of any faulty digital control equipment and any subsequent reconfiguration. In these occurrences, the period of "loss of control" must not exceed a few tens of milliseconds and there may not be time to update the system state vector when the computers regain their normal functions.

Preservation of the system state requires communication between the N channels of the control system. Typically, at the end of each cycle of computation which creates the desired digital filtering and interlocks, a new system state has been defined. Following well known practice, these successive states can be stored in some well prorected area of memory and used as recovery points if required. Progressively, subsequent inputs from sensors will update this stale state and bring the system back under normal control.

In summary, the philosophies outlined in this paper are known to be applicable to shutdown systems and control systems in which the system state may be lost in the event of error, but are not powerful enough to deal with more demanding applications where the system state must be preserved. Formal methods for the design and verification of such systems are in their infancy.

4. CONCLUSIONS

Based on existing research and development there is every reason to expect that the design and verification of real-time systems using digital control will improve in the 1990s. The introduction of formal methods of specification, the use of static code analysis to detect mistakes in computer programs and the availability of microprocessors with wholly predictable behaviour will help to produce safer equipment. Clearly these are only a few of the techniques involved in the production of programmed electronic monitoring and control systems and corresponding advances are needed in related technologies.

5. ACKNOWLEDGEMENTS

The VIPER microprocessor has been specified and developed by a team made up of Dr J Kershaw, Dr C H Pygott and the author at RSRE. Dr A Cohn and Dr M Gordon of the University of Cambridge produced the formal proofs described in Annex A.

6. REFERENCES

1 DANIELS B K   Achieving safety and reliability with
                   computer systems
                   Elsevier Applied Science Series 1987

2 RTP   MALPAS User Guide
                   Rex, Thompson and Partners, Jan 1988

3 CARRE B A   SPADE static code analysis manual
   CLUTTERBUCK D   Program Validation Ltd, June 1987

4 GORDON M   HOL A proof generating system for
                   Higher Order Logic
                   VLSI Specification, Verification and
                   Synthesis
                   Kluwer Academic Publishers, 1988

18

5   MORISON J   ELLA: Hardware description or
    et al   specification
                     Proceedings IEEE International Conf.
                     CAD-84 Santa Clara, Nov 1984

6   CULLYER W J   Implementing safety-critical systems:
                     The VIPER microprocessor
                     VLSI Specification, Verification and
                     Synthesis
                     Kluwer Academic Publishers, 1988

7   HALBERT M P   A self-checking computer module based
                     on the VIPER microprocessor
                     Achieving safety and reliability
                     with computer systems
                     Elsevier Applied Science Series 1987

8. SUFFRIN B   Z Handbook, draft 1.1
                     Oxford Programming Research Group
                     October 1985

9. JONES C B   Systematic software development using
                     VDM
                     Prentice Hall 1986

10 COHN A   A proof of correctness of the VIPER
                     microprocessor: The first level
                     VLSI Specification, Verification and
                     Synthesis
                     Kluwer Academic Publishers, 1988

11 CULLYER W J   Hardware Integrity
                     Aeronautical Journal, Royal Aeronautical
                     Society, Aug/Sept 1985

12 HSE   Guidelines on the use of programmable
                          electronic systems in safety related
                          applications
                          Health and Safety Executive June 1987

13 MOD   Draft Defence Standard 00-55
                          Director Standardization MOD July 1988

14 CULLYER W J   VIPER: Correspondence between
                          Specification amd major state machine
                          RSRE Report 86004, Jan 1986

15 COHN A   A mechanized proof of correctness of
   GORDON M   a simple counter
                          University of Cambridge Computer
                          Laboratory Technical Report No 94,
                          July 1986

16 PYGOTT C H   Formal proof of correspondence between
                          the specification of a hardware
                          module and its gate level implementation
                          RSRE Report 85012, November 1985

17 PYGOTT C H   NODEN: An engineering approach to
                          hardware verification
                          Proceedings IFIP Conference on
                          The Fusion of Hardware Design and
                          Verification, Glasgow, 4-6 July 1988

ANNEX A.

A.1 THE SPECIFICATION AND DESIGN OF THE VIPER MICROPROCESSOR

The key feature of the new VIPER processor, Figure 1, is its
simplicity.   A more complex architecture would have taken the proofs
beyond the current state of the art. As will be seen from Figure 1,
the device has an accumulator, A, two "index registers", X and Y and a
program counter, P. There is a single bit register, B, which holds the
results of comparisons and can be concatenated with registers in shift
operations. Unique to VIPER is the "stop" signal from the ALU.   Any
illegal operation, arithmetic overflow or computation of an illegal
address causes the device to stop and raise an exception on an external
pin so that corrective action can be taken by the rest of the system.

All instructions have an identical format, being split into the fields
shown in Figure 2. Decoding of the instructions is simple, as shown in
Figure 3. The available operation codes are listed in Table 1.   The
'mf' field of the instruction is used to select shift instructions when
cf = 0 and ff = 12. This minor degree of overloading is acceptable
since there is no "memory read" in this context.

TABLE 1: COMPARISON AND ALU OPERATIONS
(r = 32 - bits from register, m = 32 bits from memory)

ff	COMPARISON, cf = 1	NOT COMPARISON, cf = 0
0	r < m	NEGATE m
1	r >= m	CALL
2	r = m	READ from PERIPHERAL
3	r /= m	READ from MEMORY
4	r <= m	r + m, b := carry
5	r > m	r + m, stop on overflow
6	unsigned r < m	r - m, b := borrow
7	unsigned r >= m	r - m, stop on overflow
8	(r < m) OR b	r XOR m
9	(r >= m) OR b	r AND m
10	(r = m) OR b	r NOR m
11	(r /= m) OR b	r AND NOT m
12	(r <= m) OR b	mf = 0 : SHIFT RIGHT, copy sign
		mf = 1 : SHIFT RIGHT, through b
		mf = 2 : SHIFT LEFT, stop on oflo
		mf = 3 : SHIFT LEFT, through b
13	(r > m) OR b	illegal
14	(unsigned r<m) OR b	illegal
15	(unsigned r>=m) OR b	illegal

Some of the rationale for this architecture is as follows. One of the primary requirements was for the instruction decoder to be as simple as possible. Secondly, a wide data word was needed for high resolution in digital filter applications. Thirdly, a rich set of comparison functions was desirable, based on the setting or clearing of a single flag, B. No support has been provided for interrupts or for the manipulation of a stack. Both of these facilities lead to serious problems in software validation.

As regards address range, 20 bits may seem excessive, since critical programs should be short. However, the I/O space may need as much as 1 million words and to preserve uniformity the main memory space is made the same size, selection between the two being by a one-bit signal (MEM/IO) which essentially becomes a 21st address bit. In practice the ROM and RAM used with VIPER processors will probably be widely separated in the main memory address space, e.g. trusted ROMs at the lower end of memory and RAM at the top. Only static RAMs should be used with VIPER and the omission of any means of providing refresh to dynamic memories is deliberate.

The top level specification for VIPER has been defined in HOL, the state vector which represents the present conditions in the processor and 2 million words of memory and I/O space words of memory and I/O space being:

        state = (ram, P, A, X, Y, B, stop)

where 'ram' implies the current contents of both address spaces, P,A,X,Y and B are the current contents of registers in VIPER and 'stop' is a Boolean which indicates if the machine has stopped. The function NEXT() gives all possible transitions for VIPER in the form:

        NEXT(state) -> state

The 'state' which forms the argument is that just before the next instruction fetch. It proved possible to provide a formal specification of this processor in just 6 pages of A4, namely 5 pages of auxiliary functions and a single page definition of NEXT.

Hierarchically, the next layer of documentation defines the "major state machine" illustrated in Figure 4. This combination of elementary functions must be shown to conform precisely with the top level specification. The node 'dummy' has been included solely to act as the "primary node" for the purposes of proof. It has been established that all possible journeys round this diagram, from dummy back to dummy, produce the transformations required in the top level specification.

To do this requires an augmented vector which expresses the state of each machine :

major = ((ram, P, A, X, Y, B, stop),(t, inst))

where 't' represents the contents of an internal register not accessible to the programmer and 'inst' the current 12 bits of the instruction fields. Each of the nodes in Figure 4 produces the mapping:

MACHINE(major) -> (major, nextnode)

where 'nextnode' is the number of one of the other nodes in the diagram.

The third layer of documents specifies the so-called "electronic block model" shown in Figure 5. This is the lowest level of documentation issued by RSRE. Those wishing to fabricate VIPER in practice have to utilise their own in-house VLSI technology to produce each of the blocks shown. The specification for each of these blocks has been defined in HOL and also in the logic description language ELLA.

There were a number of reasons for changing language. As the design moves closer towards circuit level, the definition of a Boolean variable has to be extended to allow for values such as 'x' for 'irrelevant' and 'i' for 'illegal'. ELLA allows this. Secondly, before the start of the VIPER programme, ELLA had been interfaced to various VLSI CAD systems using a package called "ELLANET" which enables "net lists" for chips to be transported to alien CAD environments. In addition, the industrial teams producing the prototype chips had a specific gate level design for each block, produced at RSRE, and this aided their task in understanding the functions of each module.

The bottom level of documentation is the "circuit". This level of documentation was produced by the various VLSI companies who have fabricated VIPER in practice. In order to achieve comparison with the RSRE block model these texts were translated backwards into ELLA, using software written at RSRE. This was a vital step in the whole process of verification of the gate level design.

The above description gives an impression of "top down" design which was not wholly borne out in practice. There were several iterations of the top level specification before the final text was agreed. Since no proofs were available in the early stages of the project, confidence was built up in the various texts largely by simulation. From this experience it is fair to conclude that at least three levels of documentation (top level specification, major state machine and electronic block model) have to be iterated in harmony to achieve a practical and consistent design. Detailed design at silicon level should be postponed until these three layers of documents have been frozen.

It is interesting to note that the manufacturers of the prototype VIPER chips made comparatively little use of the top level specification or the major state machine descriptions. Their designs were completed largely on the basis of the electronic block model. This suggests that the higher levels of specification can be left in the hands of small teams of specialists, with detailed design and fabrication of chips being devolved to VLSI companies who do not necessarily need to employ experts in formal methods.

A.2. VERIFICATION OF THE VIPER DESIGN

A.2.1 Major state machine to top level specification

The informal proof of correspondence was done by the author at RSRE and took about 3 man weeks, by hand analysis, i.e. without the use of the Cambridge theorem proving tools [14]. By deriving the spanning tree of all possible transitions of the major state machine, Figure 6, it proved possible to conduct a 24-limb proof in first order logic. This established with a reasonable degree of certainty that the major state machine conformed with the top level specification.

Subsequently, Cohn and Gordon, working with HOL versions of the texts at Cambridge and using their automated theorem prover have shown that this informal proof was flawed in some minor respects but overall was sound [10]. This exercise has shown the importance of formal analysis using well founded axioms, rules and tactics to reveal the unexpected logical features of a specification. As this formal verification work in Cambridge has been completed it is safe to conclude that the major state machine is an accurate model which forms a rigorous basis for the lower levels of design [8].

A.2.2 Electronic block model to major state machine

This layer of proof was too extensive to carry out by hand and definitely required automated theorem proving. Cohn has used the Cambridge HOL tools on a SUN workstation to establish the correspondence of the electronic building blocks of Figure 5 with the major state machine. Inevitably this set of proofs is voluminous if published in full but the intention is to produce a detailed summary for review by other experts. The technique to be used relies on carrying out case–by–case analysis for the various node numbers in

Figure 4. Details of how this was done for the simpler example of a 6-bit counter are given in Reference [15].

A.2.3 Circuit to electronic block model

This proof uses the ELLA simulator and a technique devised by Pygott of RSRE. The essence of the method, which is explained in full in Reference [16], is to carry out the equivalent of exhaustive simulation on the ELLA description of one block, such as the instruction decoder, in parallel with applying the same test vectors to an ELLA description of the implementation. To avoid the combinatorial explosion and totally unrealistic run times, extensive use is made of the 'x' ie 'irrelevant' value of the type Boolean for all components of a test vector which do not affect the outcome of a particular test. By this means the quarter of a million tests which would have been required for the VIPER instruction decoder were thinned to just over 900 runs of the ELLA simulator. Indeed, the whole of the implementation of VIPER can be checked with only about 5,500 such vectors. It is worth noting that all of the tests for one chip can be completed in about 30 mill minutes on a VAX 8600.

In practice, the contractors fabricating the prototype chips made mistakes early on at circuit level when implementing particular blocks. The method outlined above proved to be powerful enough to detect the discrepancies. Both designs were corrected before net-lists were finalised and masks generated, with substantial savings in overall project timescales and costs.

A.2.4 The use of simulation

In the absence of formal proofs of correspondence in the earlier days of the project, extensive use was made of simulation to build up confidence in the various levels of documentation. Specifically, the following animations or simulations exist, running on VAX/VMS:

a. An animation of the HOL top level specification, written in ALGOL68, based on a library of HOL primitives (WORDn, BITSn etc);

b. An animation of the major state machine, written in ALGOL68;

c. A simulation of the electonic block model in ELLA, based on a library of HOL primitives written in ELLA.

The so-called 'animations' of the HOL texts proved to be very valuable. When dealing with abstract definitions, such simulators produce a great deal of engineering confidence and can be used for practical demonstrations to prospective customers for the ultimate device.

Software was written to compare the outputs from these programs automatically when the three programs are driven with the same VIPER object code.

A.3 REALISATIONS OF VIPER

A.3.1 VIPER 1

The VIPER microprocessor described in this paper is the first generation of a family of devices. At present (June 1988) the initial VIPER 1 chip is being marketed. This provides the instruction set listed in Table 1. Two realisations in different VLSI technologies are now available commercially:

a. A bipolar device from Plessey Semiconductors, UK

b. A low power CMOS Silicon On Sapphire (SOS) device from Marconi Electronic Devices, UK, which is radiation hard.

The gate level design of both devices has been checked by RSRE, using the method described in Section A.2.3 and this verification work has shown that the chips on sale are functionally correct with respect to the top level specification and the intervening layers of documentation. The devices now on sale can be clocked at 12 MHz and this gives a throughput of almost 1 MIP.

To confirm the view of RSRE that the devices are sound, a "Peer Review" group was formed in the UK, made up of 15 laboratories who had no connection with the VIPER project. Between July 1987 and January 1988 these independent laboratories examined early samples of the VIPER 1 microprocessor, running in a single board computer designed at RSRE. The chips were programmed during the Peer Review process in the structured assembly language VISTA. The reports from these independent UK laboratories are unanimous in agreeing that the VIPER 1 processor satisfies the top level specification in every respect. However, the individual companies who took part in the review were critical of some aspects of VIPER 1, notably its lack of multiplication and division instructions, and their comments have been taken into account in devising the specification for VIPER 2, as described below.

A.3.2 VIPER 1A

To allow for the possibility of chip failures in operational use, it is clear that VIPER microprocessors should be used in redundant configurations, eg duplex or triplex control systems, or in self monitoring pairs. The latter possibility has been studied in detail by the UK MOD and contractors [7]. It has been concluded that the most economic and effective design is to use a pair of VIPER processors in each channel of a control system, in such a way that one VIPER monitors the behaviour of the other. Such devices will have the same top level specification as VIPER 1 and will obey the same operation codes (Table 1).

This capability has been built into the VIPER 1A processor which is being fabricated in prototype form by Marconi Electronic Devices Ltd, under contract to the UK MOD. This new processor has comparators built into the chip so that one VIPER of a pair may act as the "master" processor, driving the data and address buses and the second as a "slave", obeying the same program and listening on the buses to try and detect any discrepancies. If there is any disagreement the pair of processors stops.

In addition, VIPER 1A has a data bus which has been extended to 40 bits, the extra 8 bits being used for error detection, down to the level of a single byte-wide memory package. It follows that all RAM used with VIPER 1A pairs will use a 5 byte wide memory and that all programs will be stored in ROM which also is 5 packages wide, the extra package holding the error detecting bits.

Assessment by an independent contractor in the UK has shown that this combination of a fault-detecting pair of VIPERs wih memory error detection will provide a standard of integrity in future control systems which is not achievable easily with present day 32-bit processors [7]. For example, a triplex architecture with a fault-detecting pair of VIPER chips in each channel would offer a very high degree of protection against random failures of devices.

A.3.3 VIPER 2

The Peer Review process in the UK has shown the clear need for multiply and divide instructions to be provided on the chip and for the performance to be improved to around 3 MIPs. This is particularly important for those involved in three-axis control problems, who require substantial computation in each digital filter "frame". At the same time, this more advanced processor must have all the features of VIPER 1A, including the ability to work in fault-detecting pairs.

A new device embodying all of these characteristics, plus the ability to handle position independent code, is being specified by RSRE at present. The top level specification is being written in HOL. The proofs that the implementations of VIPER 2 are correct will be done using a new technique, devised by Pygott of the RSRE team. This new technique is a synthetic approach and avoids the need for the generation of test vectors by hand [17].

The VIPER 2 processor will be pipelined (synchronously), will have the ability to work in fault-detecting pairs and will be clocked at some 20 to 30 Mhz, thereby offering in the region of 3 MIPs throughput. As appropriate VLSI technology already exists in the UK, it is believed that this processor will be offered in variants up to class S (space qualified) and that substantial applications will be found.

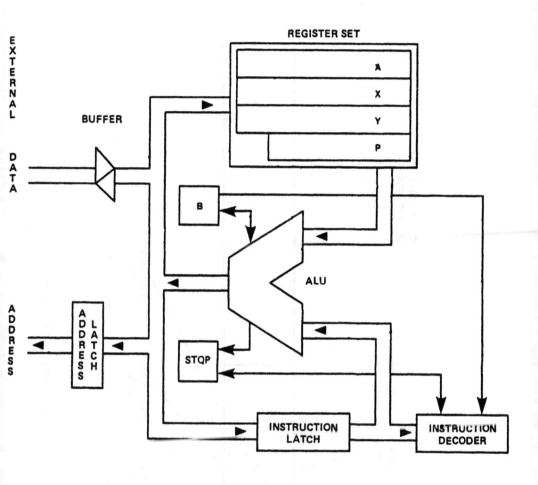

FIG 1 **VIPER** MICRO-PROCESSOR ARCHITECTURE

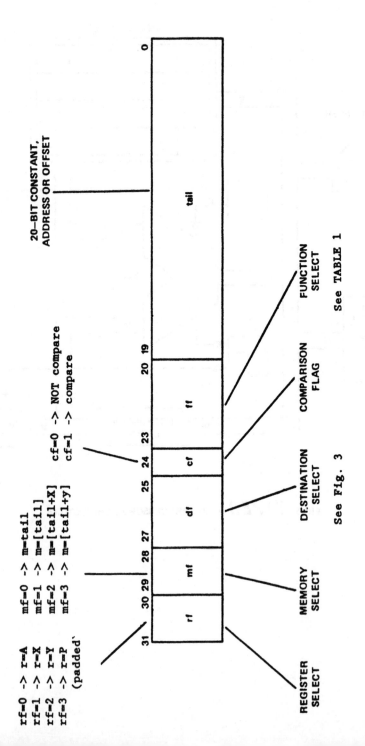

31	30 29	28 27	25	24 23	20 19	0
rf	mf	df	df	cf	ff	tail

REGISTER SELECT

MEMORY SELECT

DESTINATION SELECT — See Fig. 3

COMPARISON FLAG

FUNCTION SELECT — See TABLE 1

20—BIT CONSTANT, ADDRESS OR OFFSET

rf=0 -> r=A
rf=1 -> r=X
rf=2 -> r=Y
rf=3 -> r=P
(padded)

mf=0 -> m=tail
mf=1 -> m=[tail]
mf=2 -> m=[tail+X]
mf=3 -> m=[tail+y]

cf=0 -> NOT compare
cf=1 -> compare

FIG 2   INSTRUCTION FORMAT

33

```
df=7 -> Write to memory
df=6 -> Write to I/O
df=5 -> IF B THEN no-op ELSE destination = P
df=4 -> IF B THEN destination = P ELSE no-op
df=3 -> destination = P (unconditional)
df=2 -> destination = Y
df=1 -> destination = X
df=0 -> destination = A
```

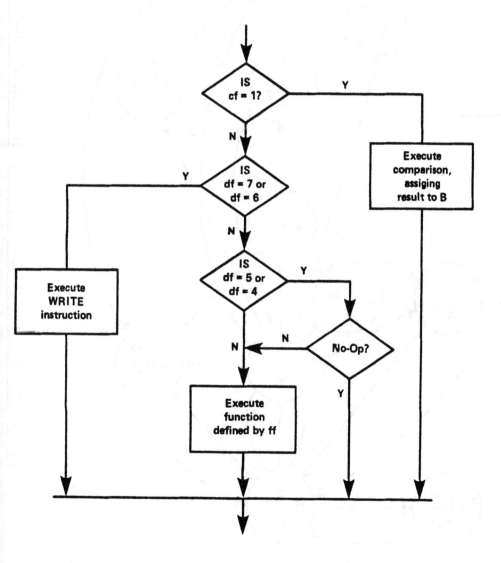

FIG 3   LOGIC OF INSTRUCTION DECODING

34

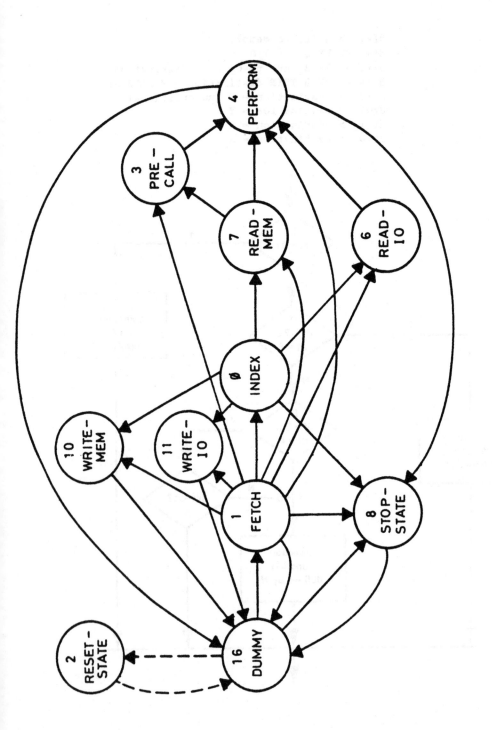

FIG.4 STATE TRANSITIONS IN MAJOR STATE MACHINE

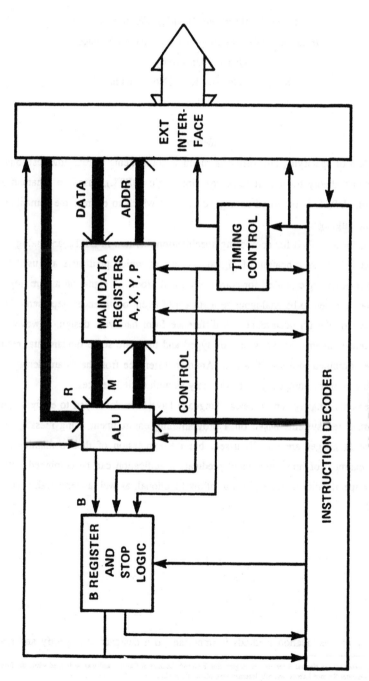

FIG 5 *VIPER* ELECTRONIC BLOCK MODEL

USING HIGHER-ORDER LOGIC FOR MODULAR SPECIFICATION OF REAL-TIME DISTRIBUTED SYSTEMS[1]

Glenn H. MacEwen, David B. Skillicorn

Department of Computing and Information Science

Queen's University

Kingston, Ontario, K7L 3N6 Canada

Abstract

The problem of specifying and verifying modular components of real-time distributed systems is investigated, and a theory for a distributed real-time logic (DRTL), based on Jahanian and Mok's RTL, is presented. DRTL is proposed as a good basis in which to express the semantics of higher level specification languages.

In looking for a method for composing specifications written in DRTL an analogy is found in Gordon's method for the specification of digital circuits, in which predicates are used to represent devices and higher-order logic is used for composition and proof. A signal on a wire, represented by a function of time, is taken to be analogous to a stream of event occurrences, represented by function that gives the time of the ith occurrence. A difference from hardware design, however, is the fact that event occurrence streams, unlike wires, are typed and there are some fundamental restrictions on how they can be combined in a specification. Another difference from hardware design is that real-time components cannot be composed quite so freely as with digital devices.

A requirements language and a design language have been developed to express specifications for real-time distributed systems based on a programming environment using message-passing and processes. These languages are not discussed, but the expression of their semantics in DRTL is presented as an example of how component predicate specification can be combined with DRTL to produce modular specifications. Extensions to allow functional, as well as temporal, specification are briefly discussed.

1. Introduction

Modularity of specification methods is important so a designer can specify and reason about

---

[1]This work is supported by the Natural Sciences and Engineering Research Council of Canada, and was performed while the first author was on sabbatical leave at the Computer Science Laboratory, SRI International, Menlo Park, CA.

the properties of a system component independently of other components to which it will eventually be combined. In this way, the process of verifying the properties of a composite component is dependent only on the properties of its parts but not on the internal structure of the parts. This is important simply to reduce the amount of verification work that must be done, to make the verification activity less complex and more tractable, and to obviate much extra verification when a system is modified. This is especially important for distributed systems, for which physically separate components can be combined in perhaps unpredictable ways.

This paper is concerned with the formal specification and verification of real-time distributed software systems. Two simple but important ideas form the basis from which the paper derives. First, an analogy to distributed systems is found in Gordon's method for the specification of digital circuits by using predicates to represent devices [7] and higher-order logic proof methods to verify designs [3]. For example, an n-transistor

is modelled by the formula

$$Ntran(g,a,b) \equiv (g \rightarrow (a = b))$$

and a structure like

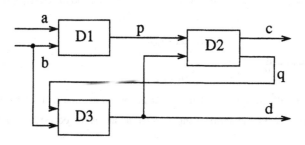

is modelled by the formula

$$D(a,b,c,d) \equiv \exists \, p,q \, . \, D1(a,b,p) \wedge D2(p,d,c,q) \wedge D3(q,b,d)$$

Notice that the components are combined by taking the conjunction of their individual specifications, given as predicates, and forming a composite predicate by using existential quantification over the "hidden" internal connections p and q. Such a formula constitutes a *design specification* for some function whose expected properties are given separately in a *requirement specification*. In other words, the requirement specification states the property or properties that the designer has been given and which are believed to be satisfied by the design. Of course, the requirements must be shown convincingly to be satisfied. If the requirement specification for the above structure is given by the predicate

$$R(a,b,c,d)$$

then the requirement verification can be completed by showing that the formula

$$D(a,b,c,d) \rightarrow R(a,b,c,d)$$

is true. It may also be necessary to show the stronger property that

$$D(a,b,c,d) \equiv R(a,b,c,d)$$

is true. However, this can be overly restrictive and is often much more difficult to do. Much of the time, we are satisfied to let the designer specify some extra things as long as the requirements are met. In the case that one of the requirements is that *no other things be done* then this should be stated explicitly as part of the requirements.

The second important idea is the use of an *occurrence function* to represent an event in a real-time system. As used by Jahanian and Mok in their *real-time logic* (RTL) [9], an occurrence function

$$f: Nat \rightarrow Nat$$

is associated with an event, and

$$f(i) = t$$

represents the fact that the ith occurrence of the event happened at time t. (For simplicity of wording, the paper occasionally uses the term event to refer to an event occurrence if the meaning is clear.)

Although it may not be immediately evident, there is an analogy between the wires in a hardware circuit and events in a distributed system. Think of a sequence of messages being sent from one node of a distributed system to another. The *sending event* is an output of one node and, in the sense that it causes a *receiving event* in the recipient node, is an input to that node. Put in another way, the sender node determines the properties of the sending event, i.e., when it happens. The behavior of the receiver node is determined by the properties of the sending event, because of course the properties of the receiving event are dependent on the sending event.

The analogy extends to other forms of communication between components of a software system. A process writing a memory variable can be modelled by an event, and a process reading the memory variable can be modelled similarly. A device interrupt is representable by an event function, and the device controller writing the device registers is modelled by an event function as well.

As with all good analogies, one can take this analogy only so far and there are some important differences between hardware specification and real-time software specification. First, software components may not be independently implemented; they can share processor control, memory space, and other resources. It may not be practical for components to refer to a common time reference. Other properties are similar to hardware systems, such as the fact that delays may be significant and, where there may be some unpredictability in such delays, bounds for them must be established if the required properties are to be realized.

Another difference from hardware design is that events, unlike wires, are typed and there are some fundamental restrictions on how they can be combined in a specification. In RTL, a set of axioms for a theory of events was presented. In this paper, an extended set of axioms is presented to describe a theory of events called *distributed real-time logic* (DRTL). The extension is necessary to recognize that in a distributed system there can be many time bases representing multiple unsynchronized clocks, and that it must be possible to reason about events in such a framework. DRTL uses the typing of events along with a *notification axiom* to provide this reasoning ability.

As with wires in hardware design, which are subjected to certain restrictions on ways in which connections can be made (fan-in and fan-out limits, for example), events in real-time system specifications cannot be connected among components in arbitrary ways. Only certain kinds of connections are meaningful. To illustrate this, Sections 3 and 4 present an extensive design method based on two languages for hard-real-time distributed system specification, and a supporting programming environment [4, 10]. The languages are RReq, for expressing requirements, and RSpec, for expressing designs. The programming environment and languages are based on message-passing and processes, but other design methods are possible with the theory to be presented.

A trivial example can illustrate some of the ideas in connecting real-time components by common event functions. Consider a component S that is to react to an external event f (an interrupt) and produce some response action g within a specified time limit. The external event never occurs during a given period of time after the previous occurrence. The component, depicted as

f
→
← S
g

has two kinds of formal requirements. The first is an *environment constraint*

$$\forall i \ . \ f(i) \leq f(i+1) - p$$

that says there are at least p time units separating consecutive occurrences of f. This is not so much a requirement as it is a property that can be assumed by the designer, and which the environment is mandated to uphold in whatever way is appropriate. The second kind of requirement is the *controller constraint* that is the actual property required of the component, which we sometimes call the controller to distinguish it from its environment (sometimes called the *plant* in the industrial control community). Here, there are two such requirements:

$$\forall i . g(i) \le f(i) + d$$
$$\forall i . f(i) < g(i)$$

The first says that the response g must follow the external event f not later that d time units after f occurs, i.e. g must meet its deadline. The second says that g occurs only after an event f causes it; i.e., there are no extraneous occurrences of g. The conjunction of these requirements will be denoted as

$$Sreq(f,g)$$

Now, what might be relevant in designing the internal structure of the component S(f,g)? We'll take a slightly simplified view and design S as comprising a *start event s* that is caused by f, and a *completion event c*. The design specification for S says that f causes s, c occurs k execution time units after s, and g occurs sometime between s and c. This is stated formally as follows:

$$Sdes(f,g) \equiv \forall i . (f(i) \le s(i)) \ \wedge \ (s(i) \le f(i) + r) \ \wedge \ (s(i) = c(i) - k) \ \wedge \ (c(i) - k < g(i) < c(i))$$

The first term in the formula says that if s occurs it must be the result of an associated f occurrence. Furthermore, the second term says that s occurs not more than r time units after f. This is rather a special kind of formula called a *scheduling assertion;* it is a statement about the run-time system supporting the software that is being specified and can best be viewed as a condition that the scheduler is mandated to enforce. Whether this enforcement is done before run-time by a static scheduler or at run-time by a dynamic scheduler is not of concern here. It is important to realize however that the method to be presented here is based on the assumption that all such scheduling assertions are correctly enforced. This provides the interface between concerns of design verification and concerns of scheduling.

The third term says that S consumes k units of processor time to execute, and the fourth says that the response g occurs sometime during the execution of S.

Notice that requirements say nothing about design issues such as execution times and scheduling delays. These are the concern of the system designer, and not of the requirements specifier.

A correctness proof for S involves establishing the truth of the formula

$$Sdes(f,g) \rightarrow Sreq(f,g)$$

This paper deals only with reasoning about real-time properties as captured by event occurrence functions. However, one of the objectives of DRTL is to allow reasoning about functional properties as well as real-time properties, but to permit these two activities to be orthogonal as much as possible. This is discussed briefly in Section 7, which describes how real-time specifications can be associated with specifications about the internal state of computations.

One final point of introduction; because of space limitations the paper does not deal with the issue of perspicuity of specifications. DRTL has a higher level of description that is also based on Jahanian and Mok's higher level description of RTL. And RSpec and RReq are successively more abstract language levels for expressing requirement and design specifications. The subject of this paper is only the predicate logic formulation of the DRTL theory that is the basis for describing the semantics of these other languages.

2. A Theory of Distributed Real-Time Logic

We first describe the conceptual model that underlies the DRTL theory and which the theory is intended to capture. After some preliminary explanation, a more precise definition is given.

An *action* represents the basic unit of computation. An action is manifested in the logic by its associated set of events; it is the unit of scheduling, the unit of specification for the requirements specifier, and is a basic unit of design. Natural numbers are used to represent time values and the ordering of event occurrences. A *node* is a unit of composition for a designer; it can be thought of as simply a set of actions. More precisely, it is the set of events associated with a set of actions. The significance of an action being associated with a node is that all such actions can be assumed to refer to a common time base. A *condition* is a statement about some aspect of the state of a component of the real-time system. It may be a condition of the internal state of a computation, of the internal state of the run-time environment, or of an external device in the environment. The logic makes no distinction about this since it is the responsibility of the designer to decide on the representation for conditions. As will be seen shortly, a condition is manifested in the logic by its associated events, one representing the condition becoming true, and one representing the condition becoming false.

An *event* serves as a temporal marker in describing the timing behaviour of a real-time system. Events are categorized into six types.

1) Activation events - an activation event represents the times at which an action is

scheduled for execution.

2) Start events - a start event represents the times at which an action starts execution.

3) Completion events - a completion event represents the times at which an action completes execution

4) External events - an external event represents the times of a physical happening in the environment.

5) Transition events - a transition event represents the times of a change in the value of a condition. There are two types; the transition of a condition to true, and the transition of a condition to false. Each condition, therefore, has two associated transition events, one of each type.

6) Notification events - a notification event represents the times at which an action becomes aware that a particular event has occurred. There are three types: the notification of a condition becoming false, the notification of a condition becoming true, and the notification of an external event. Notice that only certain events cause notifications, namely the transition events and the external events.

Each event a is represented by an uninterpreted occurrence function.

$$a(i) = \text{time of the } i^{\text{th}} \text{ occurrence of event a}$$

These occurrence functions need to be characterized by giving axiomatic restrictions on them. An informal description of these axioms is given first and later the formal axioms are stated. The first two axioms must specify that

Events occur at or after time t = 0.

Consecutive occurrences are ordered in time.

Events are also restricted according to their type so we must have

If an action completes then it must have started and have taken some time to execute.

If an action starts then it must have been activated at the same or an earlier time.

Each pair of associated transition events occur in alternation, with the initial value of the associated condition determining which occurs first.

A special uninterpreted function called the *clock skew function* is introduced to capture the notion of the multiple base times of nodes.

base(e) = a measurement of time equal to the clock skew of the node with which e is associated. These times are assumed to be measured from an unspecified global base time.

The notion of the clock skew function is used in DRTL to model different base times for each node in a system. The clock skew of a node is a measurement of time from an unspecified global base time of the entire distributed system. We want to model systems with unsynchronized clocks so we cannot know the value of base(e) nor the value of global time. However, we do specify that all clocks run at the same speed (We could easily have specified, at the price of some complexity, a weaker relationship such as one for which clocks can have constant but differing speeds.). To reflect this the clock skew axiom states that

The difference between the base times of any two nodes is a constant.

The ability to reason about events in a system in which there are multiple unsynchronized clocks is critical. Such multiple clocks are represented in the logic by the clock skew function. To reflect the fact that node clocks are unsychronized, the times of two event occurrences on different nodes are comparable only via a notification event. In terms of representing notifications by message receptions, if a message is received at time t then it can be deduced that it was sent at some earlier time t'. In order to do the comparison of course the base time of each node's clock must be taken into account. Also, such a deduction using the node base times can only occur if the event involved is a notification event. Consequently, the *notification axiom* in the logic states that

If an event occurs at time t then some other event can be deduced to have occurred at an earlier time, using the clock skew function, if and only if the former is a notification event for the latter.

To distinguish among the event types of DRTL we define nine *type predicates* that each return true for occurrence function arguments of the associated type. By convention, predicates end with the letter p after a mnemonic for the name of the type.

ap: $(N \rightarrow N) \rightarrow$ Boolean   activation

sp:	"	start
cp:	"	completion
ep:	"	external
tp:	"	true transition
fp:	"	false transition
enp:	"	external notification
tnp:	"	true transition notification
fnp:	"	false transition notification

For convenience we also define the following predicates.

notifierp(f) $\equiv$ ep(f) $\vee$ tp(f) $\vee$ fp(f)

transitionp(f) $\equiv$ tp(f) $\vee$ fp(f)

notificationp(f) $\equiv$ enp(f) $\vee$ tnp(f) $\vee$ fnp(f)

actioneventp(f) $\equiv$ ap(f) $\vee$ sp(f) $\vee$ cp(f) $\vee$ notificationp(f)

We need to capture the relation between each external and transition event with its notification event. We do this with the predicate *notifiesp*

notifiesp: $((N \rightarrow N) \times (N \rightarrow N)) \rightarrow$ Boolean

where notifiesp(f,g) is true if event g is a notification for event f, and false otherwise.

We are now ready to present the formal axioms of DRTL. The first two relate the notifies predicate with the notifier and notification predicates, and establish the uniqueness of a notifier.

Axiom A1: $\forall$ *f,g . [notifiesp(f,g) $\rightarrow$ notifierp(f) $\wedge$ notificationp(g)]*

Axiom A2: $\forall$ *f1,f2,g . [notifiesp(f1,g) $\wedge$ notifiesp(f2,g) $\rightarrow$ f1 = f2]*

We need to capture in the logic the relations among events that share a common node, a common action, and/or a common condition. That is, it is implicit that each action has an associated set of activation, start and completion events, and that each condition has an associated pair of true transition and false transition events. These three relations are captured with three associated predicates. First, we associate the predicate *mp* with each node m, that returns true for occurrence function arguments associated with m. Second, we associate the predicate *actp* with each action act, that returns true for occurrence function arguments associated with act. (We have used "act" here instead of "a" to avoid confusion with the activation predicate ap. A similar comment applies to conp in the next sentence with respect to the predicate cp.) Third, we associate the predicate *conp* with each condition con, that returns true for occurrence function arguments associated with con.

For each node mod, action act, and condition con in DRTL associate a predicate modp, actp, or conp, as appropriate for the type of object.

modp: $(N \rightarrow N) \rightarrow$ Boolean

actp: $(N \rightarrow N) \rightarrow$ Boolean

conp: $(N \rightarrow N) \rightarrow$ Boolean

where modp(ef) is true if e is associated with mod and otherwise false.

actp(ef) is true if e is associated with act and otherwise false.

conp(ef) is true if e is associated with con and otherwise false.

We also need predicates to distinguish object predicates from the other predicates in the logic, in a similar way by which we distinguish occurrence functions from other functions in the logic. The predicates npp, app, and cpp are used to distinguish respectively node, action, and condition predicates..

npp: $((N \rightarrow N) \rightarrow$ Boolean $) \rightarrow$ Boolean

app: $((N \rightarrow N) \rightarrow$ Boolean $) \rightarrow$ Boolean

cpp: $((N \rightarrow N) \rightarrow$ Boolean $) \rightarrow$ Boolean

where npp(p) is true if p is a node predicate and false otherwise.

app(p) is true if p is an action predicate and false otherwise.

cpp(p) is true if p is a condition predicate and false otherwise.

For convenience we define the predicates samenodep, sameactionp, and samecondp as follows:

samenodep(f,g) $\equiv \exists p \, . \, [\, npp(p) \, \wedge \, p(f) \, \wedge \, p(g) \,]$

sameactionp(f,g) $\equiv \exists p \, . \, [\, app(p) \, \wedge \, p(f) \, \wedge \, p(g) \,]$

samecondp(f,g) $\equiv \exists p \, . \, [\, cpp(p) \, \wedge \, p(f) \, \wedge \, p(g) \,]$

Every event is associated with some node in DRTL. However, it must follow that any actp, for some act, can only be true for events that can be associated with an action. And, of course, any conp, for some con, can only be true for events that can be associated with a condition. Consequently we have

Axiom B1: $\forall f,p . [app(p) \rightarrow [p(f) \rightarrow actioneventp(f)]]$

Axiom B2: $\forall f,p . [cpp(p) \rightarrow [p(f) \rightarrow transitionp(f)]]$

To capture the fact that there is as association among an action, its events, and the node containing them, we have

Axiom C: $\forall f,g . sameactionp(f,g) \rightarrow samenodep(f,g)$

For any event there is a unique node to which it is associated. Consequently we have

Axiom D: $\forall f . \exists p . [npp(p) \wedge p(f)$
$\wedge \forall q . [npp(q) \wedge q(f) \rightarrow q = p]]$

With the set of event occurrence functions, the nine type predicates, the notifies predicate, the function base, and the set of node predicates we can express the DRTL axioms precisely.

Events only happen at or after time zero.

Axiom E: $\forall f,i . f(i) \geq 0$

Consecutive events are ordered in time.

Axiom F: $\forall f,i,j . [i < j \rightarrow f(i) < f(j)]$

If a completion occurs it can be deduced that the associated start occurred at an earlier time.

Axiom G: $\forall g,i . [cp(g) \rightarrow$
$\exists f . [sp(f) \wedge sameactionp(f,g) \wedge f(i) < g(i)]]$

If a start occurs it can be deduced that the associated activation occurred at an earlier time.

Axiom H: $\forall g,i . [sp(g) \rightarrow$
$\exists f . [ap(f) \wedge sameactionp(f,g) \wedge f(i) < g(i)]]$

Associated transition events occur in an alternating sequence.

Axiom I1: $\forall f . [tp(f) \wedge f(1) = 0 \rightarrow$
$\exists g . [fp(g) \wedge samecond(f,g) \rightarrow \forall i . [f(i) < g(i)]]]$

Axiom I2: $\forall f . [fp(f) \wedge f(1) = 0 \rightarrow$
$\exists g . [tp(g) \wedge samecond(f,g) \rightarrow \forall i . [f(i) < g(i)]]]$

In order to characterize the function base we need to say that the base time of each occurrence function is a constant, i.e. not dependent on time. Also, it is implicit that occurrence functions associated with the same node must have the same base value. Consequently we have two axioms.

Axiom: J1 $\forall f,g$. $\exists k$. $[\mid base(f) - base(g) \mid = k]$

Axiom: J2 $\forall f,g$. $[samenodep(f,g) \rightarrow base(f) = base(g)]$

Times are only comparable via notification events.

Axiom K: $\forall f,g,i,j$. $[notifiesp(f,g) \rightarrow$
$(i \leq j \rightarrow f(i) + base(f) \leq g(j) + base(g))]$

3. Using DRTL for Requirements Specification

A requirements specification language called RReq has been developed for specifying the properties of hard-real-time distributed systems to be run in a particular programming environment based on processes and message-passing [10, 4]. As an example of the use of DRTL this section shows how the temporal semantics of RReq can be expressed; for this purpose it is not necessary to present the syntax of RReq because the entities in DRTL are very similar to those in RReq.

Actions, Events and Conditions

Each action, event, and condition in RReq is represented in DRTL by its associated event functions using a naming convention based on the RReq names; for readability all functions end in "f" to distinguish them from predicates. Nodes do not exist in RReq; they are introduced in the RSpec specifications.

Each condition c is represented by its two associated transition event functions, ctf and cff, and the condition's initial value is represented as follows:

$ctf(1) = 0$ if c is initially true
$cff(1) = 0$ if c is initially false

There are two types of actions. A *periodic action* activates with a fixed period, but only if a specified condition has a given value at the period time. A *sporadic action* activation is caused by a specified notification event, but only if a specified period has expired since the last activation. The period is optional in both cases.

For each action a represent its period p with an integer constant *aper* and an associated formula

$$aper = p$$

If no period is given, then no formula is added to the specification and aper remains a free variable.

Effect Requirements

An RReq *effect requirement* states that a particular external event or action causes a specified transition event.

The case of an external event e causing a transition of a condition c to true is represented by a formula that says "if c is false when e occurs then c becomes true at that time". The diagram below shows the situation a little more precisely, using the naming convention that ef is e's event function. If e occurs at some time t', and there was a previous transition to false at some time t with no intervening transition back to true, then the transition to true occurs at t'. The corresponding DRTL formula is shown after the diagram.

```
         cff(j)              ctf(k)          ctf(l)
                                             ef(i)
      -------|--------------------|-----------------|-----------> time
             t          does not exist        t'
```

$$\forall\ i,j\ .\ [\ cff(j) < ef(i)\ \wedge\ \tilde{}\ \exists k\ .\ [\ cff(j) < ctf(k) < ef(i)\ ]\ \rightarrow\ \exists l\ .\ [\ ctf(l) = ef(i)\ ]\ ]$$

An analogous formula is used to represent a transition to false.

An action a causing a transition of a condition c to true is represented by a formula that says "if c is false when a starts then c becomes true while a executes and c remains true until a completes". More precisely, as depicted in the diagram, if a starts and completes at some times t' and t", and there was a previous transition to false at some time t with no intervening transition back to true, then c becomes true during a's execution and no transition back to false occurs until after a completes.

```
 cff(j)            ctf(k)        asf(i)         ctf(l)        cff(k)        acf(i)
-------|--------------------|-----------------|---------------|--------------|----> time
    t          does not exist       t'                  does not exist   t"
```

$$\forall i,j\ .\ [\ cff(j) < asf(i)\ \wedge\ \tilde{}\ \exists k\ .\ [\ cff(j) < ctf(k) \leq asf(i)\ ]$$
$$\rightarrow\ \exists l\ .\ [\ asf(i) < ctf(l)) < acf(i)\ ]\ \wedge\ \tilde{}\ \exists k\ .\ [\ asf(i) < cff(k) \leq acf(i)\ ]\ ]$$

An analogous formula is used to represent a transition to false.

Activation Requirements

An RReq *activation requirement* specifies the nature of an action's activation. A periodic activation of an action a when condition c is true is represented by a formula that says "if at any potential activation time the most recent notification for c indicates true then a is activated". More precisely, if at any time t that is an integral multiple of a's period aper, the most recent transition for c was to true, then a is activated at time t. Using our naming convention this can be shown as

```
        catnf(i)             cafnf(j)        aaf(k)
    -------|--------------------|----------------|----------> time
          t'            does not exist          t
```

$$\exists \text{ aper} . \forall i,z . [\text{catnf}(i) < z \times \text{aper} \land \tilde{} \exists j . [\text{catnf}(i) < \text{cafnf}(j) < z \times \text{aper}]$$
$$\rightarrow \exists k . [\text{aaf}(k) = z \times \text{aper}]]$$

An analogous formula is used to represent an activation with condition false.

A sporadic activation involves two cases. First consider the situation in which the notification event occurs after the action's minimum period has expired. In that case, a is activated at that time. More precisely, if the notification event e for a occurs at time t' and the most recent activation for a occurred at a time t at least aper time units previous to t', then the next activation for a occurs at t'.

```
        aaf(i)              aaf(k)        aaf(i+1)
                                           ef(j)
    -------|--------------------|----------------|----------> time
          t            does not exist          t'

            <---------- ≥ aper ------------>
```

$$\exists \text{ aper} . \forall i,j . [\text{ef}(j) \geq \text{aaf}(i) + \text{aper} \land \tilde{} \exists k . [\text{aaf}(i) < \text{aaf}(k) < \text{ef}(j)]$$
$$\rightarrow [\text{aaf}(i+1) = \text{ef}(j)]]$$

Now consider the situation in which the notification event occurs before the minimum period has expired. In this case, a's activation must not occur until the period has expired. More precisely, if the notification event e for a occurs at time t', and the most recent activation for a occurred at a time t less than aper time units previous to t' then the next activation for a occurs at time t+aper.

```
      aaf(i)              ef(j)        aaf(i+1)
-------|--------------------|-----------------|----------> time
       t                    t'
```

```
            <------------- aper ------------->
```

$\exists$ aper . $\forall$ i,j . [aaf(i) < ef(j) < aaf(i) + aper $\rightarrow$ [aaf(i+1) = aaf(i) + aper]]

Latency Requirements

A *latency requirement* places a constraint on the time between two specified events. There are two types; a *deadline* and a *delay* specify an upper and a lower bound respectively. For each deadline between two events f and g represent the deadline value d with an integer constant fgdea and an associated formula

$$fgdea = d$$

For delays, the analogous naming convention is fgdel.

The meaning of a deadline {f,g} < d is more complex than might first be thought. Informally, if f and g occur at comparable times t and t' respectively, t < t', and no other occurrences of f or g exist within the interval {t,t'} then t'- t $\leq$ fgdea.

$\forall$ i,j,s,s' . [s = base(f) + ff(i) $\wedge$ s' = base(g) + gf(j) $\wedge$ s < s' $\wedge$
              $\tilde{}$ $\exists$ k . [s < ff(k) + base(f) < s'] $\wedge$
              $\tilde{}$ $\exists$ k . [s < gf(k) + base(g) < s']
    $\rightarrow$ s' - s $\leq$ fgdea]

The analogous formula for a delay is identical except that the last line is
    $\rightarrow$ s' $\geq$ s + fgdel]

4. Using DRTL for Design Specification

A design specification language called RSpec has been developed for specifying the properties of hard-real-time distributed systems to be run in a particular programming environment based on processes and message-passing [4]. As an example of the use of DRTL this section shows how the temporal semantics of RSpec can be expressed.

In DRTL there is an implicit relation on events describing the set of actions, where each action is a triple (a,s,c) of its activation, start, and completion events respectively. We now present an expanded notion of action, called the *design action,* that represents the basic unit of design composition. A design action is an implementation of an action with the activation, start, and notification events of the action hidden, but with an explicit set of *parameter events* through which the design action interacts with other design actions. A design action also has associated values for the period, execution time, and base time for the action. A design action A in its general form is depicted as

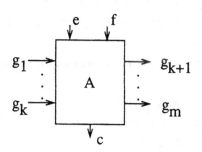

$$A (e, f, c, g_1, ... , g_m)$$

where

    e is an event constraining activation of A

    f is an event constraining the start of A

    c is the completion event for A

    g_i, $1 \leq i \leq k$, is an event causing a notification event associated with A

    g_i, $k+1 \leq i \leq m$, is a transition event associated with A

Normally, the method employs the naming convention to associate design entities with requirements entities but since this makes the formulae hard to read we'll drop the practice for event functions in this section. Consequently, the "c" in the diagram above should be understood as denoting "Acf" using the naming convention.

The notification for an input event may be delayed and so this must be specified. The problem is that the delay is dependent on the environment of the action, i.e. its node, and not on the input event. Consequently, a delay predicate must be an additional parameter of the action. Since this becomes notationally cumbersome, we use a shorthand for inputs as follows. An input parameter g actually is a pair: g.f denotes the event function and g.p denotes its associated delay predicate. For simplicity the following graphic shorthand is used:

$$\begin{array}{c} \text{g.f} \rightarrow \\ \text{g.p} \rightarrow \end{array} \quad \text{is drawn as} \quad \begin{array}{c} \text{g.f} \multimap \rightarrow \\ \text{g.p} \end{array} \quad \text{and often shortened to} \quad \text{g} \rightarrow$$

In a similar way the text A(... ,g, ...) denotes A(... , g.f, g.p, ...). Furthermore, where the meaning is clear, g can denote g.f.

A design action (we'll sometimes use the term action in the following where it is clear that we mean a design action) is a predicate representing the design specifications for an action. Its general form is a conjunction of a set of terms constraining each of the parameters.

$$A(e,f,c,g_1, \dots ,g_m) \equiv \mathbf{V}\, t \,.\, \bigwedge \text{[term for each parameter]}$$

We'll look at the case of a sporadic action first, and look at each parameter in turn to develop a precise description of a sporadic design action. A much more detailed explanation of these semantics for design actions appears in [11, 12, 13].

The event e causes the action to activate. Of course, a notification event n is associated with e, there must be an activation event a, and the precise meaning of "e causes the action to activate" must be explicated. The formula below contains these elements of specification. For simplicity, the activation event a and the start event s are assumed to be existentially quantified across all of the formulas to follow.

$$\exists\, n \,.\, \text{Ap}(n) \,\wedge\, \text{Ap}(a) \,\wedge\, \text{notifiesp}(e,n) \,\wedge\, \text{e.p}(e.f,n) \,\wedge\, \text{spor\_actp}(n,a)$$

This says that n and a must be associated with A, and e and n must be related by the notifies predicate. These predicates must, of course, be defined appropriately during the design activity. The predicate spor_actp(n,a) can be regarded as an axiom of the design method that precisely states the temporal meaning of a sporadic activation. This formula is, in fact, that same formula that was used in Section 3 to define sporadic activation for the requirements specification.

$$\text{spor\_actp}(n,a) \equiv \exists\, \text{Aper} \,.\, \mathbf{V}\, i,j \,.\, [$$

$$((e(j) \geq a(i) + \text{Aper}) \;\wedge\; \tilde{}\,\exists\, k \,.\, [\, a(i) < a(k) < e(j) \,] $$
$$\rightarrow (\, a(i+1) = e(j) \,)) \qquad \wedge$$

$$(e(j) < a(i) + Aper \rightarrow (a(i+1) = a(i) + Aper))]$$

Now we consider the precise temporal meaning of starting the action constrained by f.

$$sp(s) \wedge Ap(s) \wedge con\_startp(f,s)$$

This says that there must be a start event s associated with A, and it is constrained by the predicate con_startp. As with spor_actp above, one can think of con_startp as an axiom of the design method that precisely defines the temporal meaning of starting an action. In this case what we want to say is simply that the action is constrained to start only at or after f occurs, unless f is a special event called the *null event*, in which case there is no constraint other than the axioms. The reason for the null event provision will become clear when composition of actions is described.

$$con\_startp(f,s) \equiv (\forall i . f(i) \le s(i)) \vee nullp(f)$$

Now we consider the precise temporal meaning of an input event g. Our model does not permit an action to *block* while waiting for an input event unless the blocking operation occurs as the last event in the action. This is explained further with respect to the completion event. The meaning of an input event g then is simply that the notification can only occur during some execution.

$$\exists n . Ap(n) \wedge notifiesp(g,n) \wedge g.p(g.f,n) \wedge$$
$$(\forall i . \exists j . (s(j) \le n(i) \le c(j)))$$

Now we consider the precise temporal meaning of an output event g. As with input events, the meaning of an output event g is that it can only occur during some execution. Here, however, the event is a transition event associated with a condition and so the formula can only be given as a textual schema for some condition CON, and some predicate Bp that is either tp of fp. Note that the association of a condition with the internal state of an action in this way is one of the designer's responsibilities.

$$Bp(g) \wedge Ap(g) \wedge CONp(g) \wedge (\forall i . \exists j . s(j) \le g(i) \le c(j))$$

As noted above there are two cases for the completion. The specification (and programming) model assumes that the completion event coincides with either an attempt to receive a notification of an input transition or an output transition. Since the input transition may not have occurred then the notification may not occur (One way this can happen is for the action to execute a non-blocking receive operation on an empty port.). The input case is more interesting since the action can block waiting for the notification. Consequently, the execution time may be less than the time interval between starting and completing. If the action terminates with an output transition or a non-blocking attempt to receive a notification then the completion formula is

$$cp(c) \wedge Ap(c) \wedge (\forall i . (c(i) \leq a(i)+d \wedge c(i) = s(i)+b))$$

which says that the action meets its deadline d expressed with respect to activation time, and it consumes b time units of processor execution.

If the action terminates with a blocking attempt to receive a notification then the completion formula is

$$cp(c) \wedge Ap(c) \wedge (\forall i . (s(i)+b \leq c(i) \leq a(i)+d \wedge n(i) = c(i)))$$

We now turn to periodic actions of which the specification model has two kinds. The first has an *unconditional activation* that occurs at regular intervals. Consequently, there is no input event to cause activation.

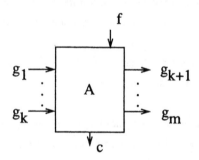

$$A (f, c, g_1, g_m)$$

The specification formula for a periodic action is

$$Ap(a) \wedge per\_actp(a)$$

where

$$per\_actp(a) \equiv \forall z . \exists k . a(k) = z \times Aper$$

The second kind of periodic action has a *conditional activation,* meaning that it activates at one of its potential interval times only if a specified condition is true. However, since in general it can't know precisely when a condition is true this means that it will activate if the last notification for that condition indicates a true value. Consequently, there are two input events to cause activation, the true and the false transitions for the condition, shown below as et and ef.

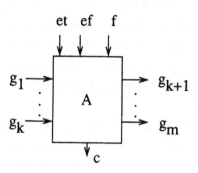

$$A (et, ef, f, c, g_1, \ldots ,g_m)$$

The specification term describing activation for the conditional periodic action is

$$\exists\, nt,nf\,.\ Ap(nt)\ \wedge\ Ap(nf)\ \wedge\ Ap(a)\ \wedge$$
$$notifiesp(et,nt)\ \wedge\ notifiesp(ef,nf)\ \wedge$$
$$et.p(et.f,nt)\ \wedge\ ef.p(ef.f,nf)\ \wedge$$
$$cond\_per\_actp(nt,nf,a)$$

where

$$cond\_per\_actp(nt,nf,a)\ \equiv\ \exists\, Aper\,.\ \forall\, i,z\,.\ [$$
$$(nt(i) < z \times Aper)\ \wedge\ {}^{\sim}\,\exists\, j\,.\ [nt(i) < nf(j) < z \times Aper\,]$$
$$\rightarrow \exists\, k\,.\ [\,a(k) = z \times Aper\,]\,]$$

all of which is to say that if at each potential activation time t, a true notification last occurred at t', and no false notification occurred in the interim, then an activation occurs.

Actions exist in a run-time environment. In particular they interact with external events through this environment. The interface to the environment seen by an action is also specified as a predicate on a software component called a *kernel* in much the same way that an action is specified. The kernel, of course, contains the run-time scheduler that is mandated to ensure that actions meet their deadlines. A kernel is very different from an action in other ways as well. Formally, it is a set of external events, along with a set of of transition events.

The nature of a kernel is much clearer if some time is taken to explain the implementation to which the design method is targeted. Each external interrupt (event) has an associated output message port in the kernel to which an input port of an action can be linked. In this way, an interrupt can cause activation of a sporadic action, for example. Actions write into device registers directly. Each device has associated with it an implicit condition that is set by an interrupt and reset by some controlling action. These are called *d conditions;* the true transition for a d condition is caused by an external event in the kernel, and the false transition is caused by some action. These are both called d transitions. The kernel true d transitions do not appear as parameters of a kernel specification; they are used for verification purposes only, having been chosen by the designer to be represented in this way but necessary to keep since they are referenced in the requirements.

The remaining kernel transitions are associated with conditions called *k conditions* which represent internal state of the kernel, and which are caused by external devices. They are used for conditional activation of actions.

In the depiction below the e's are the external events, the kt's and kf's are the true and false transitions for the k conditions, and the d's are the false transitions for the d conditions. The general form of the design specification for a kernel is shown in an informal way beside the diagram.

$$e_1 \quad kt_1 \, kf_1 \quad d_1$$

$$K(e_1, ...; kt_1, kf_1, ...; d_1, ...) \equiv$$

For each k transition g there is an e such that

$$\forall i \, . \, e(i) = g(i)$$

For each true d transition g there is an e such that

$$\forall i \, . \, e(i) = g(i)$$

What this means is that an external event (interrupt) can cause a transition event as a side effect. The interpretation is that the kernel implements k conditions and d conditions. The former are used to condition periodic activations, and the latter exist only to represent certain conditions in the requirements.

There is no statement about deadlines in the kernel design specification since the scheduling assertions simply mandate the kernel to enforce them. The question as to how one can specify a scheduler and formally verify that a kernel specification meets a set of scheduling assertions has not yet been investigated.

5. Specification Composition

Composition is of two kinds, *sequential* which forms processes from actions, and *parallel* which forms nodes (process networks) from processes, and larger nodes from smaller nodes. Sporadic actions form sporadic processes, and periodic actions form periodic processes.

A *process* is defined to be an ordered set of actions. For sequential composition, the primitive construct is to *append* an action to a process. Appending a sporadic action A to a null process to form a sporadic process P is depicted by

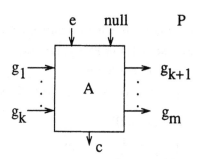

and defined by $\quad P(e,c,g_1, \dots ,g_m) \equiv A(e,\text{null},c,g_1, \dots ,g_m)$

The period of A becomes the period of P, and the deadline of A becomes the deadline of P.

Appending an action A to a process P' to form a process P is depicted by

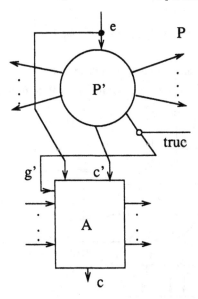

Here, the input e for P' becomes the activation input for A, the completion c' for P' becomes the start constraint input for A, and *for every transition g' in P' that is an input to A* the output from P' becomes an input to the corresponding parameter of A. All inputs and outputs for P' and A, other than those that have been hidden in the composition, become inputs and outputs for P.

The implementation significance of the composition is that A gets activated when P' activates but cannot run until the preceding action completes, and certain internal state conditions of P' can be read by A with no delay. So, taking some liberties with notation using ellipses, this is defined by

$$P(e,c,g_1, \dots ,g_m) \equiv \exists\, c',g', \dots . P'(e,c', \dots g', \dots) \wedge A(e,c',c, \dots ,g'.f, true, \dots)$$

In the case of appending an action to a process there is no notification delay. The composition P is not valid unless the period of A equals the period of P', and the deadline of A is greater than the deadline of P'. The deadline of A becomes the deadline of P.

Appending a periodic action A to a null process to form a periodic process P is depicted by

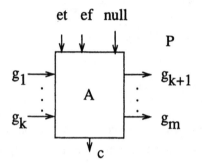

and defined by $\quad P(et,ef,c,g_1, \dots ,g_m) \equiv A(et,ef,null,c,g_1, \dots ,g_m)$

with the same equating of the deadline and period of A to those of P.

Appending a conditional action A to a conditional process P' to form a process P is depicted by

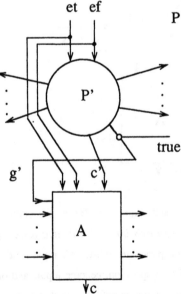

$$P(et,ef,c,g_1, \ldots ,g_m) \equiv$$
$$\exists\ c',g', \ldots . \ P'(et,ef,c', \ldots g', \ldots) \ \wedge \ A(et,ef,c',c, \ldots ,g'.f, \text{true}, \ldots)$$

The same comments apply to the deadline and period of A and P, and in addition, of course, the composition is only valid if the activation condition for A is the same as that for P.

We now turn to the composition of processes with a kernel. An *lnode* (for logical node) is a set of processes along with a kernel, and is the unit of composition for a set of processes that are to run on the same shared physical node with the same shared kernel. In the programming environment, the lnode is the basic unit of program modularity. An lnode cannot be implemented across different physical nodes, but more than one lnode can run on one physical node. However, at the time of composition, it may not be known on which physical node the lnode will run. Consequently, delay information may not be available.

The diagram below depicts an example of the composition of a sporadic process with a kernel interface. For simplicity, only one input and one output of the process are shown linked to the kernel. In this case, one delay predicate input to the lnode is needed. The result of the composition is that the lnode interface has three components: the delay predicates (see more below), the residual kernel interface (after linking some events to the process), and the residual process interface (after linking some events with the kernel). As more processes are added to the lnode, the residual kernel interface becomes smaller, and the residual process interface changes depending on how processes communicate among each other.

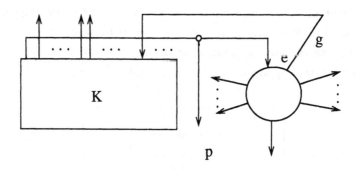

In this case the e event for the process is linked to an external event in the kernel; this is not necessarily the case since it is possible to link it later to a transition in another process, or even to an external event in another kernel (although the latter would be unlikely since interrupts normally must be processed without much delay). K transitions, however, are never used for a sporadic process.

In summary, some input transitions may be linked to external events, and some output transitions may be linked to false d transitions. The general form of the lnode specification for the example shown above is

L(p, <residual kernel interface>, <residual process interface>) ≡

∃ e.f,g . P(e.f, p, ... , g, ...) ∧ K(e.f, ..., g, ...)

The composition of a periodic process with a kernel is similar except that for a conditional activation its activation events are linked to a pair of k condition transitions.

Adding a process to an lnode is similar to adding a process to a kernel except that some linking with the processes in the lnode's residual process interface may occur. An example of this can be shown as

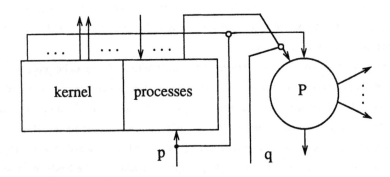

This example illustrates the use of different delay predicates. Here, and in what follows, two predicates are specified, p characterizes the delay for external notifications (interrupt handling), and q does the same for transition notifications (inter-process message handling).

Composing lnodes, having an interface for the same kernel, to form a larger lnode involves only interprocess linking along with delay predicates as needed, as shown in

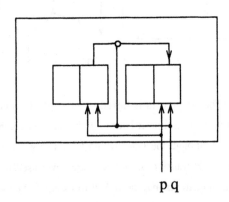

The next larger unit of composition is the *pnode* (for physical node) representing a single

physical node in a distributed system. The primitive operation is the transformation of an lnode into a pnode. This is done by creating a pnode with the same parameters but conjoined with predicates giving information about the physical delays inherent with the particular physical resources being represented. A pnode has no k transitions or d transitions. The transformation of an lnode L to a pnode P by providing the delay predicates can be written as

$$P(p, q, g_1, \dots) \equiv L(p, q, g_1, \dots) \wedge p \wedge q$$

where p and q are suitably defined.

Adding an lnode L to a pnode P' to form a pnode P is straightforward and can be written as illustrated in the following example outline in which one output g of L is linked to an input of P'.

$$P(p, q, \text{<union of residual parameters of P' and L> }) \equiv$$
$$\exists \, g.f \, . \, P'(p, q, \dots , g.f, q, \dots) \wedge L(p, q, \dots , g.f, \dots)$$

Constructing a *configuration* of pnodes can now proceed in much the same way that digital circuits are composed except that for each such composition the delay predicate for the network must be added to the conjunction of the pnode predicates. The composition of two pnodes P' and P" to form a configuration C can be written as shown in the following example in which one output of P" is linked to an input of P', and r represents the network delay predicate for inter-physical-node communication.

$$C(r, \text{<union of the residual parameters of P' and P"> }) \equiv$$
$$\exists \, g.f \, . \, P'(p', q', \dots , g.f, r, \dots) \wedge P"(p", q", \dots , g.f, \dots) \wedge r$$

where r is suitably defined.

Adding a pnode P to a configuration C' to form a configuration C can be written as shown in the following example in which, similar to the above, one output of P is linked to an input on C'.

$$C(r, \text{<union of residual parameters of C' and P> }) \equiv$$
$$\exists \, g.f \, . \, C'(r, \dots , g.f, r, \dots) \wedge P(p, q, \dots , g.f, \dots)$$

Note that one could use a different delay predicate for different kinds of connections. For simplicity, the example assumes that all inter-node communication has the same delay properties.

Finally, a well-formed completed configuration should have no input or output events remaining unlinked. The only parameter(s) is the connection delay predicate.

6. Verification

The verification problem is to show that a specification for a configuration implies the requirement constraints for that configuration. This view is taken rather than a stronger statement of equivalence of the specifications and requirements. This is likely not to be the case for practical systems, and would be much harder to do. As noted earlier, this view means that the requirements must include an explicit statement about all properties that the specifications must not exhibit. That is, the verification does not automatically guarantee that the specifications only do what the requirements say and no more; the requirements specifier must be explicit about any limitations on the specifications.

One thing that has not been discussed since it is largely a linguistic aspect is *mapping specification*. This is a statement about the representation of entities in a requirements specification by entities in the design specification. In our discussion we accomplished this by the informal use of a naming convention. In RNet, the design language RSpec contains statements for use as mapping specifications.

Our major goal has been modularity. The intent is that one can prove properties about parameterized components like Inodes independent from other components. To show that a particular requirement constraint holds one can then use only the properties of those components that are needed to complete the proof. We are just now getting to the point of addressing examples and carrying out proofs with automated assistance. The HOL system [8], the OBJ system [6] and the EHDM system [5] are all being investigated as tools for automated assistance for proofs.

7. Summary Discussion

The major effort has been the development of a design method for composing specifications using higher order-logic. This was exhibited through an extensive example of a set of design rules for expressing specifications for both requirements and design.

The method is not as clean as Gordon's method for composing hardware specifications due to the somewhat cumbersome use of delay predicate parameters. As an alternative, we could have explicitly modelled communication by specifying each medium as a discrete device rather than treating it as an environment property. The latter was chosen somewhat subjectively because it was judged to result in more readable specifications. For example, one does not want the necessity of expressing a "kernel network" linking each process in a node. This is really only a syntactic consideration since the delay predicate models a component however it is expressed. Suppression of the communication medium as an explicit component, however, seems to make the specifications cleaner. Furthermore, making the medium explicit would mean that there would be two different kinds of component, computational and communication. Finally, our treatment allows the delay predicate to be naturally deferred as a parameter.

The extent to which the complexity grows with specification size has not been addressed in detail. However, the modularity means that designs can be constructed and verified incrementally to reduce the complexity. It is also expected that, in practice, designs will be found to have repeated common structure which can be exploited to reduce the verification work.

Related work includes a class of languages intended to model synchronous systems, which are therefore unsuitable for our purposes. This includes LUSTRE [16] and ESTEREL [2]. More closely related work includes that of the Durra project [1], the work of Zwarico [17, 18], and the work of Ostroff [14].

Durra very nicely combines timing specification and functional specification, based on Mok and Jahanian's RTL and the Larch language. Non-deterministic actions are not specifiable and reasoning about timing behaviour is internal to tasks containing timing expressions. Since a common clock for tasks cannot be assumed one cannot reason about global properties of distributed systems.

Zwarico's language addresses timing behaviour only but allows non-deterministic specification. The approach is algebraic with a set of partially ordered processes and operators on processes. A process comprises a set of event traces that it can execute, along with states into which these traces can lead. A state specifies future event timing. Processes are formed from component processes such that component processes engage in common events simultaneously. Consequently, all process interaction is synchronous and assumes a common time base.

Ostroff's method is, to our knowledge, the only detailed application of temporal logic to hard-real-time reasoning. Requirements are given in RTTL, a real-time temporal logic. Design specification is given as an extended state machine (ESM). Verification requires establishing the validity of the RTTL formulae for the ESM model. Modularity seems to be a problem but recent work addresses this issue [15].

None of these projects takes the principle of separation of requirements and design specification as an explicit objective, although the separation clearly exists in Ostroff's method.

Our plan is to extend DRTL to include functional specification by generalizing the representation of an event from an occurrence function to a pair (f,p) where f is the event occurrence function as we have presented, and p is a predicate the meaning of which depends on the *type* and the *context* of f. As an example, for the case of start and completion events the context is the internal state of the associated action. The predicate associated with the start is a pre-condition, and that for the completion is a post-condition. These predicates provide the link between temporal specification and functional specification, and are intended to be used as specifications for the action implementations. Our objective is to allow reasoning about temporal aspects to proceed independently of functional aspects so that the proof process is less complex. It is believed that this can be done as long as the cleaner. Furthermore, making the medium explicit would mean that there would be two different kinds of component, computational and communication. Finally, our treatment allows the delay predicate to be naturally deferred as a parameter.

The extent to which the complexity grows with specification size has not been addressed in detail. However, the modularity means that designs can be constructed and verified incrementally to reduce the complexity. It is also expected that, in practice, designs will be found to have repeated common structure which can be exploited to reduce the verification work.

Related work includes a class of languages intended to model synchronous systems, which are therefore unsuitable for our purposes. This includes LUSTRE [16] and ESTEREL [2]. More closely related work includes that of the Durra project [1], the work of Zwarico [17, 18], and the work of Ostroff [14].

Durra very nicely combines timing specification and functional specification, based on Mok and Jahanian's RTL and the Larch language. Non-deterministic actions are not specifiable and reasoning about timing behaviour is internal to tasks containing timing expressions. Since a common clock for tasks cannot be assumed one cannot reason about global properties of distributed systems.

Zwarico's language addresses timing behaviour only but allows non-deterministic specification. The approach is algebraic with a set of partially ordered processes and operators on processes. A process comprises a set of event traces that it can execute, along with states into which these traces can lead. A state specifies future event timing. Processes are formed from component processes such that component processes engage in common events simultaneously. Consequently, all process interaction is synchronous and assumes a common time base.

Ostroff's method is, to our knowledge, the only detailed application of temporal logic to hard-real-time reasoning. Requirements are given in RTTL, a real-time temporal logic. Design specification is given as an extended state machine (ESM). Verification requires establishing the validity of the RTTL formulae for the ESM model. Modularity seems to be a problem but recent work addresses this issue [15].

Our plan is to extend DRTL to include functional specification by generalizing the representation of an event from an occurrence function to a pair (f,p) where f is the event occurrence function as we have presented, and p is a predicate the meaning of which depends on the *type* and the *context* of f. As an example, for the case of start and completion events the context is the internal state of the associated action. The predicate associated with the start is a pre-condition, and that for the completion is a post-condition. These predicates provide the link between temporal specification and functional specification, and are intended to be used as specifications for the action implementations. Our objective is to allow reasoning about temporal aspects to proceed independently of functional aspects so that the proof process is less complex. It is believed that this can be done as long as the predicates are stated independently of any considerations of scheduling. In other words, the times at which these predicates are asserted to hold follow from the event occurrence reasoning and not the reverse. Our assumption that the scheduling assertions are enforced by the run-time system conforms with this.

Functional specification forces a consideration of the issue of non-determinism. This follows because one must be able to specify input and output data for actions. Durra allows this using unbounded queues; we expect to incorporate a mechanism of unit-sized asynchronously accessed buffers for this purpose. This does not seem to be difficult if one restricts action behaviors to a model in which all input registers are read before any output registers are written. This may not be a serious restriction, and seems to yield considerable simplicity; Durra goes to complex lengths to handle a more general model.

The non-determinism occurs because it is natural for an action to read an input value and cause one of several events depending on this value. Thus the action is non-deterministic; the occurrence of the events caused is affected but not their time of occurrence. Currently, the semantics of RReq and RSpec are deterministic except for the conditional activation of periodic processes. We expect to use some form of *restriction* to introduce a more general non-determinism. Each action has an associated set of events that it causes; a restriction is any subset of these events. A way is needed to specify restrictions that allows reasonable properties to be verified.

In addition to the extensions for functional specification and non-determinism, the major remaining immediate work is to specify real examples to gain experience with the method and with the assistance of mechanical provers. Finally, the RNet system, specification languages, kernel, and other tools will continue to be developed and integrated with other tools such as the provers to provide a working prototype software engineering environment for developing real-time systems for distributed architectures.

Acknowledgement

The idea of applying Gordon's method for specifying hardware circuits to distributed systems was first suggested by John Rushby of SRI International.

References

1. M.R. Barbacci and J.M. Wing, "Specifying Functional and Timing Behavior for Real-Time Systems," *Proceedings of the Conference on Parallel Architectures and Languages*, (June 1987).
2. G. Berry, S. Moisan, and J-P. Rigault, "ESTEREL: Towards a Synchronous and Semantically Sound High Level Language for Real-Time Applications," *IEEE Real-Time Systems Symposium*, pp. 30-37 (December 1983).

3. A. Camilleri, M. Gordon, and T. Melham, *Hardware Verification Using Higher-Order Logic,* Computer Laboratory, Cambridge University (June 11, 1987).

4. M. Coulas, G. H. MacEwen, and G. Marquis, "RNet: A Hard Real-Time Distributed Programming System," *IEEE Transactions on Computers* **C-36**(8) pp. 917-932 (August 1987).

5. J.S. Crow and others, *SRI Specification and Verification System,* Computer Science Laboratory, SRI International, Menlo Park, CA (May 1986).

6. J. A. Goguen, "OBJ as a Theorem Prover," SRI-CSL-88-4, SRI International, Menlo Park, CA (April 1988).

7. M.J.C. Gordon, "Why Higher-Order Logic is a Good Formalism for Specifying and Verifying Hardware," *Formal Aspects of VLSI Design*, North Holland, (1986).

8. M.J.C. Gordon, "HOL: A Machine-Oriented Formulation of Higher-Order Logic," Technical Report 68, Computer Laboratory, Cambridge University (June 15, 1987).

9. F. Jahanian and A.K. Mok, "Safety Analysis of Timing Properties in Real-Time Systems," *IEEE Transactions on Software Engineering* **SE-12**(9) pp. 890-904 (September 1986).

10. G. H. MacEwen and T. A. Montgomery, "Expressing Requirements for Distributed Real-time Systems," *Fourth Workshop on Real-time Operating Systems*, pp. 125-128 IEEE Computer Society, (July 1987).

11. G.H. MacEwen and T.A. Montgomery, *The RNet Programming System Report 87-4: Requirements Language Semantics,* Department of Computing and Information Science, Queen's University, Kingston, Ontario (November 17, 1987).

12. G.H. MacEwen and T.A. Montgomery, *The RNet Programming System Report 87-1: Requirements Language Definition,* Department of Computing and Information Science, Queen's University, Kingston, Ontario (November 12, 1987).

13. G.H. MacEwen and T.A. Montgomery, *The RNet Programming System Report 87-3: Distributed Real-time Logic,* Department of Computing and Information Science, Queen's University, Kingston, Ontario (November 22, 1987).

14. J.S. Ostroff and W.M. Wonham, "Modelling, Specifying, and Verifying Real-Time Embedded Computer Systems," *Proceedings of the IEEE Real-Time System Symposium*, pp. 124-132 (December 1987).

15. J.S. Ostroff, "Modular Reasoning in the ESM/RTTL Framework For Real-Time Systems," Technical Report CS-88-03, Computer Science Department, York University, North York, Ontario (April 1988).

16. P.Caspi, D. Pilaud, N. Halbwachs, and J.A Plaice, "LUSTRE: A Declarative Language for Programming Synchronous Systems," *Proceedings of the ACM Symposium on Principles of Programming Languages*, pp. 178-188 (January 1987).

17. A. Zwarico and I. Lee, "Proving a Network of Real-Time Processes Correct," *Proceedings of the IEEE Real-Time System Symposium*, pp. 169-177 (December 1985).

18. A. Zwarico, "An Algebra of Time Dependent Processes," Ph.D. Thesis, University of Pennsylvania, Philadelphia (in preparation).

Timed specifications for the development of real-time systems.

Jacques JARAY

C.R.I.N

Centre de Recherche en Informatique de Nancy

Boite Postale 239

F-54500 VANDOEUVRE-LES-NANCY CEDEX

FRANCE

Abstract

The introduction of a time component in the data structures used to describe the functional specification of the behaviour of real-time systems produce statements on which time properties may be checked and from which one derive synchronized programs. This paper shows the main features of the specification language as well as the transformation rules into ADA concurrent tasks.

1 Introduction

Recent works on real-time specifications [4],[18] propose some formalisms to specify real-time systems. In both approaches the abstract data type formalism is used to specify the functional part of the specifications and the temporal properties or constraints are expressed on the execution states of the functions with a temporal logic language in [18] or a real-time logic language design by [15] in [4]. We claim that we can avoid the two levels of formalisms and introduce temporal specifications in the functional specifications. This can be done by enriching the elements in the domains of functions with an explicit time component.

Our specifications are suitable for functional or temporal verifications, we do not address the proof area. Our intent is rather to exhibit a way to specify the behaviour of real-time systems and to show how one can derive, from our temporal statements, the synchronization part of the concurrent processes which implement the system.

We want a specification language with a powerful level of expression, we think that high level constructs either functional and logical are needed, we do not give a definition of the specification language rather sketch the kind of features which seems useful to write short and easy-to-read specifications. The kernel of the language is inspired by VDM[16] or Z[2]. Functional notations are borrowed to ML [21].

As in VDM we use sequences of elements as a data structure and we introduce an important type: the *temporal sequences* which help capturing the time attributes of the data. The use of such temporal sequences is shown on an example.

We are concerned by methodology therefore we highlight the steps that lead to the specification and motivate the choices.

2 Sequences and temporal sequences to specify the behavior of systems

We feel that in many cases it is possible to describe the external behaviour of systems by exhibiting input and output sequences of data. Many people agree on the term reactive systems [13] and our view better suits transformational systems. We think that the time associated to the data is the bridge between the two classifications.

We will illustrate the way we use sequences to specify real-time systems on an example drawn from [18] and specified as follows:

Simulation of a filling station:

There are two petrol-pumps A and B and three lines in which cars are waiting for service. Cars in line L1 are only served at A, cars in L3 are only served at B and cars in L2 are served in A or B. At each pump, only one car can be tanked at the same time. The strategy of serving the three lines is as follows: Lines L1 and L2 are to be served in turns; after a car from L1, a car from L2 is to be served (in A or B) before the next car from L1 is served (except, of course, there is no car waiting in L2), and so on. The same alternating protocol is to hold between lines L2 and L3.

We introduce three sequences L1, L2, L3 to model the entrance of the cars in the station and two sequences R1, R2 to model the outputs of the station: that is the sequences of the cars served on each pump A and B.

We suppose that the sequences are finite (the station closes at night). Let *set* be the function which transforms a sequence into the set of its elements. We can state that a car can occur in only one input line :

(1) $set(L1) \cap set(L2) = set(L1) \cap set(L3) = set(L1) \cap set(L2) \cap set(L3) = \emptyset$

(2) $set(R1) \cap set(R2) = \emptyset$

states that every car entered in the L1 line leaves the station through R1 (will be served on A) :

(3) $set(L1) \subset set(R1)$
that the same holds for L3 and R2,

(4) $set(L3) \subset set(R2)$
and that the elements of L2 are dealt in R1 and R2 :

(5) $set(L2) \subset set(R1) \cup set(R2)$

And conversely, we can state that the elements of R1 "comes from" $L1 \cup L2$ and that the elements of R2 "comes from" $L2 \cup L3$.

We can prove that : $set(L1) \cup set(L2) \cup set(L3) = set(R1) \cup set(R2)$ which means that every car entering the station leaves the station.

A second series of statements state that the cars of an input queue are served in the arrival order, that is, appear in the output sequence in the same order in which they were in the input sequence.

Unless we have a "merge" operator defined on the sequences, we need express such a property on the elements of the sequences :

(6)$(\forall i, j \in \mathcal{N} | (\exists k, l \in \mathcal{N} | L1_i = R1_k \wedge L1_j = R1_l))(i > j \Rightarrow k > l)$

In order to state the criteria which govern the dispatching of the cars of the L2 line, we need to introduce some considerations about the *time*, informally speaking, one can say that if the $R1_i$ car is $L1_j$ then if the sequence LR2 is not empty $R1_{i+1} = LR2(1)$ or $R2_{k+1} = LR2(1)$ where LR2 is the subsequence of L2 whose elements are "arrived when $R1_i$ is served" and are not yet in R1 or R2.

k is the rank of the last car stored in R2 when $R1_i$ is served. The possibility that some sequences can be empty imply the need of time expression in the definition.

A more formal definition could be :

(7) $R1_i = L1_j \Rightarrow R1_{i+1} = LR2(1) \vee R2_{k+1} = LR2(1)$
   where $k = index(R2, time(R1_i))$

Now we consider that a *date* is associated to each elements of a sequence and *time* gives the date associated to the ith element of a sequence, while *index* gives the rank of the most recent element of a sequence at a certain date. The following chapter will precise this.

3 Temporal structures

For time-sensitive problems, not all the input data exist when the system starts but most of them are produced during the run-time at a rate different from the system internal computations. The data production and the computations of the system have asynchronous occurrences.

A full characterization of the input data must include informations about the dates when the data are available (birth date). The dates are modeled by a set D totally ordered by $\leq_D$. D has a minimum element START that is the *date* when the system starts.

We denote *seq E* the set of the finite sequences over E, generally their domain is $\mathcal{N}^+$ but we have found convenient to extend it with 0, the value of the sequences at 0 being $\perp \notin E$.

A *chronology* is a strict ascending sequence of dates, the type of the chronologies is denoted CHR, the value of every temporal sequence at 0 is START.

example: ch1 =[START,1515,1648,1789,1848,1945,1987]

A temporal sequence of type E denoted *t_seq E* is a sequence of the cartesian product $E \times D$ such that the sequence of the second projections forms a chronology. The value of every temporal sequence at 0 is $(\perp, \text{START})$. The two projection functions are *val* and *time*.
   example: ts1=$[(\perp, START), (37.2, 1145), (38.4, 12.50), (39.6, 1407)]$
   $val(ts1(2)) = 38.4$
   $time(ts1(1)) = 1145$
   $ts1(3) = (39.6, 1407)$
We define some functions on the temporal sequences which can be classified into several groups:

- The first group is designed to access the elements of the temporal sequences.

  1 *index* : $t\_seqE, D \mapsto \mathcal{N}$: $index(ts, d)$ is the index of the most recent element of *ts* at the date d
    : $index(ts, d) = sup\{i | time(ts(i)) \leq d\}$

  2. *item_at* : $t\_seqE, D \mapsto E \times D$: $item\_at(ts, d) = ts(index(ts, d))$

     example: $index(ts1, 1149) = 1$
     $item\_at(ts1, 1200) = (37.2, 1145)$

     As *item_at* refers to an item without referencing it with an index it is sometimes convenient to have the functions *next* and *pred* to refer to the next and previous element defined by *item_at* if they exist.

  3. *next* : $t\_seqE \times D \mapsto E \times D$:
     $next(ts, d) = item(ts, index(ts, d) + 1)$ if $index(ts, d) + 1 \in dom\ ts$

  4. *pred* : $t\_seqE, D \mapsto E \times D$:
     $pred(ts, d) = item(ts, index(ts, d) - 1)$
     if $index(ts, d) - 1 \in dom\ ts$
     And for the corresponding dates :

  5. *t_pred* : $t\_seqE, D \mapsto D$:
     $t\_pred(ts, d) = time(pred(ts, d))$

6. $t\_next : t\_seqE, D \mapsto D$:
$t\_next(ts, d) = time(next(ts, d))$

- The second group operates on the temporal sequences.

  1. $chrono : t\_seqE \mapsto CHR$
  is defined using the functional operator map of ML : $chrono = map\ time$

  2. $values : t\_seqE \mapsto seqE$:
  $values = map\ val$
  Operators are be invented in order to define temporal sequences from other temporal sequences, the most frequently used is $\_[\_,\_]$ an overloaded operator which defines a temporal sequence as a sub-sequence of contiguous elements an other temporal sequence. The bounds of the interval are indices or dates possibly mixed.

  3. $\_[\_,\_] : t\_seqE, N, N \mapsto t\_seqE$:
  $ts[i, j]$ is the empty sequence if $j<i$ and $\forall k\ 1 \le k \le j - i + 1\ ts[i, j](k) = ts(i + k - 1)$

  4. $\_[\_,\_] : t\_seqE, D, D \mapsto t\_seqE$:
  $ts[d1, d2] = ts[i, j]$ where $i=$if $time(ts(index(ts, d1))) = d1$
  then $index(ts, d1)$ else $index(ts, d1) + 1$ and
  $j = index(ts, d2)$

  5. $\_[\_,\_] : t\_seqE, N, D \mapsto t\_seqE$:
  $ts[i, d2] = ts[i, j]$ where $j = index(ts, d2)$

  6. $\_[\_,\_] : t\_seqE, D, N \mapsto t\_seqE$:
  $ts[d1, j] = ts[i, j]$ where
  $i = $ if $time(ts(index(ts, d1))) = d1$ then $index(ts, d1)$ else $index(ts, d1) + 1$

Similar operators are defined for exclusive right or/and left bound of the intervals.

- An other group of operators is designed to extract some parts of a temporal sequence or to partition a temporal sequence into a sequence of temporal sequences.

In the case of the first ones the extracted parts do not necessarily form a contiguous sub-sequence then, the target domain is more general than the temporal sequences: it is the domain of the partial functions from $N \overset{\sim}{\mapsto} (E \times D)$ such that the second projections form a chronology.

The criteria for the extraction are properties on the values or on the dates of the temporal sequences. Our interest, now, is to find the smaller set of constructs to define the criteria. We exhibit two of them:

1. $match\_date : t\_seqE, CHR \mapsto (N \overset{\sim}{\mapsto} (E \times D))$

$\forall i \in dom\ match\_date(ts, ch) time(ts(i)) = ch(i)$ and
$match\_date(ts, ch)(i) = ts(i)$

2. $match\_while : t\_seqE, CHRI \mapsto (N \overset{\sim}{\mapsto} (E \times D))$

$\forall i \in dom\ match\_while(ts, chri) \exists k \in dom\ chri$ and $first(chri(k)) \le time(ts(i)) \le snd(chri(k + 1))$

The first operator extracts the elements whose dates match the chronology. The second operator extracts the elements of ts whose dates are within the intervals of chri.

From the results of $match\_date$ and $match\_while$ we get a temporal sequence as a result of the $pack$ function.

3. $pack : (N \overset{\sim}{\mapsto} (E \times D)) \mapsto t\_seq\ E$ provided that the sequence of the second projections is a chronology.

These operators are powerful if we add to the language tools to define $chronologies$ and $chrono\_intervals$. We just investigate that domain and we think that it would be inspiring to refer to the Icon language [12]. At the present time, we do not need all the results in order to demonstrate the interest of the temporal structures in the design of programs.

4 The design phases

4.1 The specification step

Our method consists of:

- describing the different the structure of the system interface that is giving a type to the system inputs and outputs.
- defining the temporal relations which binds the sequences of results to the input data.
- defining the data values and their relations.

A similar method was studied for sequential programming in [9].

We follow such a method and we plane to design a specification environment which could help to apply it. Nevertheless, the specification editor should just propose choices and accept partial definitions as long as the specification phase is not terminated.

4.2 Transformations into more executable statements

Generally, it is not possible to transform directly our specification into a program but it can, incrementally, be transformed into an equivalent one. The transformation uses formal calculus on expressions, transformation rules and a language which describes the strategy.

One of our goal when transforming a statement is to get a recursive one which better fits to generate efficient code. The two kinds of references to the temporal sequences either by indices or by dates will give rise to two kinds of recursions.

5 Specification of an example

The optimization of the arm moves of a disc unit:

The previous tools have been used to specify different problems such as the functions of a complicated digital wrist-watch in a rather concise way. In order to illustrate our method and the tools we have preferred a rather simpler problem. This example was first specified by Abrial [2].

The goal of the system we have to design is the optimization of the disc moves when serving a sequence of access queries to the tracks. The queries may arrive more frequently than the rate of the disc end-of-services and then, the system may choose the next query to serve which needs the shortest displacement depending on the direction of the previous disc move. The problem was simplified in order to stress the essential topics. For instance, we consider that the results are a sequence of track numbers and we do not specify that different queries which compete for the same track are to be treated according to the first arrived first served order.

5.1 Specifying the structure of the system interface

At first glance, the input data consists of the queries and the results are the sequence of the ranks of the selected queries from the input stream. The aim of the specification is to define the results from the input data or to state the relation which binds them.

We notice that the selections depend on the queries arrived when the selection is done. It is reasonable to state that the selections are to be done as soon as possible and not before the completion of the previous selected query. Therefore, one must be informed of the different completions.

In the specification we represent the queries by a temporal sequence of track numbers queries together with the dates of their issue.

The signals sent by the disc drive on each completion is represented by the *chronology ready*.

72

The result selections could be a sequence of ranks of selected queries but after a first attempt we remark that each selection depends on the dates of the preceding selection.

Then, we can formally define the data structures of the interface:

queries   : *input t_seq* TRACK
ready   : *input* CHR % sequence of soonest dates when
                  the driver is ready
selections: *output t_seq(dom queries)*
                  dom gives the domain of a function

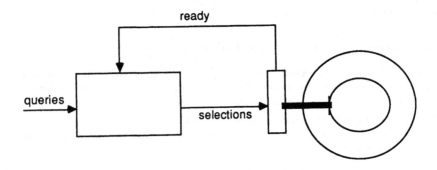

5.2   Specifying the chronology before the values

The method consists of defining the results that is the temporal sequence selections ; after some attempts we remark that the dates of the elements are relatively easy to specify : they coincide with the dates of the elements of ready when the queries issued on the dates $ready(i)$ are not all served. This could be stated : at the date of the ith ready signal the number of queries issued is greater than i, the number of selections done; otherwise they are defined by the date of the next query after the date $ready(i)$.

This could be formally stated :

$\rightarrow$ $time(selections(i)) =$
if $card(queries[1, ready(i)]) \leq i$ **then** $time(next(queries, ready(i)))$ **else** $ready(i)$

$queries[1, ready(i)]$ is the sub-sequence of queries limited on the right by the item whose date is the latest before $ready(i)$. And $card$ is the notation for the function which gives the size of a set.

$time(next(queries, ready(i)))$ is, word for word, the translation of the corresponding informal specification.

5.3   Specifying the values and their relations

Each value is selected from a set extracted from the values of *queries*. Let us introduce the sequence of the sets $e(i)$ of the indices of *queries* which have not yet been selected on $time(selections(i))$.

$\rightarrow$ $val(selections(i)) \in e(i)$

$e(i)$ is the set of the indices *queries* emitted before or on $time((selections(i))$ except the indices which belong to the values of the i-1 first selections, all this could be stated:

$$e(i) = set([1, index(queries, time(selections(i)))]) - set(values(selections[1, i - 1]))$$

where *set* is the function which transforms an interval into the set of its values.

From the definition of $time(selections(i))$ one can prove that $e(i)$ is not empty.

Some complementary properties can be stated about $val(selections(i))$:

Let us first introduce two sequences : s_dir whose items give the privileged directions of the disc moves, and *pos* whose items give the previous position of the disc arm.
The definition of *pos* is obvious :

$pos(1) = initial\_arm\_pos$

$\forall i \in domselections - \{1\}$. $pos(i) = item(queries, selections(i - 1))$

In order to define s_dir, we need to introduce two sequences of sets built from e : e_up and e_down .
$e\_up(i)$ is the set of the indices of *queries* in $e(i)$ whose corresponding item values are greater than $pos(i)$.

$e\_down(i)$ is defined in a similar way.

$e\_up(i) = \{x | x \in e(i) \text{ and } val(queries(x)) \geq pos(i)\}$

$e\_down(i) = \{x | x \in e(i) \text{ and } val(queries(x)) \leq pos(i)\}$

The first direction of the disc move is $initial\_dir$ and the direction does not change as long as there are requests for tracks in front of the actual position according to the disc move otherwise the direction is reversed. This specification can be formally stated:

$s\_dir(i) =$
if $i - 1$ **then** $initial\_dir$ **else**
if $s\_dir(i - 1) = up$ **and**
$e\_up(i) \neq \{\}$ **or**
$s\_dir(i - 1) = down$ **and** $e\_down(i) = \{\}$
then up **else** $down$

where s_dir : seq dir

type $dir = \{up, down\}$

We have sufficient definitions to state more properties of $val(selections(i))$:

Let $val(selections(i)) = k$ then :

k verifies:

$s\_dir(i) = up$ and $k \in e\_up(i)$ and $(\forall l \in e\_up(i) l \neq k \Rightarrow val(queries(k)) \leq val(queries(l)))$

or

$s\_dir(i) = down$ and $k \in e\_down(i)$ and
$(\forall l \in e\_down(i) l \neq kval(queries(k)) \neq val(queries(l))$

The whole specification is gathered in the fig. 1 .

queries : **input** *t_seq* TRACK
ready : **input** CHR
selections : **output** *t_seq(dom queries)*
time(selections(i)) =
    if $size(queries[1, ready(i)]) \leq i$ **then** $time(next(queries, ready(i)))$
val(selections(i) = k)
    $k \in e(i)$
    $e(i) =$
    $set([1, index(queries, time(selections(i)))]) - set(values(selections[1, i - 1]))$
    $k : s\_dir = up \Rightarrow k = min(e\_up(i))$
        and
        $s\_dir = down \Rightarrow k = max(e\_down(i))$
    pos : *seq* TRACK
    $pos : pos(1) = initial\_arm\_pos$
      $\forall i \in dom \ \ selections - \{1\} \ . \ pos(i) = item(queries, selections(i - 1))$
    e_up : $seq \ \wp \ \mathcal{N}^+$
    e_down : $seq \ \wp \ \mathcal{N}^+$
    $e\_up(i) = \{x | x \in e(i) \ \textbf{and} \ val(queries(x)) \geq pos(i)\}$
    $e\_down(i) = \{x | x \in e(i) \ \textbf{and} \ val(queries(x)) \leq pos(i)\}$
    type *dir* $= \{up, down \}$
    $s\_dir(i) =$ **if** $i = 1$ **then** *initial_dir* **else**
      if $(s\_dir(i - 1) = up$ **and** $e\_up(i) \neq \{\})$ **or**
        $(s\_dir(i - 1) = down$ **and** $e\_down(i) = \{\})$ **then** *up* **else** *down*

note : $\wp \ \mathcal{N}^+$ is the set of the subsets of $\mathcal{N}^+$

-Figure 1-

6 Fairness and related properties specification

For parallel programs we must add to the functional properties some fairness or promptness properties which state that the requests to a shared resource shall not be delayed for ever. They usually are stated by formulae in temporal logic which specify rules about the execution of procedures.

In our context we just need to state some temporal relations between the dates of the elements of the input data and the corresponding results:

$$time(selections(i)) - time(item(queries, selections(i))) \leq some\_max\_time$$

This statement mean a promptness condition, and for a restrictive fairness condition one could state that the ith query occurs in the sequence selections at a rank close to i.
That is : $i \leq selections(i) + Max$

The statements of fairness or justice would need more complicated expressions and it is not the main point we address in the paper.

The first kind of condition seems more natural and should be automatically added to any specification by the specification editor.

One important problem during the derivation phase is the elimination of the explicit time expressions and the second form is a step in this transformation process.

7 Analysis and transformations

The values of the sequence selections are defined by a conjunction of properties they must satisfy, one can ask if there exists a temporal sequence which verifies these properties and if there could be a solution for the specification.

We do not address these problems in this paper and we focus on the types of transformation to do in order to derive a program.

We have chosen the ADA programming language as our target language rather than a real-time oriented language which could have been looked too easy and have missed the goal of demonstrating the interest of the specification.

An other issue could have been to translate the specification into a network of communicating processes to define the properties of the exchanged data between the processes as in [16]. One advantage is that software tools are available to edit and transform the specifications in order to get the most loosely coupled network.

7.1 About the transformations

The programming language has no explicit data type representing the time. The procedures start or termination, the arrival of external signals or data, the execution of the entry calls and so on are implicit time marks. One of our tasks is to translate the explicit statements of the time into some of the preceding constructs.

The results in the specification are often defined by temporal sequences, their chronologies define the right moments when the corresponding values must be computed.

In other words, the translation of the chronology is concerned with the control part of the program, especially, the synchronisation of the concurrent activities.

7.2 Generation of the control structure of the program

For our problem, if we design our program as a collection of communicating tasks, the main task could be an infinite loop containing an accept instruction whose entry is to be called by a "timing" task which emits the entry calls according to the defined chronology of the sequence selections.

A question, now, raises up: how does the timing task "computes" the dates when it emits the entry call?

The dates depend on a condition and are defined by external events: the ready signals and the arrival of the queries. As noticed when building the specification, the chronology, sometimes, coincide with the *ready* signals and, when not, is delayed from the ready signal up to the next query. A possible frame for the timing task is an infinite loop with an accept for the ready signals and an other accept for the next-coming query under an if statement in the do part of the accept statement.

This task requires the cooperation of the task which accepts the queries. This task must emit an entry call to the timing task to signal each query arrival but must not be blocked if the timing task is not waiting. On this purpose we use a conditional entry call, this rather complicated implementation is due to ADA in which it is not possible to send a signal (an entry call) to wake-up more than one waiting task.

A squeleton of the different tasks is given in fig. 2.

7.3 Generation of the data processing part

The derivation of the data processing part of the program looks more classical and uses techniques like folding and unfolding [6] but some expressions depends on the time and this increase the difficulty. Most of the data in the specification are represented by sequences and will, generally be translated by variables.

A typical expression to transform in which it time occurs is :

$$e(i) = set([1, index(queries, time(selections(i)))] - set(values(selections[1, i - 1])))$$

The issue is to derive an algorithm to compute $e(i)$.

7.3.1 First solution : a direct translation

There exists a direct but unrealistic translation of $e(i)$ which needs to record all the queries arrived. The management of the structure which represents $e(i)$ needs the cooperation of two tasks: the one which accepts and records the queries and the one in which the selections occurs. We do not develop this solution.

7.3.2 Second solution

We aim to obtain an inductive definition of $e(i)$ on i.

One way to increase efficiency is to transform $e(i)$ into a statement depending on $e(i - 1)$. The computation of $e(i)$ will start from the value of $e(i - 1)$.

(a) **step1.** Unfolding.

$$e(i - 1) = set([1, index(queries, time(selections(i - 1)))] - set(values(selections[1, i - 2])))$$

(b) **step2.** Formal calculus on the intervals in order to exhibit the definition of $e(i-1)$ in $e(i)$.
Property 1.(on the intervals) $\forall c \in [a,b][a,b] = [a,c]+]c,b]$ where $+$ is the concatenation of intervals.

If we apply the property to $[1, index(queries, time(selections(i)))]$ we get :
$[1, index(queries, time(selections(i)))] =$
$[1, index(queries, time(selections(i-1)))] +]index(queries, time(selections(i-1)), index(queries, time(s$

and to the interval $[1, i-1]$ we get :
$[1, i-1] = [1, i-2]+]i-2, i-1].$

Property 2.(on set and some kind of intervals).

$set([I1]+]I2]) = set([I1]) \cup set(]I2])$ where $I1$ and $I2$ denotes pairs of bounds, the exclusive upper bound of $I1$ equals the inclusive lower bound of $I2$.

Then, we obtain:

$e(i) = ([1, index(queries, time(selections(i-1)))]) \cup$

$set(]index(queries, time(selections(i-1)), index(queries, time(selections(i)))]$

- $set(values(selections[1, i-2]))$

- $set(values(selections]i-2, i-1])$

We fold and get $e(i-1)$.

The sub-sequence of selections $selections]i-2, i-1]$ contains the single element $selections(i-1)$ then:
$values(selections]i-2, i-1]) = values(selections[i-1, i-1]) = val(selections(i-1))$:
Thus $e(i) = e(i-1) \cup na(i) - val(selections(i-1))$
where $na(i) = set(]index(queries, time(selections(i-1))), index(queries, time(selections(i)))])$

(c) **step3** Transformation of $na(i)$.
Here we fail applying the strategy used step 2. because $na(i) \cap na(i-1)$ is empty.
We, then try to find a recursion on the dates.
Property 3. (construction of an interval by temporal references)
$[index(ts, d1), index(ts, d2)] = \bigoplus_{t \in chrono(ts)[d1,d2]} index(ts, t)$

($\bigoplus$ is a polyadic operation which builds an interval from the values of the arguments which are consecutive integers)
Property 4.
$set(\bigoplus_{t \in chrono(ts)[d1,d2]} index(ts, t)) = \bigcup_{t \in chrono(ts)[d1,d2]} index(ts, t)$

And we apply the two rules to $na(i)$ we get :

$$na(i) = \bigcup_{t \in chrono(queries)]time(selections(i-1)),time(selections(i))]} index(queries, t)$$

(d) **step4.** Translation into an ADA program.

The definition of $na(i)$ can be obviously translated by some iterative control statement and an appropriate initialization. Let NA be the data structure which represents $na(i)$, NA is updated by the addition of a new query. This can be translated by the following piece of ADA code:

```
loop
        accept query(q) do NA.ADD(q) ; end query;
    end loop;
```

The structure NA is represented by a task in order to protected it from simultaneous accesses.

On $time(selections(i))$ the value of the structure is $na(i)$ and on $time(selections(i-1))$ NA must be reset to empty, the two operations can be combined into a single one TAKE which first copies the value and then reset the structure this is translated by :

```
            ... accept START.SELECTION do
NA.TAKE(vna); ...
```

It is worth noticing that NA is updated in different tasks of the program depending on their implicit knowledge of the time.

Similar reasonings could give the translation of $e(i)$ but a deeper study of the representation would lead to the conclusion that $e(i)$ needs not be represented explicitly. $e\_up(i)$ and $e\_down(i)$ are sufficient to represent $e(i)$ and one can choose a unique structure *struct* to represent them.

On $time(selections(i)$, this structure is increased by the value of $na(i)$ and decreased by the value $val(selections(i-1))$. This is translated by :

```
            ...accept START.SELECTION do
                    ... ADD(struct,vna);
                    DELETE(struct,selected);...
```

struct is a data structure local to the task which performs the selection.

These different constructs gathered which the structure of the ADA program given [BFig. 2 produce the following piece of ADA program:

```
task body store_requests is
begin
    loop
        accept query(q) do
            select new_query else delay 0.01*SECONDES;
            NA.ADD(q);
        end query;
    end loop;
```

end store_requests;

task body choice **is**
selection : TRACK := initial_arm_pos;
struct := empty;
vna: *type of the data exchanged with the task* NA.
begin
     loop
          accept START.SELECTION **do**
              NA.TAKE(vna);
              ADD(struct,vna);
              selection
              disc.put(selection);
              DELETE(struct, selection);
          end START.SELECTION;
     end loop;
end choice;

-figure 3-

7.3.3   Third solution

Find an inductive definition on the dates.

(a) **step1.** Transform the first sub-expression of the right hand side of $e(i)$.

There is an other way to translate $e(i)$ which avoids to introduce $na(i)$ and produces, at first appearance, a more efficient algorithm. We apply the properties 3 and 4 on the first sub-expression of the right hand side of $e(i)$ and we obtain:

$$e(i) = \bigcup_{t \in chrono(queries)[start,time(selections(i))]} index(queries, t) - set(values(selections[1, i - 1])))$$

The form of the sub-expression naturally induces the idea.

(b) **step2.** Transformation of the second sub-expression.

We apply the properties 1 and 2 and we get :

$$e(i) = \bigcup_{t \in chrono(queries)[start,time(selections(i))]} index(queries, t) - \bigcup_{j \in [1,i-1]} val(selections(j))$$

(c) **step3.** Getting a unique type of induction.

In the first sub-expression we have an induction on the dates and in the second an induction on integers we apply the definition of item_at to introduce the time and the property 3 to transform the second sub-expression and we get :

$$e(i) = \bigcup_{t \in chrono(queries)[start, time(selections(i))]} index(queries, t)$$
$$- \bigcup_{t \in chrono(selections)[time(selections(1)), time(selections(i-1))])]} val(item\_at(selections, t))$$

(d) **step4.** Getting a unique chronology.

We have the same type of induction for the two sub-expressions but different chronologies, in order to have a constructive expression we need to have a unique chronology this can be obtained by merging $chrono(queries)$ and $chrono(selections)$ on the largest of the intervals.

(e) **step5.** Getting an equivalent expression on the unique chronology.

We apply the property of commutativity of the adjunction and deletion operations on a set provided that the deletions are not applied to the empty set.

And we sort the atoms of the preceding expression on the dates of the new chronology.

We can not write the new formula but we could define the positions of the atoms and the associated operation according to the associated dates in the preceding formula.

We prefer to define $e(i)$ as the last element of a temporal sequence denoted $inter$ which, intuitively, is the sequence of the partial evaluations from left to right of the sorted formula.

$e(i) = item\_at(inter, time(selections(i)))$
$chrono(inter) = (chrono(queries) \cup chrono(selections))[start, time(selections(i))]$
$item\_at(inter, start) = \{\}$
$item\_at(inter, t) =$
if $t \in chrono(queries)$ **then** $item\_at(inter, t\_pred(inter, t)) \cup index(queries, t)$
if $t \in chrono(selections)$ **then**
$\qquad item\_at(inter, t\_pred(inter, t)) - val(item\_at(selections, t\_pred(inter, t)))$
if $t \in chrono(queries) \cap chrono(selections)$ **then**
$\qquad item\_at(inter, t\_pred(inter, t)) \cup index(queries, t) - val(item\_at(selections, t\_pred(inter, t)))$

This kind of statement is very close to a program and a transformation rule can be stated to directly generate a program.

At first glance, the resulting program seems more efficient than the one developed from the second solution but the data structure which represents $e(i)$ is more often accessed and then, a more important overhead follows and we notice that a copy of the value of $e(i)$ is needed to free the accesses from the other processes during the selection. In order to decide what is the best solution we need a difficult analysis of the complexity and this is out of the range of the paper.

A resulting part of program derived with the same arguments as above is listed :

```
task body store_requests is
task body store_requests is
begin
      loop
            accept query(q) do
```

```
          select new_query else delay 0.01*SECONDES;
          STRUCT.ADD(q);
      end query;
  end loop;
end store_requests;
task body choice is
selection : TRACK := initial_arm_pos;
local_struct : same type as the data structure in STRUCT.
begin
  loop
      accept START.SELECTION ;
      STRUCT.READ(local_struct);
      selection
      disc.put(selection);
      STRUCT.DELETE(selected)
  end loop;
```

-figure 4-

The shared data structure STRUCT representing $e(i)$ is implemented by a task and we have chosen to make a local copy of the value in the task choice when we access it to compute the selected query that avoids to block other accesses during the selection.

8   Related works

We first attempted to introduce explicit information on the time values in the specification of temporal problems in [10], Caspi and Halwachs [7] propose a model for the time in which they establish relations between the time values of the model and event counters.

The need to introduce time properties in the proof of parallel programs induceda great deal of works on the temporal logics [18]. Beyond the proof, some works start addressing the automatic generation of the synchronization of CSP programs from specifications stated by temporal logic formulae.

Other approaches in the specification field consist of specifying the functional part of the system using the abstract data types style and then introducing time constraints for the execution of the procedures which implements the functions. Kröger [18] expresses such time constraints with an extension of the temporal logic and Barbacci and Wing[4] uses RTL [15] to add timing behaviors to the interface specifications in Larch. Such approaches are a mixture of static and dynamic specifications and differ in that way from our approach.

New programming languages which integrate models of the time have been developed: LUSTRE [8] where the time is modeled by clocks. We are looking for a translation of our time expressions into LUSTRE programs. In ESTEREL [5], an other real-time language the time is considered as multi-paced, punctuated by external events and transmitted by signals, the translation of our specifications seems rather easy in ESTEREL and we have tried it successfully about the previous example. The work of J.Hooman [14] has been brought to my attention by an anonymous referee and, though it does not address program synthesis but proof, he uses the same idea of time stamps to define the denotations. And, not surprisingly, the assertion language has strong similarities with our specification language.

9   Summary

In order to specify the class of the time sensitive problems we feel that informations on the time are to be recorded. The model for the time shall be natural and the time specifications is an attribute of the data. A specification text must be short in order to represent the main features of the system it is why high order expressions are required.

An editor for the specification should implement a method by suggesting the right questions. The resulting text is a basis for derivations which use classical techniques adapted to the temporal constructs.

Acknowledgement.

I greatly benefited the advices of J.P. Finance who helped me structuring this paper and highlighting the main points. I am grateful to P. Lescanne for its advices to improve the draft of this paper. Many ideas where inspired by the fruitful working sessions in the frame of COMETE, a project supported by the C^3 CNRS program.

10 References

[1]   M. Abadi and Z. Manna. "A timely resolution."
       In *Proceedings of the Symposium on Logic in Computer Science, 1986.*

[2]   J.R. Abrial and S.A. Schuman. "Non-deterministic system specification."
       In *Proceedings of the int. conf.on semantics of concurrent computation, Evian, July, 1979.*

[3]   E.A. Ashcroft and W.W. Wadge. "LUCID, the data flow programming language."
       Academic Press, 1985.

[4]   M. R. Barbacci and J. M. Wing.
       "Specifying functional and timing behavior for real-time applications."
       In *Proceedings of the Parallel Architecture and Language Europe, LNCS 258-259, 1987.*

[5]   G. Berry and L. Cosserat.
       "The synchronous programming language ESTEREL and its mathematical semantics."
       In *Proceedings of the Seminar on Concurrency, Springer–Verlag LNCS 197, 1985.*

[6]   R.M. Burstall and J. Darlington.
       A transformation system for developing recursive programs.
       ACM Journal 24 (1), 1977.

[7][B P. Caspi and N. Halbwachs.
       A functional model for describing and reasoning about time behavior of computing systems.
       Acta Informatica 22, 595-627, 1986.

[8]   P. Caspi, D. Pilaud, N. Halbwachs and J. Plaice.
       LUSTRE: A declarative language for programming synchronous systems.
       In *Proceedings of the 14th ACM Symposium on Principles of Programming Languages,* pages 178-188. ACM January, 1987.

[9]   A. Ducrin.
       Programmation.
       Bordas, Paris, 1984.

[10]   J.P. Finance and J. Jaray.
       Towards a methodology to specify and construct concurrent programs.
       CRIN Report 80-P-09, 1980.

[11]   A. Gram.
       Raisonner pour programmer.
       Dunod, Paris, 1986.

[12] R. E. Griswold and M. T. Griswold.
      The Icon programming language.
      Prentice-Hall, Inc., Englewoods Cliffs, New Jersey, 1983.

[13] D. Harel.
      STATECHARTS: A visual formalism for complex systems.
      SCP 8(3) , June, 1987.

[14] J. Hooman.
      A compositional proof theory for real-time distributed message passing.
      In *Proceedings of the Parallel Architecture and Language Europe*
      LNCS 259, 1987.

[15] F. Jahanian and A.K. Mok.
      Safety analysis of timing properties in real-time systems.
      IEEE Transactions on Software Engineering 12(9) pages 890-904, September, 1986.

[16] C.B. Jones.
      Systematic program development using VDM.
      Prentice-Hall. C.A.R. Hoare series. 1984.

[17] J. Julliand, M. Marmonnier and G.R. Perrin.
      La conception des programmes paralleles dans le projet COMETE.
      Rapport CRIN, 1986.

[18] F. Kröger.
      Abstract Modules.
      TUM-I8601 Technische Universitaet Muenchen, January, 1986.

[19] L. Lamport.
      What good is temporal logic?
      Information Processing 83.
      R.E. Masson (ed.) Elsevier Science Publishers, North Holland, 1983

[20] Z. Manna and R. Waldinger.
      A deductive approach to program synthesis.
      ACM Transactions on Programming Languages and Systems 6(1), 1984.

[21] R. Milner.
      A proposal for standard ML.
      In *Conference record of the 1984 ACM conference on Lisp and Functional Programming*
      Austin, Texas,August, 1984.

[22] P. L. Wolper.
      Temporal logic can be more expressive.
      In *Proceedings of the 22nd Symposium on Foundations of Computer Science*, 1981.

[23] P. L. Wolper.
      Synthesis of communicating processes from temporal logic specifications.
      Technical report STAN-CS-82-925 Stanford University August, 1982.

[24] Reference Manual for the Ada Programming Language (ANSI/MIL-STD 1815 A)
      US government, Ada Joint Program Office. January, 1983.

Applications of Temporal Logic to the Specification of Real Time Systems

Amir Pnueli and Eyal Harel

Department of Computer Science

The Weizmann Institute of Science

Rehovot, Israel

Extended Abstract

1   Introduction

This paper will present a short and partial account of some of the attempts to use temporal logic, and its associated verification system, to deal with the expression and validation of real time systems.

Traditionally, temporal logic, and in particular, its application to the specification and analysis of reactive and concurrent systems, have been considered appropriate for the *qualitative* (non-quantitative) treatment of time. This can be seen by some of the abstractions that are inherent in the temporal methodology. To mention some of them, the modeling of concurrency by interleaving, the concept of *eventuality*, which guarantees an eventual occurrence of an event, but provides no bound on how soon; and the notion of *fairness* which requires that frequent attention be directed to certain components of the system, but places no bound on the frequency. All these, represent conscious efforts to deal with essentially quantitative phenomena in a qualitative way.

The benefits of this approach are obvious. The analysis and reasoning that have to be exercised are greatly simplified, by uniformly ignoring all time measures, and enable the consideration of more complex systems. Also, some of the *positive* results obtained by this approach are very robust, since they apply to a very wide family of implementations, with greatly varying ratios of speeds between the different components. For example, the conclusions drawn from a qualitative analysis of a concurrent program, are often equally valid for both a system that implements concurrency by multi-processing, allocating a separate processor to each process, as well as for a system that implements concurrency by multi-programming, allocating a task to each process, and alternately activating the tasks according to some fair schedule.

However, there are obviously many systems and applications, specifically in the area of reactive systems, for which purely qualitative specification and analysis are inadequate. Some of the clearer cases are characterized by a requirement, such as: "every p should be followed by a q, within no more than 2 seconds", which mentions real time explicitly. More subtle cases contain a requirement, such as: "no two processes may attempt to write on the channel α at the same time. This requirement does not explicitly refer to real time. However, the reason that this requirement is satisfied by a considered implementation, and therefore the proof of its satisfaction, may rely on some of the processes explicitly delaying their execution to wait for the channel to become empty.

For both of these cases, we require a logic that has the capabilities of specifying and verifying reactive systems, similarly to temporal logic, as well as the ability to express and reason about real time.

In this paper, we consider two possible real time extensions of temporal logic. The first, is the addition of a global clock as an explicit variable to which the specification may refer. The second approach, to which we refer as Quantized Temporal Logic (QTL), is more radical, and involves the introduction of qualified temporal operators, such as stating that

p will hold continuously for the next 5 seconds

or

p will occur within the next 5 seconds

This approach has been used in [RK83] and [DS84]. Both approaches call for a more specific computational model, imposing much stricter constraints than are usually included in the free interleaving model used for the qualitative version of temporal logic. Verifying a timing statement about a program requires special proof techniques, such as associating a local timer with each element that has a delay associated with it. These techniques will be illustrated on several examples. Of particular interest are the styles of reasoning induced by these extensions to the logic and their application. One of the questions, we would like to examine closely, is whether the partition of properties into safety and liveness, which is useful in the non timed methodology, still retains its meaning. The question has to be asked, since it is possible to claim that, by adding time bounds to all eventualities (which are the typical liveness property), we are turning them into safety property. Thus the statement "p will eventually happen", when we add the time bound of 5 on its satisfaction, may be expressible by the invariance property (which is a typical case of safety)

Always, when the time is beyond 5, p has already happened

In addition, we will consider several alternatives for the specification of real time systems. the main alternatives to be considered are based on state transition systems, and use the Statechart notation. We will view the use of such formalisms both as acceptors and as generators, and compare their expressive power and ease of use to that of temporal logic.

We apologize that, this being an extended abstract, but already containing some technical material, it is in a very preliminary shape, essentially intended to give a broad overview of the material we intend to discuss in the conference. We hope to correct many of the technical deficiencies in the fuller version of this paper. In particular, our list of references is almost non-existent. We will correct this omission in the full version.

2 Models

2.1 Overview

There are essentially two basic models that have been proposed for the timed temporal analysis of reactive systems.

The first model we will consider is that of *synchronous systems* in which every process performs one transition, i.e., one atomic action, at each step. This model corresponds to the case that the system possesses a global clock which drives all the individual components. In that case we usually assume that each step takes uniformly the same length of time, and hence prefer to measure time in *steps*, rather than in real clock units. This model is very appropriate for the analysis of systolic systems. It has also been successfully used for the analysis and verification of communication protocols (see [DS84]).

This model is a special case of the more general model of *maximal parallelism*, which allows many processes to perform overlapping actions, but relaxes the requirement that the initiation and termination of the parallel actions coincide.

The second model we will consider is the *interleaving* model. In this model, at each step only a single transition, chosen out of one of the processes, is executed. This is the basic model on which the non real time temporal logic is based, and it enjoys the advantage that the number of possibilities that have to be checked for each step is much smaller than the general maximal parallelism case. To make the interleaving model realistic, we have to ensure that the choice of the process which executes in each step does not consistently neglect one of the processes. In the qualitative case this is guaranteed by special fairness requirements. Here, in the quantitative case, the notion of the neglect of an enabled process can be precisely quantified. We therefore replace fairness by the much more natural requirement demanding that no process can be enabled for more than a maximal period of time (usually determined by the enabled transition) without performing (actually completing) a transition.

It is very important to realize that the model chosen to represent and then analyze a system is not necessarily uniquely determined by the actual architecture on which the system is based. The two basic requirements from a chosen model are:

1. That it can faithfully represent the relevant phenomena manifested in the actual architecture.

2. That it leads to a convenient formalization and reasoning about the relevant properties we wish to establish.

Thus, any formalization and analysis of a given system, necessarily deals with some abstraction or model of the studied system. The appropriate abstraction is determined by the type of questions we wish to ask about the system, and those features of the system which are relevant for answering these questions with an acceptable degree of accuracy. There is an obvious tradeoff between accuracy and simplicity, and the optimal choice of a model is always that of the simplest model which yields tolerable accuracy.

A typical example of this "working theory" approach to modeling, is the representation of parallelism, in the untimed case, by interleaving. While everybody admits that "this is not how things really work", the simplicity of the ensuing analysis, and the accuracy of the non-quantitative results that are obtained by this approach, make this choice of a model very attractive.

2.2 Extending The Applicability of the Synchronous Model

Before we present the formal details of the two models, we would like to illustrate how each of the models considered, can actually model a wider family of systems than originally contemplated. As already discussed above, the synchronous model can be used even for systems that are not implemented on fully synchronous architectures.

Consider, for example, a communication protocol that runs on a distributed system, with some channels interconnecting the processors. the interesting case is when the travel time of messages across the channels is not negligible. For such a distributed system, it is rarely this case that a global clock, synchronizing the operations of the separate processors, actually exists.

However, since the essential synchronization in such a system, is mainly between each processor and the channels incident on it, we will show that by relaxing the tight coupling between the process and its incident channels , we also loosen up the coupling between the different processes. We will also illustrate, on an example, a standard modeling technique which is very useful for explicitly representing the progress of an operation that takes many steps, such as the traversal of a channel by a message packet.

2.2.1 Example

Consider the program below, consisting of two processes P_1 and P_2, communicating by a buffered channel α.

$$
\begin{array}{ll}
l_0: & \alpha \Leftarrow x \\
l_1: & x := x+1 \\
l_2: & x := x+1 \\
l_3: & x := x+1 \\
l_4: &
\end{array}
\qquad\qquad
\begin{array}{ll}
m_0: & \alpha \Rightarrow y \\
m_1: &
\end{array}
$$

$$-P_1- \qquad\qquad\qquad\qquad -P_2-$$

Process P_1 sends at l_0 a message on channel α, which is the current value of x. Let us denote this value by a. Then P_1 proceeds to increment x at statements $l_1, l_2,$ and l_3. Meanwhile, P_2 is waiting at m_0 for the message to arrive. Under the assumption that it takes a message precisely 3 steps to propagate across the channel α, P_2 can read the message at exactly the same moment that P_1 is ready to execute l_3. Let us consider the sequence of states that are generated by this computation. Each state is given as a tuple of five elements, specifying the current values of the following variables:

π_1: The location pointer of process P_1.

π_2: The location pointer of process P_2.

x: The variable x, local to P_1.

y: The variable y, local to P_2.

α: Contents of the channel α, given as a list of three elements.

Note our representation of the channel as a list of elements, such that transmitted values are entered at the end of the list. In each step each element moves one position towards the beginning of the list, and read elements are removed from the head of the list.

$$
\begin{array}{ll}
\text{Initial State} & <\,l_0\,,m_0\,,\quad a\quad\,,-\,,(-,-,-)\,> \\
\text{Step 1} & <\,l_1\,,m_0\,,\quad a\quad\,,-\,,(-,-,a)\,> \\
\text{Step 2} & <\,l_2\,,m_0\,,a+1\,,-\,,(-,a,-)\,> \\
\text{Step 3} & <\,l_3\,,m_0\,,a+2\,,-\,,(a,-,-)\,> \\
\text{Step 4} & <\,l_4\,,m_1\,,a+3\,,\,a\,,(-,-,-)\,> \\
\end{array}
$$

As we see, there is a full synchronization between the execution of the two processes and the movement of the message in the channel. The danger in modeling asynchronous systems by a synchronous model is that the synchronous model admits much fewer possible executions (and hence its attractiveness to the analyst). For example, in all executions of the program above, whenever P_2 is at m_1, P_1 is at l_4, and the relation $y = x + 3$ holds. This may lull the user into a false confidence that this is indeed an invariant of his real program. If, instead of this not very interesting relation holding between the local variables of the two processes, the invariant ensured mutual exclusion of the accesses of P_1 and P_2 to some shared device or, shared item in a distributed data base, then the user may falsely conclude that his real program is safe. A typical situation would be when both l_3 and m_1 are statements accessing the shared resource. Then, the invariant stating that there is no state in which both P_1 is at l_3 while P_2 is at m_1 guarantees such safety.

In the real implementation, the assumption about the full synchronization between the travel of messages in channels and the rate of execution of the processes may be invalid. In that case the message from P_1 to P_2 may travel faster than 3 execution steps (including the writing), and lead to the unsafe situation in which l_3 and m_1 are ready to execute together.

What we need is clearly a way to slightly "asynchronize" the fully synchronous model, and loosen some of the tight coupling between the different concurrent components of the system. This can be done by introducing some elements of non-determinism into the model. For example, we may associate two transitions with the propagation of messages in a channel. One of them, similarly to our current assumption, advances one position in each step. The other, when activated, advances *two* positions. The rules of the game now are that at each step one of these propagation transitions must be activated, but the choice between them is non-deterministic. This leads to the situation that the passage of messages in the channel can take either 3 steps or 2 steps (writing included), and make the situation of the processes being at l_3 and m_1 reachable. Indeed, the formal model we represent next, will allow this possibility.

There are several possible elaborations of this idea. First, it is possible to fine tune the indeterminacy in the travel time. In the case above, we allowed two transitions. One advanced a single position at each step and the other advanced two positions at each step. If we have a relatively long channel with N positions, then the travel time can vary in the wide range between N and $N/2$ steps, i.e., an indeterminacy of almost 50%. Suppose we wish to achieve an indeterminacy of about 10%. In that case we can consider the same channel as consisting of $10 \times N$ positions, and allow the first transition to move 10 positions in a step, and the other 11.

2.3 The Synchronous Model

To be completed

3 The Timed Interleaving Model

3.1 An abstract computational model

Our generic computational model is based on the model of basic transition system (BTS). We augment the model of BTS by associating a delay time with each transition, thus the model captures the basic concepts of changing the state of the system as a function of time. We refer to the augmented model as RTTS. Let *TIME* be a time domain (nonempty) with the following operations : addition, subtraction, equality and an ordering $\leq$.

A real time transition system (RTTS) consists of the following components :

S - A set of *states* (finite or infinite set).

T - A finite set of (atomic) *transitions*. Each transition $\tau \in T$ is a function $\tau : S \longrightarrow 2^S$. Each transition τ is associated with lower and upper bounds on its delay time, $d^\tau_{min}, d^\tau_{max} \in TIME$.

S_0 - A set of *initial states*. $S_0 \subseteq S$.

If $\tau(s) \neq \emptyset$ then we say that the transition τ is enabled on the state s and if $\tau(s) = \emptyset$ then τ is disabled on s.

For a set of transitions $T_1 \subseteq T$, if for some $\tau \in T_1$, τ is enabled on state s then the set T_1 is enabled on s.

Given P (an RTTS) we define a computation of P to be a finite or infinite sequence of pairs $(s_i, t_i) \in S \times TIME$ and transitions. s_i is the state of the computation at time t_i and at all the points in the open interval (t_i, t_{i+1}) (if not empty). Thus we consider transitions between states to take zero time.

$$\sigma : (s_0, t_0) \xrightarrow{\tau_0} (s_1, t_1) \xrightarrow{\tau_1} (s_2, t_2) \xrightarrow{\tau_2} \cdots$$

The computation σ satisfies the following requirements :

Initiality : $s_0 \in S_0$.

Succession :   For each i, $s_{i+1} \in \tau_i(s_i)$ and $t_{i+1} \geq t_i$.

Termination : σ is finite and terminates in (s_k, t_k) only if s_k is terminal, i.e., $\forall \tau \in T, \tau(s_k) = \emptyset$.

Timing : The timing requirements specify when a transition τ may be taken in a computation, and when it must be taken.

     1. Every transition τ must be continuously enabled for d^τ_{min} time units before it may be taken.

     2. No transition τ is continuously enabled for d^τ_{max} time units without being taken within that time.

Note that we may have several states all bearing the same time stamp but which are still ordered in time.

3.2   Concrete models

When we speak about real time programs it is often not enough to give the program, which is under consideration, in order to specify or verify its behavior. In many cases we should also provide the hardware configuration on which the program runs, because many real time applications are hardware dependent. Thus we must know the number of processors participating in the computation, the time it takes to perform basic actions, and sometimes even the scheduling policy of the system. We present below a language having constructs useful for real time programming such as delay and suspension of certain processes. Our language is presented in a diagram style but we may as well present a text language. Next we show how to map our language on to the generic model. The communication mechanism we use in this language is shared variables, but communication channels (synchronous and asynchronous) may be used as well.

3.3   Transition diagram language

Our program P consists of m parallel processes running on k processors,

$$P : \{\varphi\}[P_1 \| \ldots \| P_m][PR_1, \ldots, PR_k]$$

Each program is associated with a set of shared variables $\overline{y} = y_1, \ldots, y_n$. φ is a formula called the precondition of P and restricts the values of $\overline{y}$.

  Each processor PR_i is represented by a set of integers s.t. $PR_i \subseteq \{1, \ldots, m\}$ and $\forall i \neq j :$ $PR_i \cap PR_j = \emptyset$. The set PR_i determine the identifiers of the processes that are served by processor i.

  Each process P_i is a sequential program represented as a transition diagram, which is a directed graph, with locations $L_i = \{l^i_0, \ldots, l^i_t\}$. l^i_0 is the entry location of process P_i. The edges of the graph are labeled by instructions, and two numbers $t_{min}, t_{max} \in TIME$, which represent the lower and upper bounds on the execution time of the instruction.

  We list below the instructions which are used in our program and explain their meanings

Guard : A guard has the form $c?$, where c is a boolean expression. The meaning of this notation is : when c holds, execution may proceed from l to l'. If it does it takes t time units where $t_{min} \leq t \leq t_{max}$.

Assignment : $u := e$, where e is an expression and $u \in \overline{y}$

Delay : $delay(T)$, where $T \in TIME$. A process that performs this instruction, must wait for at least T time units, after performing the instruction, before it can proceed to perform the next instruction. This waiting is a non busy waiting, i.e., the processor serving the delayed process may serve another process for the duration of the delay time.

Suspend : $suspend(j)$, where $j \in \{1, \ldots, m\}$. Performing this instruction causes process P_j to be suspended (not executing) until it is resumed (by another process).

Resume : $resume(j)$, where $j \in \{1, \ldots, m\}$. If process P_j is suspended then it is resumed and allowed to proceed execution.

Performing an instruction takes t time units, where $t_{min} \leq t \leq t_{max}$, i.e., executing the instruction causes the specified effect and execution reaches location l' exactly after t time units.

We augment the data variables $\overline{y}$ by control variables $\overline{\pi} = \pi_1, \ldots, \pi_m$. Each π_i is composed of two elements s.t. $\pi_i = (\pi_i.l, \pi_i.s)$.

- $\pi_i.l$ ranges over L_i and its value is the current control location in process P_i.

- $\pi_i.s$ represents the current status of process P_i. $\pi_i.s$ has one of the following values :

  1. $\pi_i.s = A$ means that process P_i is currently active and executes.
  2. $\pi_i.s = R$ means that process P_i is currently not active but is ready to become active at any time.
  3. $\pi_i.s = D(T)$, where $T \in TIME$, means that process P_i is now in a waiting state and is not executing. P_i will stay in a waiting state for at least T time units.
  4. $\pi_i.s = S$ means that process P_i is currently suspended, and will stay suspended as long as it is not resumed by another process.

We may now identify an RTTS corresponding to the transition diagram language.

S -   The set of all assignments of values to $< \overline{y}; \overline{\pi} >$. We denote by $s[u]$ and $s[e]$ the values assigned to u by state s and the value of expression e evaluated over s.

$\mathcal{T}$ -   The set of all transitions in all the processes, plus scheduling transitions. We will demonstrate only abstract scheduler and not a concrete one. The only thing we require from our abstract scheduler is that it will be able to schedule any process it wishes to. Thus we need two transitions for every process that change its activity mode, one from A to R (τ_{AR}), and from R to A (τ_{RA}). We define the following mapping from S to 2^S representing the scheduling transitions associated with process P_i :

$$\tau_{AR}(s) = \textbf{ if } (s[\pi_i.s] = A)$$
$$\textbf{then} \quad \{s[\pi_i.s \mapsto R]\}$$
$$\textbf{else} \quad \emptyset$$

$$\tau_{RA}(s) = \textbf{ if } (s[\pi_i.s] = R) \wedge (\neg \exists j, m : ((j, i \in PR_m) \wedge (s[\pi_j.s] = A)))$$
$$\textbf{then} \quad \{s[\pi_i.s \mapsto R]\}$$
$$\textbf{else} \quad \emptyset$$

The notation $s[u \mapsto a]$, for some variable u and as value a, denotes an updated version of s, which is identical to s on all variables, except for u, where its new value is a. of $\bar{e}$.) The bounds on the delay time of our abstract scheduler must satisfy the following requirements :

- For τ_{AR} : d_{min} must be large enough in order to prevent the scheduler from keep replacing active processes without performing any actions when they are able to do so. d_{max} must be determined according to the scheduling policy, and to our discussion it is enough to consider d_{max} as ∞.

- For τ_{RA} : d_{min} must be determined according to the scheduler performance and to our discussion we may consider it as ϵ or 0. However d_{max} must be small enough in order to prevent a situation of processors not doing anything for a long time. This situation, for example, may occur if we have $d_{max} = \infty$ and for some processor i, $j \in PR_i \Rightarrow s[\pi_j.s] = R$.

(From now on unless we say otherwise $d^\tau_{min} = t_{min}$ and $d^\tau_{max} = t_{max}$)

1. Guard

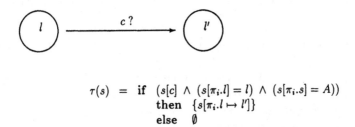

$$\tau(s) = \textbf{if} \ (s[c] \wedge (s[\pi_i.l] = l) \wedge (s[\pi_i.s] = A))$$
$$\textbf{then} \ \{s[\pi_i.l \mapsto l']\}$$
$$\textbf{else} \ \emptyset$$

2. Assignment

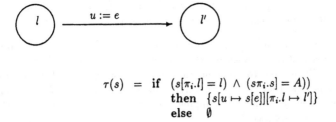

$$\tau(s) = \textbf{if} \ (s[\pi_i.l] = l) \wedge (s\pi_i.s] = A))$$
$$\textbf{then} \ \{s[u \mapsto s[e]][\pi_i.l \mapsto l']\}$$
$$\textbf{else} \ \emptyset$$

3. Delay

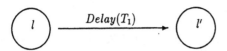

We define three transitions associated with the $delay(T)$ instruction. All three change the status of process P_i. τ_{AD} changes its status from an active process to a delayed one plus the change of its location. τ_{DD} counts down the remaining delay, and τ_{DR} returns process P_i to a ready state.

$$\tau_{AD}(s) = \begin{array}{ll} \textbf{if} & ((s[\pi_i.l] = l) \wedge (s[\pi_i.s] = A) \wedge (T_1 > 1)) \\ \textbf{then} & \{s[\pi_i.s \mapsto D(T_1)] [\pi_i.l \mapsto l']\} \\ \textbf{else} & \emptyset \end{array}$$

$$\tau_{DD}(s) = \begin{array}{ll} \textbf{if} & ((s[\pi_i.s] = D(T_1)) \wedge (T_1 > 1)) \\ \textbf{then} & \{s[\pi_i.s \mapsto D(T_1 - 1)]\} \\ \textbf{else} & \emptyset \end{array}$$

$$\tau_{DR}(s) = \begin{array}{ll} \textbf{if} & ((s[\pi_i.s] = D(T_1)) \wedge (T_1 \leq 1)) \\ \textbf{then} & \{s[\pi_i.s \mapsto R] >\} \\ \textbf{else} & \emptyset \end{array}$$

The bounds on the delay time of each transition are defined as follows :
For τ_{AD} : $d_{min} = t_{min}$, $d_{max} = t_{max}$.
For τ_{DD} : $d_{min} = d_{max} = 1$.
For τ_{DR} : $d_{min} = d_{max} = 1$.

4. Suspend

$$\tau(s) = \begin{array}{ll} \textbf{if} & ((s[\pi_i.l] = l) \wedge (s[\pi_i.s] = A) \wedge ((s[\pi_j.s] = A) \vee (s[\pi_j.s] = R))) \\ \textbf{then} & \{s[\pi_j.s \mapsto S] [\pi_i.l \mapsto l']\} \\ \textbf{else} & \emptyset \end{array}$$

5. Resume

$$\tau(s) = \begin{array}{ll} \textbf{if} & ((s[\pi_i.l] = l) \wedge (s[\pi_i.s] = A) \wedge (s[\pi_j.s] = S)) \\ \textbf{then} & \{s[\pi_j.s \mapsto R] [\pi_i.l \mapsto l']\} \\ \textbf{else} & \emptyset \end{array}$$

S_0 - The set of states satisfying $\overline{\pi} = \overline{\pi}^0 \wedge \varphi(\overline{y})$ where $\overline{\pi}^0 = \pi_1^0, \ldots \pi_m^0$. Each π_i^0 satisfies the following requirements : 1. $\pi_i^0.l = l_0^i$.
2. $\pi_i^0.s = R$.

Our model does not force the system to serve a certain process. Process P_i may be ready and its processor serves another process, thus τ_{RA} (of process P_i) is disabled. However this difficulty rises only because we have presented an abstract scheduler. When we take explicit scheduler under consideration the problem does not arise.

Dynamic allocation

So far we have presented static allocation of processes to processors. However if we want to consider also systems with dynamic allocation we need to make some changes. Each state of the computation must contain a mapping of processes to processors in addition to the former data. This can be done in two ways : either allowing each PR_i to change dynamically and be represented as a variable in the state, or treat each PR_i as before and augment the control variables in a way that will express the current mapping. We choose to augment the control variable in the following way : Each π_i is now composed of three elements s.t. $\pi_i = (\pi_i.l \,,\, \pi_i.s \,,\, \pi_i.p)$ where $\pi_i.l$ and $\pi_i.s$ are defined as in the static case. However $\pi_i.p$ contains the number of the processor to which process P_i is currently allocated. The set of states S is defined the same as in the static case but we should change the scheduler transitions and the requirements for the initial control variable $\overline{\pi}^0$. We define a transition τ_{PR} which changes the allocation of process P_i to processor j. (this transition must be defined according to the specific scheduler, and we give here only an example of it)

$$\tau_{PR}(s) \;=\; \begin{array}{ll} \text{if} & (s[\pi_i.s] \neq A) \\ \text{then} & \{s[\pi_i.p \mapsto j]\} \\ \text{else} & \emptyset \end{array}$$

We should also change τ_{RA} to the following form :

$$\tau_{RA}(s) \;=\; \begin{array}{ll} \text{if} & ((s[\pi_i.s] = R) \,\wedge\, (\neg \exists j : ((s[\pi_j.p] = s[\pi_i.p]) \,\wedge\, (s[\pi_j.s] = A)))) \\ \text{then} & \{s[\pi_i.s \mapsto A]\} \\ \text{else} & \emptyset \end{array}$$

The last change we should make is in $\overline{\pi}^0$. We require that each π_i^0 will satisfy the requirement that $\pi_i^0 = j \;\Leftrightarrow\; i \in PR_j$, together with the former requirements.

4 Specification languages

4.1 Introduction

As a specification language we examine two variants of linear time temporal logic. Temporal logic is a formalism for specifying structures of states over semi-infinite intervals of time. Real time systems, on the other hand, deal with explicit intervals of time. Hence it seems natural to augment (change) the temporal language in a way that will enable us to deal with such intervals of time, while preserving the ability to specify structures of states.

First we present our set of temporal operators and explain their meaning. Next we present our two variants of the temporal language : Global Clock Temporal Logic (GCTL), and Quantized Temporal Logic (QTL).

4.2   Temporal Logic (TL)

We use a set of symbols for the individual variables and propositions. It includes the data variables $\bar{y} = y_1, \ldots, y_n$ and the control variables $\bar{\pi} = \pi_1, \ldots, \pi_m$, as well as other variables (called logical variables), and propositions. Functions and predicates are also used in our specifications.

A state formula is any formula of first order logic constructed over the variables and propositions from our symbol set. A state formula φ may be evaluated over any single state s to give its truth value over s. The evaluation of φ over s is denoted by $s[\varphi]$. If $s[\varphi] = true$ we say that s is a $\varphi - state$, i.e., s satisfies φ.

A temporal formula is a formula constructed from state formulae and temporal operators. For simplicity we use only two basic operators : $\bigcirc$ ("next"), and $\mathcal{U}$ ("until") from which we can define other useful operators : $\square$ ("henceforth"), $\Diamond$ ("eventually") etc. (We have used here only future operators. If we want to deal also with the past we must add corresponding past operators).

Let σ : (s_0, t_0) , $(s_1, t_1) \ldots$ be a sequence of pairs representing a computation of a given program. We denote the pair (s_j, t_j) by (σ, j). If σ is finite, σ : $(s_0, t_0), \ldots, (s_k, t_k)$ then we define $|\sigma| = k + 1$. If σ is infinite we define $|\sigma| = \omega$.

Let φ be a temporal formula and σ a sequence of pairs. We inductively define the meaning of φ holding at position $j < |\sigma|$ of σ. We denote this notion by $(\sigma, j) \models \varphi$.

- For a state formula φ :
$$(\sigma, j) \models \varphi \iff s_j[\varphi] = true$$

  Since φ is a state formula we can evaluate φ over a single state.

- $(\sigma, j) \models \neg\varphi \iff (\sigma, j) \not\models \varphi$.

- $(\sigma, j) \models \varphi \vee \psi \iff (\sigma, j) \models \varphi$ or $(\sigma, j) \models \psi$.

- $(\sigma, j) \models \bigcirc\varphi \iff (\sigma, j+1) \models \varphi$.

- $(\sigma, j) \models \varphi\mathcal{U}\psi \iff \exists l : ((j \leq l < |\sigma| \wedge (\sigma, l) \models \psi)$ and
$\forall i : j \leq i < l, (\sigma, i) \models \varphi)$

Other boolean operators may be defined from $\vee$ and $\neg$ in the usual manner. We define additional temporal operators as follows :

$\Diamond\varphi = true\mathcal{U}\varphi$. This formula means that φ will eventually become true (poosibly true now).

$\square\varphi = \neg\Diamond\neg\varphi$. This formula means that φ is true now and in every future instant.

As we can see, this definition of temporal logic says nothing about finite intervals of time, and only deals with certain states in a computation (next) or with semi-infinite intervals of time.

4.3 Global Clock Temporal Logic (GCTL)

Our first specification language is Temporal Logic augmented by a global clock. This global clock of the system will be referenced via a global variable denoted by T. We assume that T has as its value the last recorded time of the system global clock. This value is updated after each transition. The way the variable T is updated is not relevant to our discussion since T is used only as a specification tool, and does not have to really exist. The interpretation of a GCTL formula is now done over pairs in the computation : $(\sigma, j)[\varphi] = (s_j, t_j)[\varphi]$.
The following formulae are examples of GCTL formulae :

- $(\varphi \wedge T = t) \Rightarrow \Diamond(\psi \wedge T \le t + 5 \wedge T \ge t + 2)$
  If φ is currently true (we identify here the current time with t) then ψ must be true at least once in the closed interval between two and five time units from now.

- $(T = t) \Rightarrow \bigcirc(\varphi \wedge T \ge t + 3)$
  φ is true in the next state of the computation and the system may be in that state not before three time units from now.

The second example shows the need for T to keep the last recorded value, and not always the current value : Consider (σ, k) and $(\sigma, k + 1)$ in the computation σ. The system is at state s_k between time t_k to time t_{k+1}, and at state s_{k+1} between time t_{k+1} to time t_{k+2}. Hence we need a convention on how to interpret T over the pair (s_k, t_k), or else it is not possible for example two to ever hold. As mentioned before we make the following (natural) convention interpreting $(s_k, t_k)[T]$ as t_k. i.e.,The global variable T is updated whenever the system moves to a new state and keeps its value until the next move. However the fact that the value of T is the last recorded value cause another difficulty : consider a situation where the program is in deadlock at (s_k, t_k) and φ holds at that point. Since T has the last recorded value we can not specify that φ holds at a time greater then t_k. To solve this difficulty we add a dummy transition (denoted by τ_c) to represent the progress of time in case of a deadlock. τ_c does nothing except for taking some time. We determine the bounds on the delay time of τ_c in a way that ensure that τ_c will be taken infinitely often in case of a deadlock. $d^{\tau_c}_{min}$ should be determined according to the granularity we wish to deal in our specifications, and $d^{\tau_c}_{max}$ should be finite.

The definition of $(\sigma, j) \models \varphi$ is the same as for TL formulae except for state formulae, in which we evaluate φ over the pair (s_j, t_j).

$$(\sigma, j) \models \varphi \iff (s_j, t_j)[\varphi] = true$$

It is important to notice that we must identify a certain point of time, with a free variable, in order to refer to certain intervals of time w.r.t. that point of time. In our examples we identify the present moment with the free variable t.

In GCTL we use a dense time domain. This is because two processes may perform a transition arbitrarily close to each other (when running on different processors). For simplicity we may choose our time domain $TIME$ to contain all rational numbers. When we speak about synchronous systems we may reduce our time domain to the integers domain.

4.4 Quantized Temporal Logic (QTL)

Our second variant of temporal logic is called Quantized Temporal Logic. When we define QTL we distinguish between synchronous systems and asynchronous systems. For the asynchronous case we need a dense time domain. For the synchronous case we may use an integer time domain since all the processes refer to the same global clock and operates only at certain points of time. For the asynchronous case we prefer to use GCTL but we may define also QTL. We think that QTL is more suitable for the synchronous case then for the asynchronous case therefore we only present the simple integer version of QTL.(from now on when we speak about QTL we refer to synchronous systems) In QTL we use one basic quantized temporal operator $\bigcirc(k)$ ("next k") where k is an integer number (positive, zero or negative). This operator will enable us to talk about specific points of time w.r.t the present moment. We define from the $\bigcirc(k)$ operator other useful operators that will enable us to talk about intervals of time and not only about points of time. The operators we use are : $< k >$ ("eventually k"), $[k]$ ("henceforth k") and $\mathcal{U}(k)$ ("until k"). The intended meaning of these operators is as follows :

$\bigcirc(k)\varphi$ φ will hold in k time units from now.

$[k]\varphi$ φ continuosly holds in the closed interval between now and k time units from now.

$< k > \varphi$ φ must hold at least once in the closed interval between now and k time units from now.

$\varphi\mathcal{U}(k)\psi$ ψ must hold at least once in the closed interval between now and k time units from now, and until then φ holds.

QTL does not refer to states of the computation and only deals with points/intervals of time. Hence we group together transitions that occur in the same time to a single transition. This grouping is done dynamically and is only for presentation purposes. Thus we present at any point of time only one state in the computation that represent all the changes that were done since the previous state.

Let φ be a QTL formula and σ a sequence of pairs. The inductive definition of $(\sigma, j) \models \varphi$ is :

- For a state formula φ :
$$(\sigma, j) \models \varphi \iff s_j[\varphi] = true$$

- $(\sigma, j) \models \neg\varphi$ $\iff (\sigma, j) \not\models \varphi.$

- $(\sigma, j) \models \varphi \vee \psi$ $\iff (\sigma, j) \models \varphi$ or $(\sigma, j) \models \psi.$

- $(\sigma, j) \models \bigcirc(k)\varphi$ $\iff \exists l : (t_l - t_j = k \wedge (\sigma, l) \models \varphi).$

- $(\sigma, j) \models \bigcirc(k)\bigcirc(k')\varphi \iff (\sigma, j) \models \bigcirc(k + k')\varphi.$

- $(\sigma, j) \models [k]\varphi$ $\iff \forall l : (0 \leq l \leq k \Rightarrow (\sigma, j) \models \bigcirc(l)\varphi).$

- $(\sigma, j) \models < k > \varphi$ $\iff \exists l : (0 \leq l \leq k \wedge (\sigma, j) \models \bigcirc(l)\varphi).$

- $(\sigma, j) \models \varphi\mathcal{U}(k)\psi$ $\iff \exists l : ((0 \leq l \leq k \wedge (\sigma, j) \models \bigcirc(l)\psi)$ and $\forall i : (0 \leq i < l \Rightarrow (\sigma, j) \models \bigcirc(l)\varphi)).$

The use of k in the above operators is only defined when $k \geq 0$ except for $\bigcirc(k)$ where k may be also negative. In QTL we do not need special operators to deal with the past. We can simply use the "next k" operator with a negative k in order to specify properties describing the past.

References

[DS84] E.Ewald D.E. Shasha, A. Pnueli. Temporal verification of carrier-sense local area network protocols. *Proc. 11th ACM Symp. on Principles of Programming Languages*, pages 54–65, 1984.

[RK83] W.P. DeRoever R. Koymans, J. Vytopil. Real time programming and asynchronous message passing. *2nd ACM Symp. on Principles of Distributed Programming*, pages 187–197, 1983.

FROM A SYNCHRONOUS DECLARATIVE LANGUAGE
TO A TEMPORAL LOGIC DEALING WITH MULTIFORM TIME

(Extended Abstract)

Daniel PILAUD, Nicolas HALBWACHS
Laboratoire de Génie Informatique - Institut IMAG
B.P. 53 , 38041 Grenoble Cedex - France

1. Introduction

Temporal logics were first used in computer science to describe the behaviour of concurrent systems [7,11,14]. More recently, some efforts [10,12,16] have been devoted to the design of temporal logics well-suited to the description of the real-time aspects of the behaviour of computer systems. These works are generally based on linear time logics, and consider the time grain of such logics as a physical time unit.

At the same time, several authors [2,4,5,8,9] have argued that *synchronous reactive systems* form a suitable framework for modelling and programming real-time systems. The basic idea is that, from a suitable level of abstraction, the only notion which is necessary for describing a real-time system is the notion of instantaneous reaction to external events. In this framework, physical time is considered as an external event, without any privileged role, and conversely, any external event may be viewed as defining a time-scale. This is the *multiform time* point of view. It encourages modularity, versatility and abstraction, since it allows a real-time process to be defined without explicit reference to physical time, and a given process description to be instantiated with different time scales.

For instance, in an actual railway regulation system, the on-board speed regulation device perceives several events: signals from the central system, beacons along the track, wheel revolutions, and milliseconds from its local clock. Now, one can consider all these events in a symmetric way. So, time can be counted in wheel revolutions as well as in milliseconds, and a "watch-dog" may be set on any event.

In this paper, we propose an adaptation of temporal logic to multiform time. For this purpose, we use temporal logic to express the semantics of the synchronous declarative language LUSTRE [3,5]. The underlying model of LUSTRE is close to that of temporal logic, since it is based on sequences: as in LUCID [1], any variable in LUSTRE is a sequence of values, and programs operate globally over sequences. Moreover, these sequences are synchronously interpreted: any variable has a *clock* associated with it, and takes the n-th value of its sequence at the n-th "tick" of its clock.

After a brief overview of LUSTRE and its formal semantics, we shall see that Pnueli's linear temporal logic is powerful enough to describe it. In this description, we shall derive new modal operators, which express the multiform time point of view. Then, the properties of these operators will be studied.

2. Overview of the language LUSTRE

2.1 Variables, Clocks, Equations, Data operators

As indicated above, any variable or expression in LUSTRE denotes a sequence of values. Moreover, each variable has a clock, and is intended to take the n-th value of its sequence at the n-th tick of its clock. A program has a cyclic behaviour, which defines its *basic clock* : a variable which is on the basic clock takes its n-th value at the n-th cycle of the program. Other, slower, clocks may be defined by means of boolean variables: any boolean variable C may be used as a clock, which is the sequence of cycles when C is true.

For instance, consider a boolean variable C on the basic clock, and a boolean variable C′ on the clock C. The following table shows the different time scales they define:

basic time	0	1	2	3	4	5	6	7
C	true	false	true	true	false	true	false	true
time on C	0		1	2		3		4
C′	false		true	false	·	true		true
time on C′			0			1		2

Variables are defined by means of equations: if X is a variable and E is an expression, the equation "X=E" defines X to be the sequence $(x_0=e_0, x_1=e_1, ..., x_n=e_n, ...)$ where $(e_0, e_1, ..., e_n, ...)$ is the sequence of values of the expression E. Moreover, the equation states that X has the same clock as E.

Expressions are built up from variables, constants (considered to be infinite constant sequences on the basic clock) and operators. Usual operators on values (arithmetic, boolean, conditional operators) are extended to pointwisely operate over sequences, and are hereafter referred to as *data operators* . For instance, the expression

if X>Y then X-Y else Y-X

denotes the sequence whose n-th term is the absolute difference of the n-th values of X and Y. The operands of a data-operator must be on the same clock, which is also the clock of the result.

2.2 Sequence Operators

In addition to the data operators, LUSTRE contains only four non-standard operators, called sequence operators, which actually manipulate sequences.

To keep track of the value of an expression from one cycle to the next, there is a memory or delay operator called "pre" (previous). If $X=(x_0,x_1,...,x_n,...)$ then

pre(X) = $(nil,x_0,x_1,...,x_{n-1},...)$

where nil is an *undefined* value, akin to the value of an uninitialized variable in imperative languages. The clock of pre(X) is the clock of X.

To initialize variables, the -> (followed by) operator is introduced. If $X=(x_0,x_1,...,x_n,...)$ and $Y=(y_0,y_1,...,y_n,...)$ are two variables (or expressions) of the same type and the same clock, then

$$X\text{->}Y = (x_0, y_1, y_2, ..., y_n, ...)$$

i.e. X->Y is equal to Y except at the first instant.

The last two operators are used to define expressions with different clocks:

If E is an expression, B is a boolean expression, and if E and B are on the same clock, then "E when B" is an expression on the clock defined by B, and whose sequence of values is extracted from the sequence of E by taking only those values which occur when B is true.

If E is an expression on a clock CK different from the basic clock, then "current(E)" is an expression on the same clock as CK, whose value at each cycle of this clock is the value taken by E at the last cycle when CK was true.

The following table shows the effect of these operators.

B = (	false	true	false	false	true	true	false	true	...	)
X = (	x_0	x_1	x_2	x_3	x_4	x_5	x_6	x_7	...	)
Y = X whenB = (		x_1			x_4	x_5		x_7	...	)
Z = current(Y) = (	nil	x_1	x_1	x_1	x_4	x_5	x_5	x_7	...	)

The rules for statically computing the clock of any expression are presented in [5]. In the following, we shall always assume that the rules of clock consistency are satisfied, and that the clock of any expression is known.

2.3 Formal Semantics [5]

The semantics of a LUSTRE program is a sequence $(\sigma_0, \sigma_1, ..., \sigma_n, ...)$ of memories, where a memory is a function from the set ID of identifiers to the set VAL of values, and where σ_n represents the state of the variables at the n-th cycle of the basic clock of the program. The set VAL contains both *nil* (the undefined value) and $\perp$, which will be used to represent the absence of value; a variable has no value when it must not be computed (its clock is false or doesn't have to be computed). Such a sequence of memories will be called a *history*, and we shall note Hist(VAL) the set of histories on the set of values VAL.

The semantics will be described by means of structural inference rules [13]. Without loss of generality, let us consider the following simplified syntax:
- an equation is assumed to involve at most one operator;
- the "pre" and "current" operators may be given an additional parameter, that records the necessary past value of their operand;
- in the case of "current", the clock of its operand (which is assumed to be known, as a byproduct of the clock analysis) is also assumed to be a parameter.

With this syntax, at a given instant, we only need to know the memory in order to compute the value of an expression . This value is assumed to be $\perp$ if the clock of the expression is not true. An equation "X=E" will be said to be *compatible* with a memory σ if and only if $\sigma(X)$ is the result of the expression E, evaluated in σ.

System of equations	Simple equation

$$\frac{eq_1 -\sigma\rightarrow eq_1' \ , \ eq_2 -\sigma\rightarrow eq_2'}{[eq_1;eq_2] -\sigma\rightarrow [eq_1'; eq_2']}$$

$$\frac{\sigma(X) = \sigma(Y)}{[X=Y] -\sigma\rightarrow [X=Y]}$$

Data operator

$$\frac{\sigma(Y)\neq\perp \ , \ \sigma(Z)\neq\perp \ , \ \sigma(X) = \sigma(Y) \ \underline{op} \ \sigma(Z)}{[X=Y \ op \ Z] -\sigma\rightarrow [X=Y \ op \ Z]}$$

$$\frac{\sigma(Y)= \sigma(Z)= \sigma(X)= \perp}{[X=Y \ op \ Z] -\sigma\rightarrow [X=Y \ op \ Z]}$$

"Previous" operator

$$\frac{\sigma(Y)=k\neq \perp \ , \ \sigma(X)=nil}{[X=pre(Y)] -\sigma\rightarrow [X=pre(Y,k)]}$$

$$\frac{\sigma(Y)=k'\neq \perp \ , \ \sigma(X)=k}{[X=pre(Y,k)] -\sigma\rightarrow [X=pre(Y,k')]}$$

$$\frac{\sigma(Y)= \sigma(X)= \perp}{[X=pre(Y)] -\sigma\rightarrow [X=pre(Y)]}$$

$$\frac{\sigma(Y)= \sigma(X)= \perp}{[X=pre(Y,k)] -\sigma\rightarrow [X=pre(Y,k)]}$$

"Followed-by" operator

$$\frac{\sigma(Y)= \sigma(X)\neq \perp}{[X=Y->Z] -\sigma\rightarrow [X=Z]}$$

$$\frac{\sigma(Y)= \sigma(X)= \perp}{[X=Y->Z] -\sigma\rightarrow [X=Y->Z]}$$

"When" operator

$$\frac{\sigma(C)=true \ , \ \sigma(Y)= \sigma(X)\neq \perp}{[X=(Y \ when \ C)] -\sigma\rightarrow [X=(Y \ when \ C)]}$$

$$\frac{\sigma(C)=false \ , \ \sigma(Y)\neq \perp \ , \ \sigma(X)= \perp}{[X=(Y \ when \ C)] -\sigma\rightarrow [X=(Y \ when \ C)]}$$

$$\frac{\sigma(C)= \sigma(Y)= \sigma(X)= \perp}{[X=(Y \ when \ C)] -\sigma\rightarrow [X=(Y \ when \ C)]}$$

"Current" operator , where C is the clock of Y

$$\frac{\sigma(C) = true \ , \ \sigma(Y)= \sigma(X)=k\neq \perp}{[X=current(Y,C)] -\sigma\rightarrow [X=current(Y,k,C)]}$$

$$\frac{\sigma(C) = true \ , \ \sigma(Y)= \sigma(X)=k'\neq \perp}{[X=current(Y,k,C)] -\sigma\rightarrow[X=current(Y,k',C)]}$$

$$\frac{\sigma(C) = false \ , \ \sigma(X)=nil \ , \ \sigma(Y)= \perp}{[X=current(Y,C)] -\sigma\rightarrow [X=current(Y,C)]}$$

$$\frac{\sigma(C) = false \ , \ \sigma(X)=k \ , \ \sigma(Y)= \perp}{[X=current(Y,k,C)] -\sigma\rightarrow[X=current(Y,k,C)]}$$

Figure 1

The rules of Figure 1 define the predicate:

$$[eq] -\sigma\rightarrow [eq']$$

which means:

"The equation eq is compatible with the memory σ and will be later on evaluated as eq' "

Let us comment some of these rules:

<u>System of equations</u>: A system of equations is compatible with a memory σ iff each of its equations is compatible with σ.

<u>Data operator</u>: From the clock consistency, the operands of a data operator "op" are on the same clock. So, either none or all of them have a value. In the latter case, the resulting value is the result of the corresponding standard operator, noted "<u>op</u>" (any data operator, except the conditional, is strict with respect to "nil").

<u>"Previous" operator</u>: There are four rules for defining the semantics of "pre(Y)". The first one applies when the clock of Y is true for the first time: then the value of pre(Y) is nil, and the value of Y is stored. The second rule applies the subsequent times the clock of Y is true: the value of pre(Y) is the stored value, and the value of Y is stored. The last two rules concern the cases when the clock of Y is not true. The same four cases are considered for the operator "current".

Now a LUSTRE program P is compatible with an history $(\sigma_0, \sigma_1, ..., \sigma_n, ...)$ if and only if its system of equations is compatible with σ_0, and must be later on considered as a new program P', which is compatible with $(\sigma_1, ..., \sigma_n, ...)$:

$$\frac{[P] -\sigma_0\rightarrow [P'] , \Sigma \vdash [P']}{\sigma_0.\Sigma \vdash [P]}$$

2.4 Example of LUSTRE program: An axle detector in a railway system

A part of a railway system must perform the following function: A track is divided into districts. At the boundary between two districts, there are two pedals which overlap each other as shown by Figure 2. The device knows the states of the pedals by means of two boolean variables P1 and P2 (Pi is true whenever a wheel is on Pi). It must compute a boolean S which is true when and only when an axle goes from the backward district to the forward district. More precisely, S is set when the axle goes out and reset just after. There can be only one axle in the zone Z. An axle may turn back within the zone Z and even oscillate on or about the zone Z.

Let us write the program which computes S. We introduce two boolean variables "last_in_b" and "out_f": the former is true whenever the last axle which entered the zone Z came from the backward district, and the latter is true whenever an axle leaves the zone Z to the forward district.

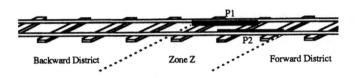

Figure 2

Now, we have

```
S = false -> out_f and lastin_b;
```

An axle enters the zone Z from the backward (resp. forward) district whenever the input P1 (resp. P2) has a rising edge when P2 (resp. P1) is false:

```
last_in _b=  if P1 and not pre(P1) and not P2 then true
             else if P2 and not pre(P2) and not P1 then false
             else pre(last_in_b) ;
```

An axle leaves the zone Z to the forward district whenever the input P2 has a falling edge when P1 is false:

```
out _f = not P2 and pre(P2) and not P1;
```

So the whole program is as follows:

```
        S =     false -> out_f and lastin_b;
last_in _b =    if P1 and not pre(P1) and not P2 then true
                else if P2 and not pre(P2) and not P1 then false
                else pre(last_in_b) ;
     out_f =    not P2 and pre(P2) and not P1;
```

3. Describing LUSTRE in Temporal Logic

3.1 Linear temporal logic

We use the logic of [7]: A formula is built from proposition symbols, usual boolean operators $(\neg, \wedge, \vee, \supset, \equiv)$, and the four modal operators $\Box$ (*always*, unary), $\Diamond$ (*eventually*, unary), O (*next*, unary) and U (*until*, binary). A model is a sequence $S=(s_0, s_1, \ldots, s_n, \ldots)$ of states, each state giving values to the proposition symbols. The semantics of a formula p is a function $|p|$ from the set of models to $\{$true, false$\}$. The semantics of modal operators are as follows:

- $|\Box p|(S)=$true iff $\forall n \geq 0$, $|p|(S^{+n}) =$ true, where S^{+n} denotes the n-th suffix $(s_n, s_{n+1}, \ldots)$ of S;

- $|\Diamond p|(S) =$ true iff $\exists n \geq 0$ such that $|p|(S^{+n}) =$ true ;

- $|Op|(S) =$ true iff $|p|(S^{+1}) =$ true ;

- $|p U q|(S) =$ true iff $\exists n \geq 0$ such that $|q|(S^{+n}) =$ true, and $\forall m, 0 \leq m < n, |p|(S^{+m}) =$ true

This logic is axiomatized by means of 8 axioms:

$$A0. \vdash \Diamond p \equiv \neg \Box(\neg p)$$
$$A1. \vdash \Box(p \supset q) \supset (\Box p \supset \Box q)$$
$$A2. \vdash O(\neg p) \equiv \neg O p$$
$$A3. \vdash O(p \supset q) \equiv (O p \supset O q)$$
$$A4. \vdash \Box p \supset (p \wedge O \Box p)$$
$$A5. \vdash \Box(p \supset O p) \supset (p \supset \Box p)$$
$$A6. \vdash p U q \supset \Diamond q$$
$$A7. \vdash p U q \equiv q \vee (p \wedge O(p U q))$$

and 3 rules of inference

R1. If f is a tautology, then $\vdash f$.

R2. (Modus Ponens) If $\vdash f_1 \supset f_2$ and $\vdash f_1$ then $\vdash f_2$.

R3. (Generalization) If $\vdash f$ then $\vdash \Box f$.

3.2 Multiform time operators

The intuitive real-time interpretation of linear temporal logic consists of assimilating logical instants with physical instants, belonging to some metric time-scale: for instance, the formula Op would be considered as meaning "p will be true at the next second". In order to handle multiform time, we must be able to define several independent time scales, so as to express in the same way, for instance, the property "p will be true at the next wheel revolution". These time scales will always be sequences of instants which are sub-sequences of the logical time. Intuitively, an event such as "second" or "wheel revolution" will be represented by a formula which is true whenever the event occurs. Now, with each time-scale defined in this way, we need to associate specific modal operators.

For any formula f, we define five abbreviations $\Box_f$ (*always when f*), $\Diamond_f$ (*eventually when f*), F_f (*at first f*), O_f (*at next f*), U_f (*whenever f until*),as follows:

$$\Box_f p \equiv \Box(f \supset p)$$
$$\Diamond_f p \equiv \Diamond(f \wedge p)$$
$$\Diamond f \supset (F_f p \equiv (\neg f \, U \, (p \wedge f)))$$
$$O_f p \equiv O F_f p$$
$$p \, U_f \, q \equiv (f \supset p) \, U \, (f \wedge q)$$

Remarks:

- When the formula $\Box f$ holds, the operators $\Box_f$, $\Diamond_f$, O_f, U_f respectively coincide with their homologues $\Box, \Diamond, O, U$. In this case F_f is the identity operator.

- The operator F_f is not completely defined; its value is only known on models satisfying $\Diamond f$. This fact is not surprising since, if f is never true, there is no information about the value of p when f is true. The same remark applies to the operator O_f.

3.3 Describing boolean LUSTRE

Here, we consider programs which only contain boolean variables and expressions. The semantics of such a program P is then a set $\Sigma(P)$ of histories belonging to $\underline{\text{Hist}}(\{\text{true, false, nil}, \perp\})$. From the semantics of LUSTRE , we have

$$\frac{[P] -\sigma_0 \to [P'] \,, \sigma \in \Sigma(P')}{\sigma_0.\sigma \in \Sigma(P)}$$

Only histories belonging to $\underline{Hist}(\{true,false\})$ can straightforwardly be considered as models for our temporal logic. So, from the point of view of logical properties, we shall consider both undefined values nil (unassigned variable) and $\bot$ (uncomputed variable) as undetermined values, which only satisfy the predicate "true". So, with each history $\Sigma=\{\sigma_0,\sigma_1,...,\sigma_n,...\}$, we associate a subset $S(\Sigma)$ of $\underline{Hist}(\{true,false\})$ defined as follows:

$$S(\Sigma) = \{\Sigma'=\{\sigma'_0,...,\sigma'_n,...\} \mid \forall n{\geq}0, \forall x{\in} ID, \sigma_n(x){\neq}nil \ \& \ \sigma_n(x) {\neq}\bot \Rightarrow \sigma_n(x) =\sigma'_n(x)\}$$

Now, we want to associate with each program P, a formula $f(P)$ such that

$|f(P)|(\Sigma') = true$ iff there exists $\Sigma \in \Sigma(P))$ such that $\Sigma' \in S(\Sigma)$

This association is inductively defined by the following rules, where c always stands for the clock of X:

$f(X{=}Y) = \square_c (X \equiv Y)$

$f(X{=} Y \text{ op } Z) = \square_c (X \equiv Y \text{ op } Z)$, for any boolean operator op

$f(X{=}pre(Y)) = \square_c (O_c (X) \equiv Y)$

$f(X{=}Y{-}{>}Z) = F_c (X \equiv Y \wedge O_c \square_c (X \equiv Z))$

$f(X{=}Y \text{ when } Z) = \square_Z (X \equiv Y)$

$f(X{=}current(Y)) = \square_c (c'{\supset}(X{\equiv}Y) \wedge O_c (\neg c'){\supset}(O_c (X){\equiv}X))$, where c' is the clock of Y

The formula associated with a system of equations is obviously the conjunction of the formulas associated with its components:

$f(eq_1;eq_2) = f(eq_1) \wedge f(eq_2)$

3.4. Correctness

Let us sketch the proof of correctness of the formula associated with the "pre" operator: The set of histories compatible with a LUSTRE program has been defined by means of a sequence of program states. Let us extend our notion of model as follows: an extended history is an infinite sequence of pairs, each pair consisting of a program and a memory. When the program is reduced to a single equation, such an extended history is a sequence

$$\Xi=(eq_0,\sigma_0).(eq_1,\sigma_1). \ ... \ .(eq_n,\sigma_n). \ ...)$$

satisfying $[eq_n]-\sigma_n\to[eq_{n+1}]$, for any n. Let us introduce the following basic predicates on extended histories:

• $[eq]$ is true for Ξ, iff $\Xi = (eq,\sigma).\Xi'$, for some σ and some Ξ'

• Let p be a basic predicate on memories; then $\{p\}$ is true for Ξ, iff $\Xi = (eq,\sigma).\Xi'$, for some eq and some Ξ', and for some σ such that $|p|(\sigma)$ holds. This notation is extended to full memories: $\{\sigma\}$ is true for Ξ iff σ is the memory part of the first pair of Ξ.

So, a rewriting predicate [eq]–σ→[eq'] may be expressed by

$$[eq] \wedge \{\sigma\} \supset O[eq']$$

and from the special form of our inference rules, a rule

$$\frac{p_1, p_2, \dots, p_k}{q}$$

may be translated into

$$\vdash \Box(p_1 \wedge p_2 \wedge \dots \wedge p_k \supset q)$$

Now, from the rules defining the "pre" operator, we get

$$\Box((\{Y \neq \perp\} \wedge [X = pre(Y,k)]) \supset \{X = k\})$$

and

$$\Box((\{Y = \perp\} \wedge [X = pre(Y,k)]) \supset (\{X = \perp\} \wedge O[X = pre(Y,k)])$$

So,

$$\Box(\Diamond\{Y \neq \perp\} \supset ([X = pre(Y,k)] \supset \{X = \perp\}U\{X = k\})$$

On the other hand, the rules provide

$$\Box((\{Y = k'\} \wedge [X = pre(Y)]) \supset O[X = pre(Y,k')])$$

$$\Box(\{Y = k'\} \wedge [X = pre(Y,k)]) \supset O[X = pre(Y,k')])$$

It follows that

$$([X = pre(Y)] \wedge \Box\Diamond\{Y \neq \perp\}) \supset \Box(\{Y = k\} \supset O\{X = \perp\}U\{X = k\}) \qquad (1)$$

Now, the following lemma results from the clock correctness:

$$[X = pre(Y)] \supset (\{X \neq \perp\} \equiv \{Y \neq \perp\} \equiv c) , \text{ where c is the common clock of X and Y}$$

So, the implication (1) becomes

$$([X = pre(Y)] \wedge \Box\Diamond c) \supset \Box(\{Y = k\} \supset O(\neg cU (c \wedge \{X = k\})))$$

or

$$([X = pre(Y)] \wedge \Box\Diamond c) \supset \Box_{\{Y=k\}} O_c \{X=k\}$$

Separately considering the cases where k is true or false, we get

$$([X = pre(Y)] \wedge \Box\Diamond c) \supset \Box_c (O_c X) \equiv Y$$

which is the desired result.

3.5. Application

Let us come back to the program of the axle detector. An expanded form of the program is:

```
        S = false -> out_f and lastin_b;
  last_in _b = (P1 and not pre_P1 and not P2) or
                    (not(P2 and not pre_P2 and not P1 ) and pre_last_in_b );
      out_f = not P2 and pre_P2 and not P1;
     pre_P1 = pre(P1);
     pre_P2 = pre(P2);
pre_last_in_b = pre(last_in_b);
```

From this program and the rules of §3.3, we get the following formula, where b stands for the basic clock of the program:

$$F_b(\neg S \wedge O_b \, \Box_b \, (S \equiv (\text{out\_f} \wedge \text{last\_in\_b}) \wedge$$
$$\Box_b \; \text{last\_in\_b} \equiv ((P1 \wedge \neg \text{pre\_P1} \wedge \neg P2) \; \vee (\neg(P2 \wedge \neg \text{pre\_P2} \wedge \neg P1) \wedge \text{pre\_last\_in\_b})) \wedge$$
$$\Box_b \; \text{out\_f} \equiv (\neg P2 \wedge \text{pre\_P2} \wedge \neg P1) \wedge$$
$$\Box_b \, (O_b \, (\text{pre\_P1}) \equiv P1 \; \wedge \; O_b \, (\text{pre\_P2}) \equiv P2 \; \wedge \; O_b \, (\text{pre\_last\_in\_b}) \equiv \text{last\_in\_b})$$

Let us call this formula *axles* . The program is intended to work under the assumption of synchrony: it runs at a suitable rate so as to perceive any change in the state of its inputs. Let us call *chg* the formula which is true whenever the state of a pedal changes:

$$\neg(P1 \equiv OP1) \vee \neg(P2 \equiv OP2)$$

The assumption of synchrony may be written as the following formula, *sync* :

$$\Box(chg \supset b)$$

Moreover, it is assumed that the state of only one pedal, as perceived by the program, may change at a given instant. This assumption is expressed by the following formula, called *excl* :

$$\Box_b \, (\neg(P1 \equiv O_b \, P1) \supset (P2 \equiv O_b \, P2))$$

The proof of an expected property P of the program consists of proving the theorem

$$\vdash (axles \wedge sync \wedge excl) \supset P$$

For instance, P may express that whenever a train straightly crosses the zone Z from the backward district to the forward one, the output S is true. Such a property is simpler to write on the clock *chg* . The straight crossing of a train from the backward district to the forward one, is expressed by the formula *b-f-cross* :

$$\neg P1 \wedge \neg P2 \wedge O_{chg}P1 \wedge O_{chg}O_{chg}P2 \wedge O_{chg}O_{chg}O_{chg}\neg P1 \wedge O_{chg}O_{chg}O_{chg}O_{chg}\neg P2$$

and the theorem to be proven is

$$\vdash (axles \wedge sync \wedge excl) \supset \Box_b \, (b\text{-}f\text{-}cross \supset O_{chg}O_{chg}O_{chg}O_{chg} \, S)$$

4. A logic to deal with multiform time

Our multiform-time operators have been shown to be quite useful. Let us now examine their specific properties.

First, we can adapt the axioms of standard temporal operators to our operators. The following properties have been shown, for any formulas f,p,q:

B0. $\vdash \Diamond_f p \equiv \neg \Box_f (\neg p)$

B1. $\vdash \Box_f (p \supset q) \supset (\Box_f p \supset \Box_f q)$

B2. $\vdash O \Diamond f \supset (O_f (\neg p) \equiv \neg O_f p)$

B3. $\vdash O \Diamond f \supset (O_f (p \supset q) \supset (O_f p \supset O_f q))$

B4. $\vdash \Box \Diamond f \supset (\Box_f p \supset (F_f p \wedge O_f \Box_f p))$

B5. $\vdash \Box_f(p \supset O_f p) \supset (F_f p \supset \Box_f p)$

B6. $\vdash p \cup_f q \supset \Diamond_f q$

B7. $\vdash \Box \Diamond f \supset (p \cup_f q \equiv F_f q \vee (F_f p \wedge O_f (p \cup_f q)))$

B8. $\vdash \Diamond f \supset (F_f(\neg p) \equiv \neg F_f p)$

B9. $\vdash \Diamond f \supset (F_f(p \supset q) \equiv F_f p \supset F_f q)$

A comparison of properties B0-B7 and axioms A0-A7 shows that they only differ in that properties B2, B3, B4 and B7 need an additional premise which states that the formula f must be true infinitely often. So, a good property for an event defining a time-scale is to occur infinitely often (*time never stops*). When time-scales satisfy this property, one can change the time-scale of a system, and adapt all the formulas proven for the initial system only by changing the time-scale (subscript) of the modal operators.

Now, the following properties allow a formula to be projected onto a finer time-scale:

B10. $\vdash \Box(f' \supset f) \supset (\Box_{f'}(p) \equiv \Box_f(f' \supset p))$

B11. $\vdash \Box(f' \supset f) \supset (\Diamond_{f'}(p) \equiv \Diamond_f(f' \wedge p))$

B12. $\vdash (\Box(f' \supset f) \wedge \Diamond f') \supset (F_{f'} p \equiv (\neg f' \cup_f (p \wedge f')))$

B13. $\vdash (\Box(f' \supset f) \wedge \Diamond f') \supset (O_{f'} p \equiv O_f F_{f'} p)$

B14. $\vdash \Box(f' \supset f) \supset (p \cup_{f'} q \equiv (f' \supset p) \cup_f (f' \wedge q))$

These properties express that, if f is more frequently true than f' (that is, if the formula $\Box(f' \supset f)$ holds) then the modal operators on f' may be defined in terms of the modal operators on f, in exactly the same way as they were defined in terms of the usual operators (on *true*).

Conclusion

In this paper we have shown that the synchronous, data-flow language LUSTRE may be viewed as a subset of a linear temporal logic. This fact is an argument showing the cleanness of the semantics of LUSTRE. Moreover, it suggests that standard decision procedures can be used for proving boolean LUSTRE programs.

On the other hand, translating LUSTRE in temporal logic led us to introduce some abbreviations, which are used as new temporal operators, dealing with multiform time. The usefulness of these operators for expressing properties of real-time systems has been illustrated.

This work must be continued in several directions:
- Of course, non boolean computation must be introduced in the logic. This does not raise serious problem, but involves the loss of decision procedures.
- The same construction must be done in a branching time logic, thus allowing non-deterministic inputs to be taken into account.
- Ultimately, this work should lead to an environment for specifying and verifying LUSTRE programs, similar to some tools [6, 15] developed for imperative languages.

References

1. Ashcroft E.A., Wadge W.W.: *LUCID, the data-flow programming language* . Academic Press, 1985.

2. Austry D., Boudol G.: *Algèbre de processus et synchronisation* . TCS 30, april 84.

3. Bergerand J-L., Caspi P., Halbwachs N., Pilaud D., Pilaud E.: *Outline of a real-time data-flow language* . 1985 Real-Time Symp., San Diego, dec. 85.

4. Berry G., Cosserat L.: *The ESTEREL programming language and its mathematical semantics* . RR nr. 327, INRIA, 1984. To appear in Science of Computer Programming.

5. Caspi P., Pilaud D., Halbwachs N., Plaice J.: *LUSTRE: a declarative language for programming synchronous systems* . 14th ACM Symp. on Principles of Programming Languages, Munich, january 87.

6. Clarke E.M., Emerson E.A., Sistla A.P.: *Automatic verification of finite-state concurrent systems using temporal logic specifications* . ACM TOPLAS, 8(2), 1986.

7. Gabbay D., Pnueli A., Shelah S., Stavi J.: *On the temporal analysis of fairness* . 7th ACM Symp. on Principles of Programming Languages, Las Vegas, january 80.

8. Harel D.: *Statecharts: A visual approach to complex systems* . Advanced NATO Institute on Logics and Models for Verification and Specification of Concurrent Systems, La Colle-sur-Loup, 1984.

9. Le Guernic P., Benveniste A., Bournai P., Gautier T.: *SIGNAL: a data-flow oriented language for signal processing* . RR nr. 378, INRIA, 1985.

10. Koymans R., DeRoever W.P.: *Examples of a real-time temporal logic specification* . In The analysis of Concurrent Systems, LNCS nr.207, august 83.

11. Manna Z., Pnueli A.: *Verification of concurrent programs: the temporal framework* . In The Correctness Problem in Computer Science (R.S.Boyer and J.S.Moore, eds), International Lecture Series in Computer Science, Academic Press, London, 1982.

12. Moszkowski B.C.: *Reasoning about digital circuits* . PhD Thesis, Report STAN-CS-83-970, Dept. of Computer Science, Stanford University, july 83.

13. Plotkin G.D.: *A structural approach to operational semantics* , Lecture Notes, Aarhus University, 1981.

14. Pnueli A.: *The temporal logic of concurrent programs* . 12th ICALP, LNCS 194, 1977.

15. Queille J-P., Sifakis J.: *Specification and verification of concurrent systems in CESAR* . 5th Int. Symp. on Programming, Springer-Verlag 1981.

16. Schwartz R.L., Melliar-Smith P.M., Vogt F.H.: *An interval logic for higher-level temporal reasonning: language definition and examples* . Technical Rep. CSL-138, Computer Science Lab., SRI International, february 83.

A Specification Language for Reliable Real-Time Systems

Hanno Wupper and Jan Vytopil
Computer Science and Technical Applications
Catholic University Nijmegen
Toernooiveld, 6525 ED Nijmegen, The Netherlands

1. Language support during systems development — the current state

For the development of correct programs, methods and languages based on formal theories are becoming increasingly popular. Though it must be admitted that hardly a system of some serious size has ever been result of completely formal development or subject to watertight formal verification, formal methods have proved valuable in practice: They provide immense guidance during the development and verification process to those programmers who know and understand them, and this guidance is of importance—not the continuous but blind application of formalisms.

The vehicles to transport the necessary knowledge and understanding are specification and programming languages based on a sound theory which (a) provide the right constructs to inspire the informal part of development, (b) support formal transformation, (c) allow to express anything necessary for a formal correctness proof as completely *as desired* , and (d) encourage the generalization of particular solutions to re-usable algorithms not restricted to a particular data type or storage model or class of operations.

In the evolution of language constructs we can distinguish three "generations" with respect to language support in systems development. Constructs of what we here will count as first generation give no support at all, they merely allow to *somehow* achieve any necessary computation. Constructs here called second generation allow or enforce automatic inclusion of "run-time checks", synchronization, garbage collection, stack administration, etc. to help to detect design errors or avoid error-prone programming. They are always accompanied by powerful "run-time systems" i. e. collections of precompiled algorithms for anticipated problems. Third generation constructs, to the contrary, *syntactically enforce consistency* to make run time checks unnecessary. Examples are static typing, module structure, polymorphism. Third generation constructs syntactically restrict the expressive power of a language in such a way that it is difficult to use error-prone structures but easy to use approved ones. Construction errors are likely to be detected as "syntax errors" rather than to give rise to inconsistent systems. The more these constructs support the derivation of consistent systems, the less will the necessary syntactic restrictions and enforced redundancy be taken as an obstacle. Third generation constructs do not rely on run-time systems with precompiled general solutions: they allow effective special solutions to be tailored for each individual application.

As long as we are interested in pure functionality ("which output for a given input?"), we find several sound third generation languages at our disposal—though most existing languages are a mixture of constructs from all three generations.

Distributed computer systems which control physical processes must not only be functionally correct; they must, moreover, meet *timing and reliability requirements*. Their development therefore involves another dimension of problems.

Timing requirements may be *qualitative* statements about the necessary temporal order of activities. While older languages at most provided some first generation communication and synchronization primitives, languages like Ada® offer second generation means to meet such requirements. — In the case of real-time systems we also have *quantitative* requirements with respect to physical time (e.g. the duration of an activity in seconds or a moment—"epoch"— in absolute time). Second generation language constructs often are disastrous in their consumption of physical time; therefore, many programmers prefer to use purely first generation languages for real-time applications. Some newer specification languages allow to state real-time requirements next to the specification of functionality, as it were in a second layer of specification.

The term "reliability" in computer science is often defined as the probability that a certain system component functions correctly over a certain period of time. This definition gives rise to four questions: (1) Does it cover 'Reliability' in the sense of natural language (i. e. is it a sufficient basis to allow to decide whether we can "rely" on a system)? (2) If we accept the definition: How do we obtain the reliabilities of the building blocks of systems (in other words: what does "to function" mean)?   (3) How does a system's reliability depend on its structure and the reliabilities of its components. (4) How can we formulate reliability requirements for the overall system?

Question (1) is extra-mathematical and shall not be addressed here. In any case this probabilistic approach is widely accepted to tribute enough to Reliability to justify further research. For hardware components, engineering disciplines have contributed a lot to (2) [Birolini 85]. (3) is purely intra–mathematical and has been studied well: If components of known reliabilities and known average repair times are assembled in a given way, the overall reliability can be computed by statistical means. This has lead to approved methods to include redundancy in systems in order to increase reliability. The requirement that redundant components be really independent is usually not checked formally, however. Analysis of accidents often reveals that their cause was not an unforeseen failure of a basic component but an illegal interference between components assumed to be independent [Leveson 86]. Though reliability is a probability, (4) cannot simply be dealt with by stating one number for a whole system. It is more realistic—and common practice—to separately require reliabilities differing in order of magnitude for different sub-functions of a complex system. Reliability requirements are in itself something complex, closely linked to the system structure.

Take for example a modern fully automated railway train: Certain ones of its functions, think of the brakes, must be close to being absolutely reliable at almost any cost. For other functions it is simply not realistic and not necessary to strive for nearly 100%; a door that fails to open automatically at the station does no harm as long as some doors do indeed open and none opens automatically outside the station; if in an emergency situation all computing power is needed elsewhere it is no problem if the heating has to be neglected for a certain time. Thus, "overall system reliability" is in itself something complex. For systems such as telephone exchanges it is common practice nowadays to list different reliability requirements for the different functions or subsystems. Particular connection paths are allowed to be relatively unreliable as long as the system contains enough redundant substructures that it can compensate the breakdown of such paths. To this end, a few control modules and message lines must be some orders of magnitude more reliable than the rest. Systems to meet such requirements have been implemented successfully, using well-understood techniques to introduce redundancy, but always on the basis of informal or semi-formal reasoning.

Though some theoretical aspects of reliability have been studied and several reliability-improving algorithms have been developed, a complete formal framework for development and verification does not exist[1]. Consequently, the few existing second generation constructs for reliable programming ("exception handling") are not very well founded theoretically. Third generation constructs to our knowledge have not been investigated at all.

2. Towards unified treatment of correctness, timing, and reliability

To design correct algorithms we have been taught to pay less attention to *how* a result is computed than to *what* the result is and to prefer "slow" but obvious algorithms to "efficient" but obscure ones. Moreover, we have been taught to assume that hardware always functions correctly[2]. This may hold for compiler construction in an ideal educational environment; for embedded systems, however, correct timing and predictable reliability are as essential as functional correctness.

Often we hear that verification of temporal and reliability aspects of systems is possible only with respect to concrete hardware, as opposed to functional correctness. Timing and reliability are regarded second class citizens in the world of system development and verification. We wish to show that this view is based on historical coincidence rather than theoretical necessity. Correctness, timing, and reliability are issues of great similarity and we can hope to treat them in common, with formal systems for development and verification which pay equal right to all three of them. — Look at the symmetries:

Functionality. The function an algorithm computes is a consequence of the algorithm's structure, although two algorithms of very different structure may compute the same function. Functional correctness can be treated by formal methods based on nothing but the simplest axioms of computability. If we have developed and verified an algorithm, we know nothing but that the function under discussion *could* be mechanically computed if we had hardware

---

[1] "In 20 years of watching attempts to prove programs correct, I have seen only one attempt at proving that a program would get the correct answer in the event of a hardware failure. That proof made extremely unrealistic assumptions. ... We have no techniques for proving the correctness of programs in the presence of unknown hardware failures..." [Parnas 85]

[2] "We can dismiss this problem as not our concern: machines that are unreliable ... are of no interest to computing science (except as objects that we return to the manufacturer with a note asking that they be replaced)." [Turner 84]

exactly modelling our theory of computability. Concrete hardware, however, always has its limitations, and an implementation can only be verified with respect to particular hardware assumptions. To enable such verification, algorithms have to be adapted to these limitations. Functionally equivalent algorithms of different structure (for example recursive vs. iterative ones) can differ considerably in use as soon as hardware limitations are taken into account.

Timing. The time an algorithm consumes equally is a consequence of its structure. Time consumption is treated in complexity theory on the basis of very few simple axioms reflecting the properties of physical time. If we have developed and verified an algorithm of a certain complexity we know no more than that it could be computed mechanically in a certain time if we had hardware of certain temporal properties. For hardware with given properties, the algorithms often have to be adapted considerably, before the temporal behaviour of an implementation can be verified.

Reliability. The reliability of a system is a consequence of its structure and of the properties of a particular execution mechanism in much the same way as its temporal behaviour is. Functionally equivalent algorithms may, when implemented on particular hardware, give rise to systems drastically differing in reliability. Less obvious is whether reliability of algorithms can be discussed without reference to specific hardware in the same framework as their functionality and temporal complexity. We will give evidence that this indeed is possible.

3. A specification language for reliable hard real-time systems

We have developed a specification language for hard real-time systems [Wupper 88] which treats both functionality and timing in the same formal framework. Temporal requirements are taken into the design process by means of *types* in exactly the same way as functional requirements are. At present we are extending the language to cover reliability requirements as well. Here the new language shall be sketched.

It consists of two interwoven languages, the *type language* and the *algorithmic language*. The algorithmic language is a very simple functional language. It is used to describe *how* the system has to work. The type language is a subset of predicate calculus. It is used to specify *what* the system has to do, i. e. which input values it may expect when and which values it has to deliver at what time. If a is a valid expression in the type language and x is an algorithm or a piece of an algorithm (a system or a system component) which fulfils the condition defined by a we say: $x :: a$ ("x is of type a").

An essential difference to typed functional languages like Miranda [Turner 85] and Tale [Barendregt 86] is that statements about temporal behaviour and reliability are parts of the types in the same way as statements about data domains are.

In the present paper we merely explain some of the essential basic constructs and principles. Of course, the language also provides the necessary "syntactic sugar", which we shall not, however, attempt to present here. Also, the problem of *notation* shall not be addressed here. The reader is asked to understand the symbols used in this paper as preliminary. At this state, the *abstract* language is the more important issue.

3.1. Types. Following the ideas of constructive type theory[3] we regard types as predicates stating properties of systems or system components. Types can be built from four kinds of elementary predicates by means of logical junctors and quantifiers as described below. They can be given names by means of *type declarations*.

As far as data types and functionality are concerned, our type system is slightly more general than that of FUN [Cardelli 85][4]; moreover, two new "dimensions" allow to address timing and reliability properties.

Data predicates. The language allows to distinguish between arbitrarily many different data objects, each to be denoted by a capitalized identifier like *True, Error* , or *XOFF*. To express that a value must or will be *XOFF* and nothing else, we write the data predicate: *"!XOFF"*.

Such elementary data predicates may be joined by "logical or" (written: *"| "*); the result corresponds to a Pascal "enumeration type" and may be given a name:

$$bool := (!True) \mid (!False)$$
$$digit := (!Zero) \mid (!One) \mid (!Two) \mid (!Three)$$

Whenever in the sequel we use data predicate names such as *"bool "*, *"result"*, *"number"* we assume that these have been suitably defined.

Elementary timing predicates. The language allows to refer to moments in Real Time. For the purpose of this paper it is not interesting to dwell upon conventions of time denotation; we will use symbolic constants like $t, t1, t2$, etc. and assume they have been defined to denote suitable moments in absolute time. Points in time may be addressed relative to already defined ones by formulae like *"t + (t2 – t1) "*. — To express that something happens after $t1$ but not later than $t2$ we write the timing predicate: *"@t1 \t2"*. When $t1$ is not relevant we shall abbreviate this to *"\t2"*. Beside such *quantitative* timing predicates, two *qualitative* ones may be used: *"\#"* indicates that an event will happen before some unknown but finite moment, *"\?"* indicates that it may not happen at all.

These timing predicates are sufficient for the treatment of *hard real-time* systems with *static timing*. Many safety-critical process control systems belong to this class. They measure physical variables other than time and must be guaranteed to react at certain moments or within certain time intervals; their temporal behaviour follows a pattern known prior to execution. Our language is less useful for the development of systems with *dynamic timing*, i. e. such systems which measure the time between events or which compute durations.

---

[3]See [Nordström 84] for an introduction and for further references.

[4][Cardelli 85] shows that the FUN type system covers and exceeds the essentials of conventional function, record and variant types (like those in Pascal and Algol 68) as well as some other concepts like modules, generic packages, or objects. The reader interested in the flexibility and simplicity of the type system we based ours on will find extensive discussion and many examples in [Cardelli 85]. The notations rely as follows:

FUN record types:	{f1: Int, f2: Real, ...}	our notation:	*(int F1) & (real F2)*
FUN variant types:	[a: Int, b: Bool]		*(int A) I (bool B)*

Elementary reliability predicates. As simplest prototype for predicates covering aspects of Reliability we will choose the probability that a result is incorrect. The notation is: "*~r* ", where *r* is some real value between 0 and 1 or "*#* ". The latter is used to express "some unreliability" which cannot be quantified; it allows to use the language for *qualitative* treatment of system, distinguishing only between absolutely reliable and unreliable results. — Though these predicates will not allow to express predicates like mean time between failures, mean time to repair, etc., our type system can already be used to verify whether certain system functions remain reliable if unreliability is introduced in some place.

Throughout the remainder of this article, "reliability" is to be understood as: "Reliability, as far as it is covered by our elementary reliability predicates."

Locations. Arbitrarily many locations in a system may be distinguished by means of *labels*, denoted by capitalized identifiers such as *SensorPort*. Whether a label is implemented as channel, record component, storage location, area on the screen, file, or whatever is an implementation decision. The advantages of labels are manifold; some discussion and interesting application examples can be found in [Cardelli 85].

Atomic types. Atomic types each consist of one data, timing, and reliability predicate and a label, as in:

!XOFF \t ~0 TerminalPort

Taken as a system requirement, this reads: "An *XOFF* must be produced at *TerminalPort* not later than *t* and with absolute reliability." Once we have succeeded in building a system *x* of this type, we may write:

x::(!XOFF \t ~0 TerminalPort)

Now the same atomic type tells us: "An *XOFF will* be produced at *TerminalPort* not later than *t* and with absolute reliability." — All our types can be interpreted likewise as requirements that something must happen or as statements that something will happen.

Our type system boils down to conventional static data typing if all timing predicates are set to \? and all reliability predicates to ~0 . This shows an interesting asymmetry in the conventional approach: There, absolute reliability is assumed, whereas with respect to timing the worst, namely non-termination, is admissible.

From atomic types, composite types can be formed by means of disjunction, conjunction, implication, and quantification.

Disjunction. Any two (atomic or composite) types can be joined by "logical or" to express that at least one of two conditions must or will be fulfilled. — This is a typical specification of a "realistic" implementation:

(result \t ~#) | (!MemoryOverflow \# ~0) | (!Loop \? ~0)

(To be read as: "Some unreliable *result* (as defined elsewhere) not later than moment *t* or a memory overflow at some unpredictable moment, possibly later than *t*—but if it will occur, then definitely after finite time—or, worst of all, an endless loop which may be undetectable in finite time.") Note that the reliabilities given are independent of each other. They need not add up to 1 and are not meant to express with which probability which of the three possibilities will hold. We are not dealing with probabilistic results but with the probabilities that a result is wrong. The above type has to be read as: "If a *result* is delivered, this will not necessarily be the correct one. (For example, a memory overflow might go undetected under certain circumstances, leading to an erroneous result.) If, however, a *MemoryOverflow* will be reported, this will always indicate that a memory overflow has occurred indeed."

Conjunction. Two types can also be joined by "logical and" to express that two conditions must or will both be fulfilled. This allows to formulate what in other languages is called record types, e. g.:

$$(string \setminus t \sim 0 \ Name) \ \& \ (string \setminus t \sim 0 \ Address)$$

But, of course, the timing and reliability predicates of the two components may differ, as may the data predicates:

$$(result \setminus t \sim 0 \ Screen) \ \& \ (dayfile \setminus \# \ \sim r \ File)$$

A system fulfilling this requirement produces two values (which in a particular implementation may be written to the terminal screen and a file respectively). The value at *"Screen"* will definitely be available not later than moment t; the other value will be available at some finite, but yet unknown, point in time, with error probability r.

Implication. The third junctor for types is "logical implication":

$$a \Rightarrow b$$

Here, a and b may be atomic or composite types. A system is of type $a \Rightarrow b$ if it produces a result of type b *provided it is given a result of* a. Implication types cover what in many languages is known as function types. a specifies the (data, timing, and reliability) requirements the "input" or "actual parameter" has to fulfil to allow an "output" or "result" fulfilling b to be established. (Notice that any effectively computable function mapping a domain *dom* to a range *rg* can indeed be interpreted as a proof for the implication: *If* an $x::dom$ can (constructively) be shown to exist *then* a $y:: rg$ can (constructively) be shown to exist as well.) In regard to time, note that we do not have a primitive concept for the "duration" of a computation (or "function execution"). Instead, the atomic types in a and b contain timing predicates for all individual input and output components.

Universal types. The universal quantifier may be used to express predicates not bound to a specific data object, point in time, or error probability. To express that an input, whatever it may be, has to be duplicated immediately and without loss of reliability to two "channels", we might write:

$$FOR \ ALL \ a. \ a \setminus t \sim r \ Input \Rightarrow ((a \setminus t \sim r \ Channel1) \ \& \ (a \setminus t \sim r \ Channel2))$$

Here, a is a data variable bound by the universal quantifier; t and r are assumed to be defined elsewhere.

Quantification over time allows to describe activities which may happen at any time but have a constant duration. A function which may be "called" at any time to compute a real number (*real* being suitably defined) from another real number, but consuming not more than a microsecond, could be of type:

$$FOR\ ALL\ t.\ real \setminus t \sim 0\ Input \Rightarrow real \setminus (t+1\mu s) \sim 0\ Output$$

This is to be read: "For any given *t*, if a *real* argument of absolute reliability is available not later than *t*, a *real* result of absolute reliability will be available not later then *t+1µs*; otherwise, nothing can be guaranteed."

If we need a general algorithm that, given a function that computes its result with a certain reliability in a certain amount of time, delivers a function which does so with improved reliability but using a greater amount of time, we might ask for an algorithm of type:

$$FOR\ ALL\ d, r. \quad (FOR\ ALL\ t.\ real \setminus t \sim 0\ In \Rightarrow real \setminus (t+d) \sim r\ Out) \Rightarrow$$
$$(FOR\ ALL\ t.\ real \setminus t \sim 0\ In \Rightarrow real \setminus (t+d+d) \sim (r^*r)\ Out)$$

This example shows that universal quantification allows to express requirements like durations of functions, not supported by our elementary predicates, and to establish relations between the reliabilities of different functions.

Existential quantification, as described in [Cardelli 85] is also present, but shall not be discussed in this paper.

3.2. Algorithms. The algorithmic part of our language is a simple functional language. Every construct has a type; the types of composite constructs are defined in terms of the types of their constituents. The most important constructs are:

Constants. The algorithm producing a value *NACK* at moment *t* at location *Reply* is written:

$$!NACK\ @t\ Reply$$

(In the algorithmic part of the language, "*!*" can be read as "produce" and "*@*" as "at moment", while in type expressions they should be understood as "is"/"must be" and "after", respectively.) The type of above algorithm is, of course:

$$!NACK\ @t \setminus t \sim 0\ Reply$$

Thus:

$$!NACK\ @t\ Reply :: (!NACK\ @t \setminus t \sim 0\ Reply)$$

Store and wait. Consider an algorithm *x* of type $((!True) | (!False)) \setminus t1 \sim r\ Loc$ which will produce either *True* or *False* at some moment not later than *t* at point *Loc*. If we want to know, at a moment *t2* later then *t1*, whether the value was *True* or *False*, we need *memory* : The result must be *stored* until *t2* .

This is achieved by writing:

$$x @ t2$$

The type of the resulting algorithm is $((!True) | (!False)) @t2 \setminus t2 \sim r \; Loc$, provided that $t2$ is a type level constant statically known. If tx were a value computed at run time, we would only be able to derive:

$$x @ tx :: (((!True) | (!False)) \setminus \# \sim r \; Loc)$$

This store-and-wait operation will hardly ever be written explicitly: Due to our subtype algorithm it can always be inserted automatically where necessary, as will be described later.

Functions.   Like in typed lambda calculus, if e is a piece of text containing free occurrences of a name x such that, for all $v::a$, $e[x:=v]$[5] would be an algorithm of type b ,

$$FUN \; x::a \; . \; e$$

is an algorithm of type:

$$a =\!\!> b$$

Information about time consumption and reliability of functions (which is derived from the structure of the function "body" e) is manifested in the types of its domain and range. Our function types do not read: "a result is computed in so and so many seconds with such and such reliability" but: "*if* a (composite) value fulfilling the data, timing, and reliability requirements of a can be offered, *then* the required result can be produced and guaranteed to fulfil the requirements of b".

To write a function which takes more than one argument, we can make a a conjunction type. Similarly, the body e may consist of collaterally joined algorithms as described below, to deliver more than one result (i. e. a result of a conjunction type).

Not all components of a function parameter or a function result need to be equally reliable or available at the same time. This allows us to express communication between processes without anything like *send* and *receive*. Any sequential, non-iterative section of a process can be written as a function whose domain is a conjunction type with one component for every input interaction and whose range is a conjunction type with one component for every output interaction. (Of course, language constructs are needed to express iteration and the connection of several communicating processes. Our present language does not yet provide them and therefore is suitable only for the treatment of iteration steps *inside* separate processes.)

Function application.   If $f::(a=\!\!>b)$ and $x::a$, we may apply the function f to the argument x by writing:

$$f(x)$$

The whole then is an algorithm of type b . Function application is *sequential composition* of algorithms: f is applied to the result of x . But it should not be understood too literally as: "first compute x , then apply f to the result." If the domain of f were:

---

[5] e, with all occurrences of x replaced by v

$$\textit{(input } \backslash t \sim r1 \textit{ Channel1)} \quad \& \textit{ (input} \backslash (t+d) \sim r2 \textit{ Channel2)}$$

for some $d > 0$, the "execution" of f might well start before component *Channel2* of its argument provides an *input* value. The syntax of the language will, however, ensure that inside f in the period up to $t+d$ the value from Channel2 may not be assumed to be available.

Collateral algorithms. Two algorithms $x::a$ and $y::b$ may be joined collaterally:

$$x \& y :: (a \& b)$$

This describes an algorithm executing x and y independently; its result consists of the result of x and that of y. Nothing is said about the further processing of the results. In particular, it is not implied that they be moved to adjacent storage locations like "record components". Collateral algorithms may be used to model records values, but they are much more general. The timing and reliability predicates in the types of the two algorithms normally do not require that both results be available at the same time or be equally reliable.

Selection and relabelling. A component of a collateral algorithm (i. e. an algorithm of some conjunction type) can be selected and relabelled by writing:

$$x \$ \textit{ Label1 Label2}$$

provided that the type of x guarantees this component to be available, i. e. provided that $x::((a@t1 \backslash t2 \sim r \textit{ Label1}) \& b)$ for some b . Then:

$$x \$ \textit{ Label1 Label2} :: (a \ @t1 \ \backslash t2 \sim r \textit{ Label2})$$

Note that timing and reliability of the selected result component are not influenced by the presence or absence of differently labelled components: We may use the result from one system component even if some other system components are still "busy". Note furthermore that selection and relabelling is not a dynamic operation that consumes time or influences reliability: It rather is a renaming at conceptual level.

Polymorphic algorithms. Algorithm schemata which do not depend on a particular type may be expressed in terms of a formal type parameter, as customary in polymorphic languages. Such polymorphic algorithms have *universal types*. Before they may be used, they must be *instantiated* . This allows us to formulate, e. g., a sorting algorithm independently of the type of the objects to be sorted. It also allows us to express algorithms in general terms of time, like the following:

> *POL d.*
> > *FUN f :: (FOR ALL t. real $\backslash t \sim 0$ In $\Rightarrow$ real $\backslash (t+d) \sim 0$ Out).*
> > > *POL t.*
> > > > *FUN x :: (real $\backslash t \sim 0$) . f [t+d] (f [t] (x) \$Out In)*

This example—which as a whole is of type:

FOR ALL d. $\quad$ *(FOR ALL t. real \t ~0 In =› real \(t+d) ~0 Out) =›*
$\qquad\qquad$ *(FOR ALL t. real \t ~0 In =› real \(t+d+d) ~0 Out)*

shows both how polymorphic algorithms are written and used.

The conventional view of polymorphism is biased. Polymorphism with respect to data types is rather considered a luxury. Computer programs usually are not data-polymorphic, and instantiation is an expensive compile-time operation. They are, however, naturally time-polymorphic: Any function subprogram may be "called" at any time. Instantiation just happens unnoticed at the moment of calling. The same holds for reliability: One and the same function subprogram can handle input of any reliability; it will simply produce output of a corresponding reliability. But we should not base a specification language too much on these properties of a particular execution mechanism for two reasons: (1) Many functions in the "real world" are *not* time-polymorphic; think of the postal mail service[6]. (2) As soon as we need more parallel processes than we have hardware processors available or are interested in temporal precision down to the order of magnitude of machine cycli, time-polymorphism of computer programs turns out to be illusionary.

There are other specification formalisms which use the *duration of an operation* as a basic concept. This allows to avoid reference to moments in real time, but it has serious disadvantages: Without reference to absolute (or, if we use polymorphism, relative) time, it becomes clumsy to formulate dependencies such as:

$\qquad$ *((data1 \1 ~r1 Chan1) & (data2 \t2 ~r2 Chan2)) =›*
$\qquad$ *((data3 \t3 ~r3 Chan3) & (data4 \t4 ~r4 Chan4))*

or:

POL r. POL t. $\quad$ *((data1 \t ~r Chan1) & (data2 \(t+d2) ~r Chan2)) =›*
$\qquad\qquad$ *((data3 \(t+d3) ~r Chan4) & (data4 \(t+d4) ~r Chan4))*

and relate them to algorithms without loss of structure. Note that both can be realized by single functions in our language, with all benefits of statically typed functional languages.

Tests. $\quad$ Only one construct serves as a basis for all necessary tests: The collateral combination of two or more functions, called: *function bundle* . If we have two functions *f1::(a1=›b1)* and *f2::(a2=›b2)*, their collateral combination *f1 & f2 :: ((a1=›b1)&(a2=›b2))* is not a function. Nevertheless we may apply such a bundle to an argument *x* if *x::(a1 | a2)* :

$$(f1 \& f2) (x)$$

When evaluated, *x* will yield a result of type *a1* or of type *a2* . That result will be tested. If it is of type *a1* the result of *(f1 & f2) (x)* will be equal to *f1(x)* ; if it is of type *a2* the overall result will be *f2(x)* . — Semantically, function bundles are equivalent to Dijkstra's guarded if...fi [Dijkstra 76] extended with **await** and **delay** guards (cf. [Koymans 85]); syntactically,

---

[6]Not "electronic mail" is meant but ordinary letters for which the mailbox is cleared at fixed moments not triggered by the user's needs.

they are third rather than second generation: Each branch is joined with its corresponding guard to a function to allow better type check and more effective code generation. A discussion of function bundles can be found in [Wupper 88].

3.3. Timing and reliability of algorithms. The type derivation rules for algorithms must take the laws of Time and Reliability into account. Consider the simple case of a function with atomic domain and range, i. e. a function of some type:

$$(d1 @tl1 \setminus tu1 \sim r1) =\rangle (d2 @tl2 \setminus tu2 \sim r2)$$

Assume that for the computation of the result of that function the value of its parameter is actually needed. Then $tl2$ must be determined in accordance with these rules:

(1) $tl2$ must be at least $tu1$ (because the result cannot be guaranteed to be available before the parameter can).
(2) If the computation of the result involves general recursion, $tl2$ becomes ? (because termination cannot be guaranteed).
(3) In absence of general recursion, if the computation involves primitive recursion (which can be guaranteed to terminate) and $tu1$ is not ? , $tl2$ becomes #.
(3) $tu2$ must be at least $tl2$, of course.
(4) In absence of recursion and if $tu1 < \#$, concrete moments $tl2$ and $tu2$ with $tu1 \le tl2 \le tu2 < \#$ can be determined from the types of the functions involved in the computation.

Similar rules must be given for the propagation of error probabilities. As long as only the three qualitative values $0, \#$, and 1 are involved, this is straightforward and left as an exercise to the reader. Quantitative treatment will have to be based on probability theory.

If the range of a function is not atomic, these rules must be followed for each component of the result. If the domain is not atomic, each component of the result may depend on more than one parameter component; in this case we must replace $tu1$ by $max\{ tu1_i \}$ over all relevant parameter components.

How must the type derivation of our language be defined in accordance with these rules?

The only place where values are actually inspected is the function bundle $(f \mathrel{\&} g)(x)$. Only here, these rules will have to be taken into account. We shall explain how this is achieved for atomic values, i. e. for x being of some atomic type $dx @tlx \setminus tux \sim rx$ and the domains of f and g being of some atomic $df @tlf \setminus tuf \sim rf$ and $dg @tlg \setminus tug \sim rg$.

To be able to do so we must make some *assumptions about the properties of execution mechanisms* . We shall keep these assumptions as weak and general as possible. Let v be the value delivered by x. We assume:

(1) v becomes available at a certain moment $v_t \le tux$. Before that moment, it is at any time and without delay possible to detect that it is not yet available.
(2) If (at v_t) it can be detected without delay whether v has been computed correctly or not:

Let v_r be 0 if it has been computed correctly and 1 if an error has been detected.

If no error detection is possible, let v_r be rx.

v_r can be compared against rf and rg without delay.

(3) If $v_r = 0$, at v_t, the correctly computed value v_d of v can be compared with df and dg without delay.

Under these assumptions it is always constructively decidable whether a value fulfils a condition stated as a type, and our function bundle can be implemented by means of a dynamic test. To take nature of Time and Reliability into account, we must define the type of its result according to the rules given earlier. We observe: The value to be inspected is not available until v_t; but if $v_t > tuf$, f will not be used to compute the result; likewise, if $v_t > tug$, g will not be used. On the other hand, the syntax allows such a function bundle to be applied to x only if $x::(df\ @tlf\backslash tuf\ \sim rf\ |\ dg\ @tlg\backslash tug\ \sim rg)$, which means that, whatever the value of x may be, one of the functions will be applicable. Thus, $min\{tux, tuf, tug\}$ is the moment at which the decision can definitely be taken.

The overall type of $(f\ \&\ g)(x)$ therefore cannot simply be the disjunction or the ranges of f and g: the timing predicates must be adjusted to $min\{tux, tuf, tug\}$ to take into account that an implementation must wait until the test is possible.

For bundles of more than two functions whose domains, moreover, are composite types, the definition of type derivation rules becomes a rather dull exercise in combinatorial logic; it can be found worked out in [Wupper 88].

3.4. The subtype relation.

From mathematical viewpoint, writing an algorithm of a given type p is nothing but proving *constructively* that the p, regarded as a logical predicate, can be fulfilled. In general, predicate calculus is undecidable,—which means that program construction necessarily involves intelligence and creativity. Nevertheless we can leave a lot of routine work (mind the word!) in program development to machines:

Any effectively computable procedure S which, for *some* pairs of types (a, b), can produce an algorithm of type $a \Rightarrow b$, shall be called a *subtype algorithm*. If S succeeds for a particular pair of types (a, b), we call a a *subtype* of b (with respect to S) and write: $a \sim > b$. In other words: Whenever $a \sim > b$, the construction of an algorithm of type $a \Rightarrow b$ can be left to the subtype algorithm.

We had restricted function application in our language: For $f :: (b \Rightarrow c)$, we allowed to write $f(x)$ only if $x :: b$. When we use a subtype algorithm, we may allow f to be applied to x whenever $x :: a$ with $a \sim > b$. We write $f(x)$, whereupon the subtype algorithm constructs a function $g :: (a \Rightarrow b)$ and translates $f(x)$ to $f(g(x))$.

Example: A subtype algorithm handling $d\ \backslash t1\ \sim\#\ Loc\ \sim >\ d\ @t2\ \backslash t2\ \sim\#\ Loc$, for $t2 > t1$ simply has to insert the necessary store-and-wait operation:

$$FUN\ x:: (d\ \backslash t1\ \sim\#\ Loc).\ x\ @t2$$

Going a little further than [Cardelli 85], we have implemented a straightforward subtype algorithm which, amongst others, handles the cases:

$$
\begin{array}{lll}
d@\,t1\backslash t2\text{~}r\ L & \text{~>} & d@\,u1\backslash u2\text{~}s\ L & \text{if } u1 \leq t1,\, u2 \geq t2,\, s \geq r, \text{ for all } d,L \\
a & \text{~>} & a\ |\ b & \text{for all } a,b \\
a1\ |\ b1 & \text{~>} & a2\ |\ b2 & \text{if } a1 \text{~>} a2,\, b1 \text{~>} b2 \\
a\,\&\,b & \text{~>} & a & \text{for all } a,b \\
a1\,\&\,b1 & \text{~>} & a2\,\&\,b2 & \text{if } a1 \text{~>} a2,\, b1 \text{~>} b2 \\
a1 \Rightarrow b1 & \text{~>} & a2 \Rightarrow b2 & \text{if } a2 \text{~>} a1,\, b1 \text{~>} b2 \\
\end{array}
$$

The usefulness of these relations is explained in [Cardelli 85]; more discussion can be found in [Wupper 85].

4. Developing hard real-time systems

Our language can be useful in several stages of the development and verification process. We shall briefly describe some typical applications.

4.1. From requirements to algorithms. Even though the presentation given here views types from an unfamiliar standpoint, our type system essentially contains the type systems of languages like Pascal or Ada® (but makes far less assumptions about the execution mechanism). Anybody used to letting data types of such languages help him to derive correct programs may use our types, with little further knowledge, for the derivation of hard real-time algorithms of predictable reliability. But our type system also supports a more systematic development methodology, as described by [Petersson 86]. It shall be sketched briefly:

One begins by formulating the requirements as type. This will lead to a large composite type expression; let us call it a. The task to be solved then is to find an algorithm x, $x::a$. In some cases this will be straightforward: If a is of form $a1\,\&\,a2$, it can be refined to the task of finding two algorithms $x1::a1$ and $x2::a2$ and combining them collaterally to $x1\,\&\,x2$. If a is of form $a1\ |\ a2$, any algorithm of either type $a1$ or type $a2$ will do. If a is of form $a1 \Rightarrow a2$, a suitable body of type $a2$ for a function starting with "*FUN z::a1 .*" has to be developed. When such a schematic approach does not lead anywhere, creativity is needed: One must search for an intermediate step p such that $p \Rightarrow a$. If such a p can be found, our task may be refined to finding both an $y::p$ and an $f::(p \Rightarrow a)$, and combining them sequentially to $f(y)$.

A user acquainted with that development methodology may use our language without further knowledge of, say, temporal logic, compositional semantics, or proof theory: Results from these and other disciplines have been moulded into type derivation and subtype rules; users apply them without noticing them as such.

4.2. From algorithms to types. Our language supports static typing: The type of each algorithmic expression can be *derived* automatically from the types of its components. Types thus derived state the strongest properties which can be guaranteed for the described algorithms. Wherever a function is applied to an argument, types must be *checked*: The syntax allows application of a function $f::(a \Rightarrow b)$ to an expression $x::c$ only if x can be guaranteed to fulfil *a*, which is the case if *c=a* or if *c~>a* due to a subtype algorithm. — Automatic type derivation and type checking have three benefits:

Consistency check. A successfully type-checked specification describes an implementable system which is guaranteed to be consistent with respect to what is covered by our elementary predicates: Never will a function be applied to an argument for which it is not defined; never will a value be inspected before it is defined; nowhere does a system component rely more on another one than is justifiable, be it directly or indirectly.

Interface analysis. The type derived from the specification of a system or system component describes the interface with the environment and with the assumed execution mechanism in terms of predicate calculus, including assumptions made about temporal and reliability properties. The type does not tell us *how* an algorithm works, but it tells us to a certain degree *what* it does. This information can be used in the validation process.

Improvement analysis. As already said, inconsistencies can be discovered by a mechanical check. More interesting, however, is analysis of a *correct* specification: A mechanical analyzer based on the subtype relation can point out—qualitatively and quantitatively—where and to which degree system components are "better", e. g. perform their function faster or earlier or with a smaller error probability than required by their environment. Furthermore, for any given time interval the degree of parallelity necessary during that interval can be determined automatically. The information so obtained be used to develop optimizations.

4.3. From specification towards implementation: Taking specific hardware into account.

Our language is based on very general assumptions about computability, the passage of physical time, and the propagation of reliability between system components. Beyond these, no assumptions are made about execution mechanism properties. Any consistent specification can be implemented on a sufficiently large, sufficiently fast, and sufficiently reliable machine. Miracles are not required. But it cannot be promised that every specification can be implemented on arbitrary hardware.

When a system has to be implemented by means of a particular execution mechanism, we may proceed as follows. First, the properties of the execution mechanism are specified—at the required level of abstraction—in form of a type, usually a large conjunction type with a component for every function the mechanism provides, containing many machine-dependent constants:

> (FOR ALL t. FOR ALL r.
>   ((byte\t~r AndIn1) & (byte\t~r AndIn2)) => (byte\(t+d1)~(r *r1) AndOut)
>) & ...

The original specification is then transformed to an equivalent one which (a) depends on a function bundle parameter "*machine*" of just that type and (b) consists of nothing but applications of functions from that bundle. This transformation may be done and verified by any suitable technique—manually, or by means of a program. If the resulting specification is consistent, the specified system can be implemented on that *machine* in such a way that no checks on data values, time, or reliability need to be built into the implementation except those contained in the translated form of the specification.

During this stage of development, improvement analysis based on type checking becomes a particularly useful tool. It allows, for example, to detect "time gaps" during which certain *machine* resources are definitely not needed. Such information may be used to merge two originally unrelated functions in "static scheduling".

4.4. Generalization. We can write polymorphic algorithms and functions which depend on functions or yield functions. This allows special solutions to be generalized. If, for example, a solution has been found to increase the reliability of a certain function in a system, the essentials can in many cases be re-formulated as a general algorithm not depending on a particular data type, functionality, or on specific values of error rates or time constants. If such an algorithm later is instantiated with particular types and parametrized with particular functions, the type check will confirm whether it is suitable under those circumstances.

5. Conclusion

The described prototype of a specification language can be used for the development and verification of such real-time systems which have to react at fixed moments or within a fixed period of time with predictable error probability. It has mainly been developed to show that a consistent language based on the principles of static typing of timing and reliability can indeed be defined and that such a language will be useful in several stages of the development and verification process. Our present type system is not yet powerful enough to express all reliability requirements needed in practice; moreover, algorithmic constructs like such to describe incorporation of redundancy are still lacking.

Nevertheless, the development and evaluation of this language prototype has given evidence that—
- it is possible to treat such different issues as functionality, timing, and reliability of systems in a common framework;
- constructive type theory and strong polymorphic typing provide such a framework and can help us to find specification languages which—
  - help to design a system,
  - support validation of specifications,
  - allow automatic verification of specifications at various levels of abstraction, also with respect to particular hardware,
  - support improvement analysis and transformation;
- type derivation rules should not make assumptions about the properties of execution mechanisms (e. g. "maximum parallelism") beyond the most general assumptions about the nature of Time;
- special properties of a particular execution mechanism can best be specified be means of the language together with the system to be implemented (rather than be built into the language).

To obtain a more general language, we will have to investigate results from temporal, real-time, and probabilistic logic and from reliability theory, to be able—
- to define more powerful elementary predicates about temporal behaviour and reliability, and

– guided by these, to define suitable (third generation) algorithmic constructs to describe improvement of timing (like: "take the *first* result available from one of several collateral algorithms") or reliability (i. e. constructs to describe redundancy and independence).

Acknowledgements

The authors owe many thanks to Henk Barendregt, Luca Cardelli, Dave Harrison, and Willem-Paul de Roever for helping to take the right decisions in the project and to Marco Huysmans, Dick de Reus, Louis Vuurpijl, and Freddy Zwerus for their thorough reading of the manuscript and numerous suggestions for improvement.

References

Barendregt 86 H. P. Barendregt, M. van Leeuwen: *Functional Programming and the Language TALE*, in: Current Trends in Concurrency (J. W. de Bakker et al., eds.), LNCS 224, Berlin 1985

Birolini 85 A. Birolini: *Qualität und Zuverlässigkeit technischer Systeme*, Berlin, New York, Tokyo 1985

Cardelli 85 L. Cardelli, P. Wegner: *On Understanding Types, Data Abstraction, and Polymorphism* , ACM Comp. Surv. 17 (1985), Nr. 4, pp. 471-522

Dijkstra 76 E. W. Dijkstra: *A Discipline of Programming* , Englewood Cliffs, N. J. 1976

Koymans 85 R. Koymans, R. K. Shyamasundar, W. P. de Roever, R. Gerth, S. Arun-Kumar: *Compositional Semantics for Real-Time Distributed Computing*, Report No. 68 (1985), Sectie Informatica, Kath. Univ. Nijmegen, 1985

Leveson 86 Nancy G. Leveson: *Software safety: Why, What, and How* , Comp. Surv., 18, No. 2, June 1986, pp.125-163

Nordström 84 B. Nordström, J. M. Smith: *Proposition, Types, and Specifications of Programs in Martin-Löf's Type Theory*, BIT 24 (1984), pp. 288-301

Parnas 85 D. C. Parnas: *Software Aspects of Strategic Defense Systems*, C.ACM 28 (1985), No. 12

Petersson 86 K. Petersson, J. M. Smith: *Program Derivation in Type Theory: A Partitioning Problem*, Comput. Lang. 11, No. 3/4 (1986), pp. 161-172

Turner 84 D. A. Turner: *Functional Programs as Executable Specifications*, Phil. Trans. R. Soc. Lond. A 312 (1984), pp. 363-388

Turner 85 D. A. Turner: *Miranda: A non-strict functional language with polymorphic types* , Proc. Conf. in Fun. Lang. and Comp. Arch., Nancy, Sept. 85

Wupper 88 H. Wupper, J. Vytopil, M. Wieczorek, D. de Reus: *A Simple Language with Static Typing of Hard Real-Time Constraints* , Rep. no. 88-3 (1988), Informatica, Kath. Univ. Nijmegen

Timed Acceptances: A Model of Time Dependent Processes [1]

Insup Lee and Amy Zwarico
Department of Computer and Information Science
University of Pennsylvania
Philadelphia, PA 19104

Timed Acceptances is a process model for describing and reasoning about processes with explicit timing constraints (real-time processes). A process is an entity that interacts with other processes and makes internal decisions that affect its subsequent behavior. An interaction corresponds to synchronization or communication among processes. An internal or unobservable decision is not affected by any other process. In a real-time process, the actions that can occur are constrained both logically and temporally. A sequence of interactions and internal decisions occurring at particular times constitutes an execution of a real-time process.

To model execution, we use a temporal extension of Hennessy's Acceptance Trees and characterize a real-time process by the set of all its possible executions. The interactions of a process are represented by *events*. An event is an instantaneous visible action in which a process engages during its execution. The state of a process controls the possible interactions of the process and the times at which the interactions can occur. The internal decisions represent the *nondeterministic* behavior of a process. They affect the subsequent behavior of the process by changing the *internal state* of the process. Thus, the possibility of an internal decision is represented by the set of states which a process may be in at a given time.

We now give the formal description of an execution, which consists of a *timed trace* and the possible states the process may be in after executing the trace. We assume that the choice of state is made immediately upon executing the last event in the trace. A timed trace is a finite sequence $\langle (a_1, n_1), (a_2, n_2), \ldots, (a_m, n_m) \rangle \in (\Sigma \times N)^*$ where N is the nonnegative integers. Each (a_i, n_i) represents the occurrence of the ith event in the execution of the process. The time n_1 is the time between 0 and the occurrence of a_1. For $i > 1$, n_i represents the relative time between events a_{i-1} and a_i.

A state is represented by a set of event-time pairs $\{(A_1, n_1), \ldots, (A_m, n_m)\} \subseteq \mathcal{P}(\mathcal{P}(\Sigma) \times N \cup \{(\emptyset, \infty)\})$ where Σ is the set of events, $\mathcal{P}(A)$ is the set of all finite subsets of A and A_i is either $\{a_i\}$ or $\emptyset$. Each $(\{a_i\}, n_i)$ represents the possibility of event a_i occurring n_i time units after a process enters the state. The pair $(\emptyset, n_i)$ represents the possibility of the process stopping at time n_i. If $n_i = \infty$, the state represents the process *diverging*. A divergent process is one that continues to execute, but does not engage in any further useful computation.

The set of all executions of a process is its acceptance set, $\mathcal{A}(P)$. Formally, a process is represented by a pair $(\bar{\alpha}P, \mathcal{A}(P))$ satisfying the following six constraints. First, the empty trace is a trace of P since it represents the behavior of P the moment it is *switched on*, but before it engages in any action. Second, the trace set of P is prefix closed because if P has executed a trace s, it must have executed all prefixes of s first. Third, all events in a nonempty

---

[1]This research was supported in part by NSF DCR 8501482, NSF DMC 8512838, NSF MCS 8219196-CER, ARO DAA6-29-84-k-0061, and a grant from AT&T's Telecommunications Program at the University of Pennsylvania.

trace are in the alphabet of P. Fourth, if $s\hat{}\langle(a,i)\rangle$ is a trace of P then there is a state reachable by s from which a may be executed at time i. Fifth, for every event-time pair (a,i) in a state reachable by executing s in P, $s\hat{}\langle(a,i)\rangle$ is a trace of P. Finally, the state set associated with a trace s of P is saturated.

The set of all pairs consisting of a set of events (an alphabet) and a set of acceptances and satisfying the six properties of a process forms the domain. It is partially ordered by *process containment*. Process containment formalizes the notion of one process being more defined than another. We say that $P \sqsubseteq Q$ (P contains Q) if Q is more deterministic than P. That is, P can make more internal decisions during its execution. Since process containment is a partial ordering, it induces an equivalence relation on processes. This relation, process equivalence, corresponds to the intuitive notion of process equality. That is, two processes are equal if they behave identically in all situations.

We also define a set of operators on the domain. They are the CSP operators defined with respect to time and represent the passage of time, choice, concurrency and interaction, repetitive behavior and abstraction mechanisms for representing nondeterminism, hiding and generic process instantiation. Each operator is defined denotationally by the process it represents. The operators possess a variety of algebraic properties. Since they are time dependent versions of the CSP operators, most of the algebraic properties of the CSP operators also hold for the timed acceptances operators. In addition, the operators also satisfy properties that reflect the temporal nature of their definitions.

Timed Action: Instead of representing the passage of time by a wait statement and associating an execution time with each event, we represent the passage of time by the timed action operator, $a \stackrel{i}{\leadsto} P$. This process engages in event a at time 0 and, after delaying for exactly i time units, executes the process P. It is used to model the occurrence time of events, the execution time of program actions, the simultaneous occurrence of events and the initial delay in a process' execution. The initial delay is represented by introducing an event ϵ that acts as a temporal marker. Thus $\epsilon \stackrel{i}{\leadsto} P$ is a process that starts behaving like P after a delay of i time units. The algebraic properties of timed action represent the invisibility of ϵ, $a \stackrel{i}{\leadsto} \epsilon \stackrel{j}{\leadsto} P = a \stackrel{i+j}{\leadsto} P$ and $\epsilon \stackrel{0}{\leadsto} P = P$; and the ability to represent simultaneously occurring events in any order, $a \stackrel{0}{\leadsto} b \stackrel{i}{\leadsto} P = b \stackrel{0}{\leadsto} a \stackrel{i}{\leadsto} P$.

Parallel Composition: $P\|Q$ represents the concurrent execution and interaction of P and Q. $P\|Q$ executes only those events that either P or Q can execute and only at the times that P or Q can execute them. Furthermore, if $P\|Q$ executes an event that both component processes may execute, then both must be able to execute it *at that time*. When this occurs, we say that P and Q interact or synchronize on that event. The set of events that both P and Q can execute are called *shared events*. $P\|Q$ also makes the same internal (nondeterministic) choices made by P and Q. Thus, when observing the execution of $P\|Q$, we are actually observing the interleaving with respect to time of an execution of P with an execution of Q. The concurrent execution of P and Q may lead to *deadlock*. $P\|Q$ is deadlocked if both P and Q only prepared to execute shared events, but not at the same time. As demonstrated in the following example, the parallel operator does not force the execution of either P or Q. $P\|Q =$

$((\epsilon \overset{1}{\leadsto} a \overset{1}{\leadsto} \text{STOP}) \square (\epsilon \overset{3}{\leadsto} c \overset{1}{\leadsto} \text{STOP})) \| ((\epsilon \overset{2}{\leadsto} b \overset{1}{\leadsto} \text{STOP}) \square (\epsilon \overset{3}{\leadsto} c \overset{1}{\leadsto} \text{STOP}))$ is equivalent to the choice between three processes, $\epsilon \overset{1}{\leadsto} a \overset{1}{\leadsto} b \overset{1}{\leadsto} \text{STOP}$, $\epsilon \overset{2}{\leadsto} b \overset{1}{\leadsto} \text{STOP}$ and $\epsilon \overset{3}{\leadsto} c \overset{1}{\leadsto} \text{STOP}$. The first process represents $P\|Q$ choosing to execute a at time 1. It can then execute b 1 time unit later because Q can still execute b at time 2. The second process represents $P\|Q$ initially choosing to execute the event b at time 2. After doing so, $P\|Q$ stops since P can only execute the shared event c, but Q cannot execute any other events. This execution of $P\|Q$ occurs if, for some reason, P does not execute a at time 1. The final process represents the two synchronizing on event c at time 3. After doing so, they stop. Note that the shared event on which two processes synchronize is not internalized by the synchronization. This allows the representation of synchronization time and, more importantly, allows another process to synchronize on this event.

Concealment: Concealment is an abstraction mechanism used to isolate the relevant events from the surrounding details of a process' execution and to preserve their occurrence times. Concealment does not eliminate any potential execution sequences of a process. For example, $P = (a \overset{2}{\leadsto} b \overset{3}{\leadsto} c \overset{1}{\leadsto} \text{STOP}) \backslash \{a\}$ is equivalent to $\epsilon \overset{2}{\leadsto} b \overset{3}{\leadsto} c \overset{1}{\leadsto} \text{STOP}$. As in CSP, concealment may introduce nondeterminism and divergence. Nondeterminism arises if an event used in determining which branch of a process to follow is hidden. Divergence occurs if all of the events in an infinite process are hidden. Although the process continues executing, we are unable to see what it is doing and consider it to be diverging. The concealment operator is continuous because we treat a process that delays infinitely long before executing an event as a divergent process. As an illustration, consider the chain of processes $\{P_i | i \geq 0\}$ defined as follows.

$$P_0 = (\epsilon \overset{1}{\leadsto} a \overset{1}{\leadsto} \text{CHAOS}) \square (\epsilon \overset{1}{\leadsto} b \overset{1}{\leadsto} \text{STOP}), \quad P_{n+1} = \epsilon \overset{1}{\leadsto} a \overset{0}{\leadsto} P_n$$

Process P_{n+1} performs n a events and then either executes b and stops or executes a and then behaves chaotically. The limit of this chain of processes, P, can execute any sequence of a's occurring every 1 time unit. Each execution leaves P in the state $\{(a,1)\}$. If we conceal a from P, $P\backslash\{a\}$, the resulting process has a single acceptance $(\langle\rangle, \{\{(\emptyset, \infty)\}\})$ representing divergence. On the other hand, each process in the chain, $P_i\backslash\{a\}$, either executes b at time $i+1$ and then stops or begins behaving chaotically at time $i+2$. The limit of this chain also is a divergent process since the only acceptance that is common to all processes in the chain is the acceptance in which the process does nothing and then after an infinite delay behaves chaotically. By definition, this is $(\langle\rangle, \{\{(\emptyset, \infty)\}\})$ which represents divergence.

Currently, we are showing that the denotational semantics are fully abstract with respect to operational semantics that correspond to our description of real-time execution. We are also developing and automating analysis techniques based on the algebraic properties of the operators for verifying real-time processes. Finally, we are comparing our representation of processes and semantics of parallel composition to those in ECP, Timed Stability, CSP-R and SCCS.

Responsive Sequential Processes

Neelam Soundararajan   and   Roger L. Costello

Computer and Information Science Department
Ohio State University
Columbus, OH 43210, U. S. A.

In this paper we propose a new model/language for real-time systems. Our proposal, while in no sense an *extension* of CSP [1], is nevertheless heavily influenced by it. Thus each process of a real-time system in our approach runs on its *own processor* and interacts with other processes exclusively by means of communications. We do not make any attempt to share processing power between the various processes. Thus our approach is quite different from many others that (use complex scheduling algorithms in the underlying OS to) execute the various processes on a *common pool of processors*. Given current (and expected future) costs and performance of microprocessors, our (or rather the CSP) approach seems reasonable.

While processes of real-time systems do not need to share processing power with each other, they *do* need to share other resources, examples of such resources in practical systems being robot arms, tv cameras, and the like. Consider an example: Suppose a process Q needs a robot arm controlled by another process P to be moved in a certain manner within, say, 2 seconds. One approach, the one used in such languages as Occam [2] and Ada is to use a 'time-out' mechanism; if P does not interact with Q within 2 seconds, Q *times-out* and tries other alternatives (such as trying a different robot arm controlled by a different process, say, P'). While this may be appropriate in some situations, in general it does not seem very useful: Q needed the service (movement of the robot arm) in 2 seconds, and when the 2 seconds expire it is very likely too late for Q to try any alternatives such as requesting the service of P'. We cannot get around this by having Q time-out earlier for then it might time-out even if P would have provided the service in a timely manner. Alternatively we could use two CSP-like output guards (P!.., P'!..) in Q to send the request to whichever one of P, P' will accept it. However, this does not allow Q to prefer P to P'; and if neither P nor P' accepts the request within two seconds, Q has again lost valuable time waiting. A better solution, the one underlying our approach, is to use a *responsive* communication mechanism; *as soon as* Q tries to send the request (or any messages in general) P either *rejects* the request or *accepts* it (for processing at a later time but, presumably, within the constraint specified in the request). If P accepts the request, Q can proceed immediately with its other actions, confident that P will perform the requested service in a timely fashion. If P rejects the request, Q can try other alternatives such as trying the request on P'. P may reject the request because it is already committed to too many other requests, or because the robot arm is jammed, or because of any other reason; it does not really matter to Q *why* P rejected the request; what does matter is that Q be informed (of the rejection) immediately so that it can try other alternatives.

But how can P accept or reject Q's request if it is busy with some local computations? We assume, in our system model that there are *two* (not just one) processors associated with P. One processor, $\mu1$, executes P's local code. The second processor, $\mu2$, receives the messages sent by other processes. $\mu2$ accepts some messages[1] and rejects others and in either case the sender knows whether the message was accepted or rejected. If $\mu2$ accepts a message, it adds the message to a buffer it maintains; when $\mu1$ executes the next input command, it will read in the entire buffer, i.e all the messages received and accepted by $\mu2$ since the last time $\mu1$ executed an input command. If $\mu2$ rejects the message, no trace of the message remains in $\mu2/\mu1$ (i.e., P has no way of even knowing that the message was rejected). Thus $\mu2$ provides the quick response needed by processes that send messages to P, while $\mu1$ continues to execute P.

----

[1] As in CSP, *what* a message means is decided by the programmer; thus whether a message is a request, a piece of data or something else is up to the (code of the) sender and receiver.

How does μ2 decide which messages to accept and which to reject? As part of the process P, the programmer is required to write an *'acceptance condition'*, a boolean function of the incoming message, the messages accepted since P's last input command or guard (i.e., the contents of μ2's buffer), and the state of P at its most recent i/o command (or guard). When a message comes in, μ2 evaluates the acceptance condition; if it evaluates to true, the message is accepted (and the sender informed), and added to μ2's buffer, else the message is rejected. Note that the state of P used in the acceptance condition is *not P's current state*; that is constantly changing as P (or rather μ1) executes its local actions and μ2 has no access to that state.

'Responsive communications' can, of course, be simulated in CSP. All we need do is associate, with P, a buffer process B to do precisely what our μ2 does. Of course, this buffer process and the sender would have to go through additional communications to inform the sender whether the message was accepted or rejected, but that is a relatively minor detail. While this is true, given that in real-time systems all processes are required to be responsive to communications from other processes, it seems more reasonable to make the communication mechanism provided by the language a responsive one, instead of setting up an explicit buffer process each time.

In addition, our approach also allows us to deal with an important class of *'emergencies'* in a very natural fashion. Consider again the robot arm example: suppose the robot arm process P accepts Q's request (to move the robot arm in a certain manner within 2 seconds), but before it is able to carry out this request, the robot arm jams. At the very least what P should do now is to send a message informing Q that it will not provide the service needed by Q despite its previous commitment to do so. There is no problem in *P's sending such a message*; P does not even care whether Q accepts or rejects the message. The problem is that Q is proceeding on the assumption that P will provide the service it agreed to, and the message from P reneging on that commitment might signify an emergency for Q calling for *immediate* corrective action. Our solution is to associate an 'emergency condition' with each process. The *emergency condition* of a process, like its acceptance condition, is a boolean function of the incoming message, the contents of the buffer (of μ2), and the state of the process at the last i/o. When a process receives a message, μ2 (of the process) first evaluates the emergency condition of the process; if this evaluates to false, μ2 then evaluates the acceptance condition and proceeds as described earlier. If the emergency condition evaluates to true, we have an emergency! The message is accepted (and the sender informed), and added to the buffer. Suppose the most recent i/o executed by the process was an input command, say, ?h. When this input is executed, the contents of μ2's buffer, i.e., all the messages received and accepted since the previous input, are read into h (a *sequence* variable), the buffer cleared, and μ1 continues execution of whatever statement immediately follows the input command ?h. Also, μ2 records the state of the process (including the value of h) at this point since this will be needed in evaluating the acceptance and emergency conditions to decide which messages to accept and which to reject. The accepted messages are, of course, added to the buffer until finally the 'emergency message', i.e., the one that causes the emergency condition to evaluate to true, arrives, and is added to the buffer. μ1 then stops, control (in μ1) is backed up to the point immediately after the input command, the state restored to what it was at that point, and the contents of the buffer, *including the "emergency message" that triggered it all* concatenated to h, (and the buffer cleared), and μ1 again starts execution. The programmer has no way of knowing that any of this 'backing up' took place. For all he can tell, the process just waited in front of the command ?h until the emergency message arrived and then executed the input. Of course, it is the programmers responsibility to write appropriate code following ?h to take corrective action if h contains an emergency message, but he does not have to, in the code corresponding to the non-emergency case, constantly check if an emergency message has just been received. In the case of the robot arm example, the emergency condition of the process Q requesting the service of the robot could evaluate to true if a message of the form "reneging on previous commitment" comes from P (the robot arm controller). Q would then be backed up to the most recent i/o command (which we have assumed is an input), the input reexecuted, and Q can take appropriate corrective action.

Note that our emergencies are very different from standard *exceptions*. Exceptions are problems caused by the action, say division by 0, of a particular process, say, Q, and have to be taken care of by Q. In our case, however, it is *P, not Q*, that is responsible for the emergency for Q; Q learns about the emergency only beause of the message from P. This kind of situation is quite common in real-time systems, hence an emergency mechanism such as ours seems essential in real-time languages. Note also that our emergencies are quite different from interrupts. Interrupts are useful in situations where the interruptor, say, P needs the 'services' of the interruptee, say, Q urgently, and after this need is met, Q can continue with its own work. In our example on the other hand, the message from P to Q signifies an emergency not for P but for Q. P does not even care whether Q accepts or rejects the message. Our mechanism allows Q to identify the messages that it might receive that signify emergency situations, and to react quickly when such a message is received and take corrective action. Since the emergency condition is a function of the incoming message, as well as the contents of the buffer, and the state of Q at the most recent i/o, Q can be very selective about what messages constitute an emergency for it and when. Thus it is easy to program Q so that a message is treated as an emergency while a second identical message received immediately after the first one, is accepted as a normal message, or even rejected altogether. We have not, of course, explained what happens if the most recent i/o when an emergency message is received is an output rather than an input. This, as well as a simple system architecture that provides a very effecient method for saving (by $\mu 2$) of the state of a process following an i/o and the backing up to this state if an emergency message is received, are described in the full paper [3].

In summary, the motivations and concepts underlying RSP are:

1. Processing power is not a critical resource in real-time systems, and does not have to be shared between the different processes; however, other resources do need to be shared.

2. Processes have to be *responsive* to communications from other processes, hence the communication mechanism provided by the language must be a *responsive* one.

3. The language must provide an *emergency mechanism* that allows a process to identify messages that signify emergencies for it and to react quickly to the receipt of such messages and take corrective action.

Before concluding, it is worth remarking that our emergency mechanism seems to be a useful programming paradigm even in 'non-real-time' systems: if a number of processes are cooperatively engaged in some task and *one* of them discovers that the particular path that they are trying is useless, it can send a message to that effect to the others which can treat this as an 'emergency' message and abandon this path and try another. The full paper [3] contains an interesting algorithm for computing prime numbers using this paradigm.

References:

1. C. A. R. Hoare, Communicating Sequential Processes, CACM *21* (1978) pp. 666-677.

2. OCCAM programming manual, INMOS corporation, Prentice-Hall, 1985.

3. N. Soundararajan, R. Costello, Responsive Sequential Processes, tech. report, Ohio State University, September 1987.

Static Analysis of Real-Time Distributed Systems

Leo YuHsiang Liu and R. K. Shyamasundar
333 Whitmore Laboratory
Department of Computer Science
The Pennsylvania State University
University Park, PA 16802, U.S.A.
(lyliu@GONDOR.CS.PSU.EDU, shyam@PSUVAX1.CS.PSU.EDU)

1. Related Works and Motivation

Static analysis for concurrent programs has been carried out by Apt [1, 2] and Taylor [19]. However, Apt does not discuss algorithms for the parallel composition of CSP programs, and Taylor does not consider real time for Ada programs. Wolper [20] proposes Extended Temporal Logic (ETL) to specify and verify program properties which can be described with regular expressions (in fact, ETL is equivalent to transition systems with appropriate acceptance conditions [14]). Jahanian and Mok [6, 7] have done the safety analysis of timing properties using Real-Time Logic (RTL) based on the refutation approach.

We propose a *systematic* way following [18] to reason about the temporal behaviors of real-time distributed systems in CSP-R [8] under the *maximal parallelism* model [16]. One of the distinctive features of our method is that it is *compositional* and thus provides a basis for compositional specification and verification techniques. Although our approach only provides an approximate timing behavior by ignoring the state information, we can identify many interesting properties such as possibly synchronized pairs, deadlock behavior, termination of processes, possible parallel actions, and detection of possible temporal errors (violating timing constraints) and failures. Our method not only leads to efficient algorithms for the static analysis of CSP programs but also applies to many other languages. Furthermore, the approach can be used to infer timing properties of real-time programs statically, and suitably augmented, to consider various run-time features.

2. Language CSP-R

CSP-R has been derived from CSP [5] with additional real-time features which allows the modeling of Ada programs. The syntax of the language is given in Appendix A. The interpretation of CSP-R follows essentially on the lines of CSP except for the following: (i) the addition of the real time construct "**wait** d" and the hiding of the network "[N]" (hiding is not discussed in this paper), (ii) processes communicate via unidirectional channels which connect exactly two processes, and (iii) the alternative command may have input/output (i/o) guards as well as wait guards. The formal semantics and the informal interpretation of CSP-R can be found in [8].

3. Maximal Parallelism Model

The behavior of a program can be characterized by a global transition system based on the pure maximal parallelism model (referred to as $MAX_0(0, 1)$ model [8]). The model is realistic in the sense that *concurrent actions can and will overlap in time unless prohibited by synchronization constraints* and *no unnecessary waiting* of processors is modeled. For example, let cset be a set of channel names. Then, the alphabet corresponding to cset, written Σ_{cset}, is defined by:

$$\Sigma_{cset} \stackrel{\text{def}}{=} cset \cup \{R(D)|\ D \in cset\} \cup \{\Box\}$$

Here, symbol D reflects the actual communication via channel D; symbol R(D) denotes the readiness of the process to communicate over channel D; symbol $\Box$ represents a local computation which is invisible outside. To model the proper termination of processes for terminating systems, we further introduce the terminal symbol, τ, into the alphabet to denote the action that just awaits the ticking of the clock, and this enables us to study behaviors of incomplete computations such as deadlocks and distributed terminations as well as other eventuality properties. In $MAX_0(0, 1)$ model, a discrete-time model is used; we assume that each action symbol of the alphabet takes one time unit, and it takes no time to recognize a communication request. The behavior of a process is modeled as possible histories which are sequences of sets of action symbols. Real-time is modeled in the histories by relating the i-th element of a history with the i-th tick of a conceptual global clock.

4. Global Transition System

The characterization procedure can be summarized as follows. Firstly, the behavior of each component process is characterized by a (regular) behavior expression over the possible histories. An equivalent Deterministic Finite Automaton (DFA) can then be derived from the behavior expression as it is regular. Secondly, we provide a merging algorithm (see Appendix B) to do the parallel composition of processes (the global transition system can be obtained by merging all the component processes involved in a program). Actually, the parallel composition of processes merely drops inconsistent histories. Two histories (of different processes) are *consistent* (with respect to their joint channels) if and only if they are (i) *communication compatible*: at any instant, if one process claims a successful communication via some channel D, then the other process should make the same claim, and (ii) *no unnecessary waiting*: both processes should not wait for communication over the same channel at the same time. The parallel composition of processes is modeled as a composite machine computed by the merging algorithm. In fact, we have proved that the merging operation is *compositional* in the sense that it is commutative, associative, and preserves the regularity (i.e., the composite machine is also a DFA).

5. Reduction of Complexity

The complexity of the composite machine (i.e., the number of states and transitions) is proportional to the product of those of the component processes in the worst case. Many times the complexity of the composite machine becomes unacceptable when the component processes have large cycles. To overcome the explosion of the complexity, we further extend the DFA (inspired by [12]) to include a guard and an assignment action so that we can count the number of occurrences of some action symbols. This not only significantly reduces the complexity of the composite machine but also makes the reasoning of the system easier.

6. Specification and Verification of Timing Properties

The need of our technique can be highlighted by the following example. Consider a producer-consumer system consisting of two producers and a consumer. The consumer can receive an item from either producer 1 or producer 2. Upon the receipt of an item, the consumer operates on the item for 3 seconds and then is ready for another item. Producer 1 takes 4 seconds to produce a new item while producer 2 only needs 2 seconds. The goal of the design of this system is to ensure that *the consumer is receiving at least an item every 4 seconds*. To determine if such a system can achieve the above goal, obviously, one would like to specify/verify the system.

The classes of timing constraints which can be specified in CSP-R are limited to the maximal and the minimal timing constraints of i/o commands; however, using the behavior expression along with the projection operation we are capable of deriving various interesting classes of properties that can be expressed in RTL as well as in ETL for both reactive systems [15] and terminating systems. Given a system supposedly satisfying some timing property, one can derive the composite machine and then check whether the composite machine satisfies the property or not. Another way is to introduce exceptions into the program, and the detection of temporal errors amounts to examining if the composite machine contains any exception symbols. As our method is compositional (the associativity and regularity of the hiding operation is proved elsewhere [10]), this feature enables us to reason about timing properties incrementally. In fact, we need to consider only the joint channels of the processes, and hence the verification of the property will be less tedious than considering the whole alphabet. The algorithms for verification of properties can be captured through efficient pattern matching algorithms for regular expressions as well as by efficient reachability algorithms in the global transition system.

7. Concluding Remarks

Our approach not only can easily extend to the general maximal parallelism model (referred to as $MAX_\gamma(\delta, \epsilon)$ model [8]), but also can apply to other languages such as Ada, Occam [13], and RT-CDL [9]. Furthermore, the analysis can be refined in a variety of ways such as associating i/o commands with distinct labels and associating assertions with the labels. Such enrichments enable us to prove several interesting properties such as priority, and to compute *statically matched communication* pairs (cf. [2]).

Our main interest has been in real-time embedded systems in which the system and the environment interact, but yet are autonomous. Currently, we are working toward the development of an automatic system using the above described framework for the verification of timing properties in real-time distributed programs. Further work is in progress toward analysis of the complexity of static analysis and toward algorithms for the verification of timing properties. Furthermore, we are working toward identification and limitation of various real-time properties that can be established by our approach. The relationship of such an analysis toward the development of proof systems for real-time distributed programs has been discussed in [18]. As the classes of timing properties that can be expressed in CSP-R are very limited, therefore, CSP-R cannot be used in many real-time applications. We are currently investigating the extension of our analysis to some more powerful languages such as asynchronous languages [17] as well as strong synchronous languages (e.g., Esterel [3, 4] and RT-CDL [9, 11]), which are capable of broadcasting and expressing various timing constraints.

References

1. Apt, K. R., Proving Correctness of CSP Programs - A Tutorial, *Control Flow and Data Flow Concepts of Distributed Programs, Edited by M. Broy*, 1984, 441-474.

2. Apt, K. R., A Static Analysis of CSP Programs, *LNCS 164*, 1984, 1-17.

3. Berry, G., Moisan, S. and Rigault, J., ESTEREL: Toward a Synchronous and Semantically Sound High Level Language for Real Time Applications, *IEEE Real-Time Systems Symp.*, 1983, 30-37.

4. Berry, G. and Cosserat, L., The ESTEREL Synchronous Programming Language and its Mathematical Semantics, *LNCS 197* (1984), 389-448.

5. Hoare, C. A. R., Communicating Sequential Processes, *Comm. of the ACM 21*, 8 (Aug. 1978), 666-677.

6. Jahanian, F. and Mok, A. K., A Graph-Theoretic Approach for Timing Analysis in Real Time Logic, *IEEE Real-Time Systems Symp.*, 1986, 98-108.

7. Jahanian, F. and Mok, A. K., A Graph-Theoretic Approach for Timing Analysis and its Implementation, *IEEE Transaction on Computers C-36* (Aug. 1987), 961-975.

8. Koymans, R., Shyamasundar, R. K., de Roever, W. P., Gerth, R. and Arun-Kumar, S., Compositional Semantics for Real-Time Distributed Computing, *Proc. Logics of Programs, LNCS 193 (Extended full version to appear in Information and Computation)*, 1985.

9. Liu, L. Y. and Shyamasundar, R. K., Specification of Real-Time Programs in RT-CDL, *IEEE Fourth Workshop on Real-Time Operating Systems*, Cambridge, MA., July 1987, 110-119.

10. Liu, L. Y. and Shyamasundar, R. K., *Temporal Behaviors for Real-Time Distributed Systems*, Technical Report, Penn. State University, CS-87-38, University Park, PA 16802, Dec. 1987.

11. Liu, L. Y. and Shyamasundar, R. K., *Programming for Real-Time Reliable Reactive Systems*, Technical Report, Penn. State University, University Park, PA 16802, 1988.

12. Ostroff, J. S., Real-Time Computer Control of Discrete Systems Modelled by Extended State Machine: A Temporal Logic Approach, *Technical Report, University of Toronto*, Jan. 1987.

13. Pitassi, T., Narayana, K. T. and Shyamasundar, R. K., A Compositional Denotational Semantics for Occam, *Penn. State University CS-86-19*, June, 1986.

14. Pnueli, A., Specification and Development of Reactive Systems, *Information Processing 86, H.J. Kugler (ed.)*, 1986, 845-858.

15. Pnueli, A., Applications of Temporal Logic to the Specification and Verification of Reactive Systems: A Survey of Current Trends, *LNCS 224*, 1986, 511-584.

16. Salwicki, A. and Muldner, T., On the Algorithmic Properties of Concurrent Programs, *LNCS 125*, 1981.

17. Shyamasundar, R. K., Narayana, K. T. and Pitassi, T., Semantics for Nondeterministic Asynchronous Broadcast Networks, *14th International Colloquim on Automata, Languages and Programming*, Karlshruhe, July, 1987.

18. Shyamasundar, R. K., Hooman, J. and Gerth, R., Proof Systems for Real-Time Distributed Programming, *Penn. State University CS-87-19*, June, 1987.

19. Taylor, R. N., A General-Purpose Algorithm for Analyzing Concurrent Programs, *Comm. of the ACM 26* (May 1983), 362-376.

20. Wolper, P., Temporal Logic Can Be More Expressive, *Information and Control 56* (1983), 72-99.

Appendix

A. Syntax of CSP-R

- Program P :: S | N
- Statement S :: **skip** | x := e | **wait** d | α | A | *A | $S_1; S_2$ | [N]
- i/o command α :: D?x | D!e
- Alternate command A :: $[\ \overset{n}{\underset{i=1}{\|}}\ g_i \rightarrow S_i\ ]$
- guard g :: b | α | **wait** d | b; α | b; **wait** d
- Network N :: $S_1 \parallel S_2$

Here, x is a variable; e is an expression; d is a duration; D is a channel name.

B. Merging Algorithm

Let $M_1 = \ <2^{\Sigma_1}, N_1, i_1, F_1, T_1>$ be the DFA for process 1,

and $M_2 = \ <2^{\Sigma_2}, N_2, i_2, F_2, T_2>$ be the DFA for process 2,

where Σ_k is the alphabet of action symbols, N_k is the set of states, i_k is the initial state, F_k is the set of final states, and T_k is the set of transition rules for process k. Then, the composite machine M after merging M_1 and M_2, written $M = M_1 \parallel M_2$, can be computed by

$$M = \ <2^{\Sigma_1 \cup \Sigma_2}, N_1 \times N_2, <i_1, i_2>, F_1 \times F_2, T>$$

where, T can be computed as follows.

    $SP = \{<i_1, i_2>\}$ -- set of states to be processed.

    $T = \emptyset$ -- set of transition rules.

    $N = \{<i_1, i_2>\}$ -- set of states reached.

    while $SP \neq \emptyset$ **do**

        select an element $<j_1, j_2>$ from SP

        for every $<j_1, A_1, k_1> \in T1$ **do**

            for every $<j_2, A_2, k_2> \in T2$ **do**

                if A_1 and A_2 are *consistent* with respect to cset

                    -- A_1 and A_2 are sets of parallel action symbols

                    -- cset = chan(P1) $\cup$ chan(P2), R = $\{R(D)| D \in cset\}$

                    -- A_1 and A_2 are consistent iff $A_1 \cap cset = A_2 \cap cset \wedge A_1 \cap A_2 \cap R = \emptyset$

                then do

                    $T = T \cup \{(<j_1, j_2>, A_1 \cup A_2, <k_1, k_2>)\}$

                    if $<k_1, k_2> \notin N$ **then do**

                        $SP = SP \cup \{<k_1, k_2>\}$

                        $N = N \cup \{<k_1, k_2>\}$

                  end if

                end if

            end for

        end for

        $SP = SP - \{<j_1, j_2>\}$

    end while

Low Level Synchronisation Problems in Digital Systems

J. A. McDermid
G. Morgan

Department of Computer Science
University of York

1. Introduction

This paper is concerned with synchronisation errors in otherwise fault-free digital computer systems. This problem is of particular importance in fault-tolerant multicomputer systems where the individual processors are very closely synchronised in order to read identical input data and perform identical calculations. Empirical and theoretical evidence [Kacprzak1987] suggests that even closely matched components which are operating in concert will behave differently, hence *generating* faults in a redundant system, not masking them. However there are well known techniques for avoiding these problems, eg through the use of wired-or synchronisation circuits.

It is now widely accepted that it is appropriate to use formal techniques in the development of High Integrity Systems. Consequently we would like to use formal techniques to demonstrate the absence of synchronisation faults, such as those described above, in fault tolerant computer systems. This formal approach would be particularly appropriate for a modified VIPER [Cullyer1987] chip suitable for use in TMR or NMR applications.

2. Issues of Formalism

2.1. Introduction

For the purposes of this discussion, we will assume that the main technical requirement is to demonstrate that the synchronisation mechanisms guarantee that the components in an NMR system see identical values. This can only be achieved, in general, by use of wired-logic synchronisation signals. Thus we need to be able to give a formal treatment of wired logic and the necessary additional data communications logic and synchronisation software. We will further assume that the design for the synchronisation logic is the result of a conventional hierarchical specification where refinement between each level in the hierarchy is verified for adequacy.

2.2. Relevant Specification Approaches

Existing formal specification approaches such as Z [Hayes1986] are well suited to specifying system *functionality* and can be used whether the implementation is in hardware or software. Techniques such as the variant of LCF used for VIPER [Cullyer1985] are more directly suited to hardware, but are still oriented towards specification of functionality.

In general, even where formal techniques are used to design hardware [Shepherd1988], other techniques (usually simulation) are used to verify timing properties. For High Integrity Systems the synchronisation mechanisms are critical - indeed if these are ill-designed they could result in the use of redundancy *generating*, not masking, faults. Consequently it is appropriate to consider formal techniques which deal with timing.

Time based logics such as Temporal Logic (see for example Rescher[Rescher1971]) takes a discrete, state-based, view of time. Similarly techniques such as Petri Nets represent a discrete, albeit concurrent, world.

However, in order to deal with synchronisation issues, we need to treat time on a continuous basis not on a discrete, i.e. post-synchronisation, basis. Thus, at first sight, it seems impossible to treat these issues formally - which implies that we cannot carry out design and verification of an NMR system completely within a formal system. In fact it seems that the desire to treat time continuously is at variance with the use of logics which are essentially discrete.

By considering the hierarchical approach to system development, it is possible to set the problem in the design context, which will enable us to see how to (partially) solve it.

2.3. Hierarchical Development.

It is now accepted that it is appropriate to carry out formal development in a hierarchical fashion. The guidelines for transformation from one level of description to the next are known as refinement paradigms, and there are several sets of rules for verifying the adequacy of refinements [McDermid1988].

In our case we would expect to produce high-level specifications of the structure and functionality of an NMR system. We would not expect high-level specifications to identify synchronisation issues - this would be inappropriate at this level of abstraction. Technically we would expect to see functions representing each replicated resource, where each function had the same input domain, and each set of invocations of the replicated function took the same input value. This we could specify within a language such as Z [Hayes1986] or perhaps more naturally via traces in CSP [Hoare1985].

The important point here is not the detail of the specification, but the fact that we can specify synchronisation at an abstract level, albeit implicitly, independent of implementation mechanisms for achieving synchronisation. We can now return to the main theme of our argument.

Using conventional paradigms for data and algorithm refinement we could proceed towards an implementation of the NMR system, verifying the adequacy of the refinement at each stage. However nothing in our refinement process would guarantee the absence of low-level synchronisation faults of the type described above. Consequently it would be possible to produce a verified implementation which suffered from synchronisation faults. Clearly this problem can be avoided by application of knowledge of the appropriate engineering techniques - but it is very unsatisfactory to be unable to treat this critical design issue within the formal framework.

2.4. Specifications and Models

The problem we have identified is, in essence, that we wish to design using, and verify against, properties which we cannot articulate within a given logical framework. However it is possible to specify the *solution* to the problem, i.e. we can produce a formal description, which we shall call a model, of the circuits necessary to achieve synchronisation. We can then *validate* a low level specification against this model, as well as verifying it against the higher level specifications. This validation will show that the system (the specification) avoids the synchronisation problem.

It may seem that we have achieved very little as we still have to validate the model and we have already seen that this is not possible within available logical frameworks. However we have made some useful progress. The implementation model will apply to many systems, indeed a synchronisation model should apply to any system using static redundancy. Thus we can show the validity of the model once, e.g. by simulation and testing, then formally validate many specifications against this model. Thus we have brought more of the design verification and validation into the formal development process, and thus gained greater confidence in our design work. To put it another way, we have reduced the likelihood of there being residual design faults by building a formal model encapsulating the engineering decisions which are needed to solve the synchronisation problems.

In general we would expect to use models to deal with aspects of design solutions which are generic, and/or which involve non-functional information which is outwith the purview of our formal specification notations. This idea is also applied in other domains, e.g. military security, where system specifications are verified against formal security policy models (see for example Boebert [Boebert1985]). The concept of using environmental models for specifying requirements of real-time safety critical systems has recently been discussed [Esp1987].

In general it seems appropriate to have a hierarchy of models, linked to a hierarchy of specifications. Space does not admit a detailed discussion of the arguments in favour of this approach. However, intuitively, it is appropriate because we make particular decisions, based on non-functional information, at different levels of abstraction, eg logical and physical views of memory. The approach suggested above represents a new paradigm for formal development of dependable systems and, to the authors' knowledge, it is not one which has been employed in practice.† However there seem to be a number of benefits of this

---

† That is, employed, explicitly. Clearly designs are actually based on intuitive understanding of the relevant engineering issues at each level of abstraction.

approach, not least the ability to re-use well tried design and implementation concepts which are encapsulated in the models.

We believe that this will prove to be an effective way to design High Integrity Systems. Recent work on VIPER has been concerned with the use of the processor in conventional NMR systems, and some suggestions have been made for modified synchronisation circuits. Consequently it would be instructive to attempt to design an NMR VIPER system both with the current synchronisation logic and with redesigned logic following the above approach. We are currently investigating such uses of VIPER and other possible applications of the above techniqurs.

3. Summary and Conclusions

We have briefly discussed a class of low level synchronisation faults which can occur in digital systems. Further we have shown the necessity of solving, or avoiding, this problem in static redundant fault-tolerant systems in order that the redundancy masks faults rather than generates them.

It is generally accepted that it is desirable to use formal techniques in the development of High Integrity Systems, hence we turned out attention to the issue of formally designing systems so that they can be shown to be free from the above synchronisation problems. We outlined the difficulties of expressing such problems, and verifying their absence, in existing (and possibly any future) formal specification notations. In particular we discussed the difficulty of showing that an implicit specification of synchronisation can be refined to an explicit one, via the normal refinement paradigms.

We concluded by suggesting that an alternative paradigm is required in the formal development of High Integrity Systems. This involves a hierarchy of models, as well as a hierarchy of specifications, where the models represent generic solutions to implementation problems (such as synchronisation) which are outwith the purview of the specifications notation.

Whilst this is a novel concept which has not been validated in practice, it can be seen by analogy with the development of other critical (e.g. secure) systems, that this proposed approach warrants further study.

4. References

Boebert1985.   B W Boebert et al, "Secure Ada Target: Issues, System Design and Verification", *Proceedings of the 1985 Symposium of Security and Privacy*, IEEE (1985).

Cullyer1985.   W J Cullyer, "VIPER Microprocessor: Formal Specification", RSRE Report 85013 (1985).

Cullyer1987.   W J Cullyer and C H Pygott, "Application of formal methods to the VIPER microprocessor", *Computers and Digital Techniques*, IEE (1987).

Esp1987.   D G Esp, "Environment Based Specification of Real-Time Interlock and Control Systems", CERL Report TPRD/L/ECS152/M87 (1987).

Hayes1986.   I Hayes (Editor), *Specifcation Case Studies*, Prentice Hall International (1986).

Hoare1985.   C A R Hoare, *Communicating Sequential Processes*, Prentice Hall (1985).

Kacprzak1987.   T Kacprzak and A Albicki, "Analysis of Metastable Operation in RS CMOS Flip-Flops", *IEEE Journal of Solid State Physics* SC-22(1), pp. 57 - 64 (February 1987).

McDermid1988.   J A McDermid (Editor), *Proceedings of Workshop on Theory and Practice of Refinement*, 1988.

Rescher1971.   N Rescher and A Urquart, *Temporal Logic*, Springer-Verlag (1971).

Shepherd1988.   D Shepherd, "Using Formal Methods in VLSI Design", in *Proceedings of Workshop on Theory and Practice of Refinement*, ed. J A McDermid (1988).

Reasoning about Uncertainty in
Fault-Tolerant Distributed Systems*

Michael J. Fischer   Lenore D. Zuck

Yale University
New Haven, Connecticut

Abstract

We present a temporal logic for reasoning about uncertainty in distributed systems that contain both probabilistic and nondeterministic transitions. Probabilistic transitions model randomness in the processes of the system and in the fault model. Nondeterministic transitions model lack of information about the true faulty behavior of the system and the progress of the computation. We demonstrate the naturalness of our approach by offering new analyses and solutions to some classical fault-tolerant distributed computing problems, namely the coordinated attack problem and authenticated Byzantine agreement problem.

1 Introduction

1.1 Uncertainty in Distributed Systems

Uncertainty is inherent in distributed systems and is what distinguishes their study from the study of "parallel computation". Uncertainty arises from many factors:

1. Lack of knowledge of system configuration.

2. Lack of knowledge of the protocol being run by other processors.

3. Lack of knowledge of inputs received at other sites.

4. Unreliability of hardware components of the processors or communication system.

5. Variability of processor step times.

6. Variability of message delivery times.

7. Unpredictability of random coin tosses.

8. Unpredictability of future external inputs.

9. Lack of compute power to extract knowledge from the available information.

---

*This work was supported in part by the National Science Foundation under grant DCR-8405478 and by the Office of Naval Research under Contract N00014-82-K-0154.

The first three items concern uncertainties of an individual agent (process) in the system; these uncertainties are of facts that *are* known to an external agent with a global view of the entire system. Items 4–8 concern uncertainty about the system as a whole, i.e., what course the run of the system will take in the future. From the agent's local point of view, all of these items have the potential of introducing error into a computation, and all force the agent to view its own knowledge with a degree of skepticism. In this work, we introduce a formal system that enables one to reason about the knowledge of an agent in a system that has elements of 1–8. Item 9 is of a slightly different nature as it concerns issues of computational complexity. It is unimportant in many distributed systems where the amount of retained information is small, but it is a major issue in cryptographic systems [HMT88,FZ87,GMR85,TW87]. In the interest of simplicity we do not treat it in this paper, although we believe the formal system of reasoning about knowledge, probability, and time presented here can be extended to encompass the notions of relative knowledge and belief presented in [FZ87].

If the uncertainty is caused by a random process, independent of the operation of the system, then we say that it is *probabilistic* and model it as a random variable. Otherwise, we say that the uncertainty is *non-deterministic* and are forced to consider worst-case scenarios. Namely, we view the uncertainty as if it were controlled by an "adversary" who wants to cause the system to behave as "badly" as possible.

1.2 Formal Treatment of Uncertainty

The goal of this paper is to define a formal system adequate to describe the kind of "knowledge" possessed by agents in distributed systems that involve elements of uncertainty. Our approach is similar to that of [FH88,HMT88], but it differs in two major respects:

1. Our system treats uncertainty due to lack of information and uncertainty due to the unpredictability of future random events in a uniform way. Thus, we can give an exact characterization of the "probabilistic knowledge" possessed by an agent at the end of a protocol as well as at the beginning.

2. We handle non-determinism explicitly in our model, rather than trying to allow for it implicitly by making certain sets unmeasurable.

Consider a simple 2-party protocol between agents p and q in which p flips a private unbiased coin *and nothing further happens*. q cannot see the outcome of the coin toss. There are only three global states in the system: the initial state s_0 before the coin has been flipped, the state s_h in which the coin has landed "heads", and the state s_t in which the coin has landed "tails". Because the coin is unbiased, the probabilities of reaching s_h from s_0 and of reaching s_t from s_0 are both $1/2$.

In state s_0, q knows that the coin will land heads with probability $1/2$. Halpern, Moses, and Tuttle (cf. [HMT88]) would express this fact by the formula

$$K_q^{1/2} \diamondsuit \text{heads}$$

which says that q knows that with probability at least $1/2$, the statement "at the next state (after the coin has been flipped), the coin will be heads" holds. The probability here is taken over the possible future extensions of the run. In this example, there are two equally likely runs, one ending in s_h and the other in s_t. Since heads is true at the end of the first run and false at the end of the second, q reasons in s_0 that heads will hold at the next step 1/2 of the time.

After the coin has been flipped, q still does not know the outcome (since p has not told him). From q's perspective, it is still just as likely that the coin landed "heads" as it is that it landed "tails". Intuitively, the statement

$$K_q^{1/2}\text{heads}$$

should now hold and reflect this uncertainty in q's knowledge. However, the [HMT88] logic does not permit this uncertainty to be expressed, for the only uncertainty it can accommodate is that resulting from future randomness. After the coin has been flipped, the outcome is determined and there is no more future uncertainty. The global state is now either s_h or s_t. In s_h, heads holds with probability 1, and in s_t it holds with probability 0, but in neither state does it hold with probability 1/2. Since q does not know which is the true state, the formula $K_q^\alpha\text{heads}$ only holds for α equal to the minimum of those two probabilities, which is 0.

In our system, we *can* formalize the fact that at the end of this protocol q considers the two states s_h and s_t to be equally likely and therefore has confidence 1/2 that the coin has landed heads. Confidence, the way we use it, is well defined; its intuitive meaning is that, if q bets even money on heads and the game is repeated many times, then its expected loss is zero. To avoid confusion with true knowledge, we call our notion of knowledge with a possibility of error *implicit belief*, and we denote it with the symbol B instead of K.

In the above example, the formula

$$B_q^{1/2}\text{heads}$$

holds at both s_h and s_t. It should be read, "q believes with confidence 1/2 that the coin has landed heads". It might seem that in s_t the formula should not hold. However, q has no clue whether the real state is s_t or s_h as it cannot distinguish one from the other. The only additional information q obtained about the outcome of the coin flip is that it had been determined. Therefore, q reasons that 1/2 of the times in which it finds itself in this situation (of the coin having been flipped but not knowing the outcome), the true state is s_h and the other half of the times it is s_t. Since heads is true in s_h, it is quite reasonable for q to believe with confidence 1/2 that the coin is "heads".

More generally, i has only partial information about the true global state s of the system, so i must consider any state s' possible for which its local view is the same as for s. Let $[s]_i$ be the set of all such states. Even though i cannot distinguish those states, it does have some a priori knowledge about the *likelihood* of being in each of those states (assuming for the time being that we are considering a purely probabilistic system, i.e., with no non-determinism). Namely, since the probability distribution on the runs of the system is common knowledge to all agents, i can determine for each state $s' \in [s]_i$ the probability of the system being in s', given that the system is in some state of $[s]_i$ and can therefore determine the probability α_φ of being in a state in which φ holds.[1] If $\alpha \leq \alpha_\varphi$, we say that

---

[1] More precisely, there is a well-defined probability of the system *passing through* s' when started from s. Our analysis is valid if one has extra knowledge that the "current state" is s' whenever the system passes through s'.

agent i believes φ with confidence at least α in state s, which we write as

$$s \models \mathsf{B}_i^\alpha \varphi.$$

When we add temporal operators, we obtain formulas such as ◇**heads** mentioned above which are neither true nor false at a given state but rather have a certain probability of being true there. Defining belief with confidence α of such formulas requires a slight generalization of the above definition. Details are presented in Section 3.

Non-determinism presents a special problem in reasoning about probabilistic protocols, for how can one talk about the probability of a statement being true when that probability is affected by non-deterministic choices? The answer is that one can't, for the probability then is not expressed by a single number but rather by a *function* of the non-deterministic choices. However, once *all* the non-deterministic choices are fixed, the resulting system is purely probabilistic, thereby reducing this case to the simpler one of pure probabilistic protocols. Without loss of generality, we fix all possible non-deterministic choices as if made before the protocol is run and before the outcomes of any of the coin tosses are known.

The need to fix all the non-deterministic chioces as if made at the beginning was realized in many previous works that dealt with asynchronous probabilistic distributed systems ([Pnu83,PZ86,VW86]), where non-determinism arises due to scheduling choices. The general system is modelled as a two player game in which each transition consists of a source state and a probability distribution on possible destination states. To determine the next state, the non-deterministic player (scheduler) chooses a transition and the probabilistic player (coin-tosser) chooses a destination state of the transition according to the probability distribution. In the verification process, one shows that for *all* schedulers, the program is correct, say, with probability 1. Thus, one arbitrarily fixes the scheduler by selecting one transition from each state and then verifies the resulting probabilistic program which no longer involves non-deterministic choices.

Fagin and Halpern [FH88] define a formal logic for reasoning about knowledge and probability which is based on Kripke structures that have been extended to include a "subjective" probability space for each agent i at each global state s. Subjective probability generalizes the indistinguishability relationship of classical knowledge logic and tells for each set of states S the agent's belief that the true state belongs to S when in fact the true state is s. Because of non-determinism, it does not make sense to assign probabilities to all possible sets of states. Fagin and Halpern note that it is okay to leave such problematic sets unmeasurable since a probability space does not require that all sets be measurable. For example, in game G_1 of the next section, the probability of ending up in the set $\{s_1, s_3\}$ is either 0.5 or 0.8, depending on the initial non-deterministic choice, so there is no single "right" measure to assign to it.

The [FH88] model allows additional generality that can be used in trying to capture the non-determinism more exactly. For example, it permits an agent to have different subjective probability spaces in different global states which are indistinguishable to it. While this additional generality may make the logic more expressive, we also find it very unnatural that an agent's subjective probabilities should depend on information not available to it.

The main contributions of this paper are the following:

1. We present a formal system to reason about "knowledge" in probabilistic systems, where knowledge is subject to a probability of error. Our system treats uncertainty

due to lack of information and uncertainty due to unpredictability of probabilistic events uniformly. This allows one to make probabilistic statements about a random event *after* its occurrence and before information about its outcome has been obtained.

2. The degree of confidence expressed by our notion of implicit belief corresponds exactly to the worst-case conditional probability of a fact holding, given only the information in the local view of the agent, for the particular "adversarial game" we define. Thus, we have captured all of the probabilistic knowledge available to the agent in the worst case, that is, all that the agent can count on in the face of adversity.

3. Our system sheds light on some classical problems of distributed computing. Namely, by requiring only high confidence rather than certainty in the outcome of a protocol, we can obtain easy solutions to a large variety of problems, some of which are are otherwise provably insoluble. We demonstrate our approach on the coordinated attack problem. We also show that implementations of the simple authenticated Byzantine agreement protocol of [DS83] using digital signatures do not attain either common knowledge or certain agreement. All they attain is agreement with a high degree of confidence.

2 The Computational Model

2.1 Probabilistic Distributed Systems

We model a *terminating probabilistic distributed system* by a set of node-disjoint Markov processes, denoted by T. Each Markov process represents the system that results from a particular set of nondeterministic choices that could be made in the system. In this paper, we restrict each Markov process to be a finite tree $T \in T$.

2.1.1 Paths and Runs

Let S denote the set of nodes appearing in the trees. These nodes represent the *global states* of the system. For every $s \in S$, let *tree(s)* $\in T$ denote the tree that s resides in. If $T \in T$, we denote the set of all states in T by S_T; thus, $S = \bigcup_{T \in T} S_T$. The initial state of a Markov process T is its root, denoted by *root(T)*.

Let $s \in S$ and $T = tree(s)$. We denote by π_s the unique path in T from *root(T)* to s. Formally, π_s is a sequence of nodes $\pi_s(0), \pi_s(1), \ldots, \pi_s(m)$ in T such that $\pi_s(0) = root(T)$, $\pi_s(m) = s$, and for each $0 \le i < m$, there is a directed edge from $\pi(i)$ to $\pi(i+1)$ in T. We call $|\pi_s| = m$ the *length* of π_s, and we let *last(π_s)* $= s$ denote π_s's last node. We say π is a *rooted path* if $\pi = \pi_s$ for some $s \in S$. We let $\Pi_T = \{\pi_s \mid s \in S_T\}$ be the set of rooted paths in T, and we let $\Pi = \{\pi_s \mid s \in S\}$ denote the set of all rooted paths. A rooted path $\pi \in \Pi$ is a *run* if *last(π)* is a leaf node. Let Ω_T be the set of all runs in T, and let Ω be the set of all runs.

Given a run r and a state $s \in S$ that appears in r, we refer to the pair (r, s) as a *point*. Let (r, s) be a point. The set of s's successors on r (including s itself) is denoted by *succ(r, s)*. The immediate successor of s on r is denoted by *next(r, s)*. Note that both s and *next(r, s)* are in *succ(r, s)*.

2.1.2 Transition Probabilities

Each edge $e = \langle s, s' \rangle$ in a tree T is labelled by some *strictly positive* real number $pr(e)$ which is the probability that the *next state* of the Markov process will be s', given that the current state is s. Let $s \in S$, and let $e_1 = \langle s, s_1 \rangle, \ldots, e_k = \langle s, s_k \rangle$ be all of the outgoing edges from s. The edge labels satisfy $\sum_{i=1}^{k} pr(e_i) = 1$.

We extend pr to rooted paths in the natural way. Namely, if π is a rooted path, then

$$pr(\pi) = \prod_{0 \leq i < |\pi|} pr(\langle \pi(i), \pi(i+1) \rangle).$$

We define $pr(\pi) = 1$ if $|\pi| = 0$. Thus, if $s \in S$, then $pr(\pi_s)$ is the probability that the Markov process *tree*(s) passes through state s when started at *root*(*tree*(s)). For convenience, we define $pr(s) = pr(\pi_s)$.

A set $A \subseteq S$ is called *independent* if $A \subseteq S_T$ for some tree $T \in T$, and no two states of A lie on the same path of Π_T. We extend pr once again to independent sets $A \subseteq S$ by defining

$$pr(A) = \sum_{s \in A} pr(s).$$

Let $A' \subseteq A \subseteq S$. We say that A' is a *maximal independent subset* of A, written $A' \lhd A$, if A' is independent, and for every independent A'', if $A' \subseteq A'' \subseteq A$, then $A'' = A'$. It follows from our definitions that if $A \lhd S$, then $pr(A) = 1$.

The set of endpoints of the runs in Ω_T is a maximal independent subset of S_T. The function pr gives rise to a natural probability space on Ω_T. Namely, all subsets of Ω_T are measurable, and if $B \subseteq \Omega_T$, we define

$$\mu(B) = \sum_{\pi \in B} pr(\pi).$$

It is easily verified that $\mathcal{P}_{\Omega_T} = (\Omega_T, 2^{\Omega_T}, \mu)$ is a probability space.

The following shows a simple relation between the probability $pr(s)$ of reaching a node and the measure of the set of all runs through that node.

Observation 1 *Let $s \in S$, let $T = $ tree(s), and let $B_s \subseteq \Omega_T$ be the set of all runs that pass through s. Then $pr(s) = \mu(B_s)$.*

2.2 A Temporal Logic

We assume a set Φ_0 of *basic facts*, and an evaluation $I: S \to 2^{\Phi_0}$ that maps each state $s \in S$ to $I(s)$, the set of basic facts that are true in s.

We use a temporal language over the propositional formulas in Φ_0 using the boolean connectives $\neg$ and $\vee$, and the *temporal operators* $\diamondsuit$ (*next*) and $\diamondsuit$ (*eventually*).

Temporal formulas are constructed by the following:

- true and false are temporal formulas.

- Every proposition $Q \in \Phi_0$ is a temporal formula.

- If φ is a temporal formula, then so are $\neg\varphi$, $\diamondsuit\!\!\!+\,\varphi$, and $\diamondsuit\!\!\!>\,\varphi$.

- If φ_1 and φ_2 are temporal formulas, then so is $\varphi_1 \vee \varphi_2$.

The set of all temporal formulas so constructed is denoted by Φ.

We define a satisfiability relation $\models$ between a point (r, s) and a temporal formula as follows:

$$(r, s) \models \text{true}, \qquad (r, s) \not\models \text{false}$$

For a basic fact $Q \in \Phi_0$, $(r, s) \models Q$ iff $Q \in I(s)$. Let $\varphi, \varphi_1, \varphi_2 \in \Phi$. Then

$$
\begin{aligned}
(r, s) &\models \neg\varphi & &\text{iff } (r, s) \not\models \varphi; \\
(r, s) &\models \diamondsuit\!\!\!+\,\varphi & &\text{iff } s \neq last(r) \text{ and } (r, next(r, s)) \models \varphi; \\
(r, s) &\models \diamondsuit\!\!\!>\,\varphi & &\text{iff for some } s' \in succ(r, s), (r, s') \models \varphi; \\
(r, s) &\models \varphi_1 \vee \varphi_2 & &\text{iff } (r, s) \models \varphi_1 \text{ or } (r, s) \models \varphi_2.
\end{aligned}
$$

Additional boolean connectives (such as $\wedge$, $\rightarrow$, $\equiv$) can be defined in the usual way.

For every $s \in \mathcal{S}$, we denote by $r_s(\varphi)$ the set of all runs which have (r, s) as a point and that satisfy φ at (r, s). Formally,

$$r_s(\varphi) = \{r \mid (r, s) \models \varphi\}.$$

2.3 Probabilistic Truth

We next define an evaluation function α that maps every state $s \in \mathcal{S}$ and every temporal formula $\varphi \in \Phi$ to a real number $\alpha_s(\varphi) \in [0, 1]$, which we term the *degree of confidence in* φ *at* s. Intuitively, $\alpha_s(\varphi)$ is the probability that a randomly chosen run r in $tree(s)$ that passes through s satisfies $(r, s) \models \varphi$. Formally,

$$\alpha_s(\varphi) = \frac{\mu(r_s(\varphi))}{pr(s)}.$$

This follows since $\mu(r_s(\varphi))$ is the probability that a random run r in $tree(s)$ goes through s and satisfies φ at the point (r, s), and $pr(s)$ is the probability that a random run in $tree(s)$ passes through s. (Note that $pr(s) = \mu(r_s(\text{true}))$.) Their quotient is the conditional probability that a random run r satisfies φ at the point (r, s), given that it goes through s.

We extend the degree of confidence α to independent subsets $A \subseteq \mathcal{S}$. We want $\alpha_A(\varphi)$ to expresses the degree of confidence that φ is true, given a randomly chosen point (r, s) such that $s \in A$. Thus, we define

$$\alpha_A(\varphi) = \sum_{s \in A} \frac{\mu(r_s(\varphi))}{pr(A)}.$$

The following is immediate from the definitions:

Observation 2 $\alpha_A(\varphi)$ *is the expected value of* $\alpha_s(\varphi)$. *Thus,*

$$\alpha_A(\varphi) = \sum_{s \in A} \alpha_s(\varphi) \cdot \frac{pr(s)}{pr(A)}.$$

Finally, we extend the degree of confidence α to arbitrary sets A. Because of non-determinism, there is in general no natural probability distribution defined over A. Thus, we consider the worst case and let $\alpha_A(\varphi)$ be the greatest lower bound on $\alpha_{A'}(\varphi)$, where A' ranges over maximal independent subsets of A. Formally,

$$\alpha_A(\varphi) = \inf\{\alpha_{A'}(\varphi) \mid A' \triangleleft A\}.$$

Discussion Our handling of non-determinism is embodied in the notion of independent set. In our formalism, there are two sources of non-determinism that affect the "current" global state of the system: the choice of tree T in $\mathcal{T}$, and the choice of how far the execution has proceeded. A maximal independent set $M \subseteq S$ specifies both—all of its states belong to the same tree T, and it intersects every run in T at a unique point.

If we take the point of view that the system is playing a game against an adversary, the adversary gets to choose M. This determines T. The system then runs randomly according to the transition probabilities in T, starting from $root(T)$, and thereby generates a random run r. That run intersects M at a unique state s, yielding a point (r, s). We thus obtain a set of possible points (r, s) with an associated probability distribution which describes the behavior of the system under adversarial choice M. By considering "worst-case" behavior, we are just saying that we are interested in universal truths—statements that hold for all suitable M.

In general, we will have some partial information, both about the set of possible current states and also about the actual one. For example, in example G_2 below, we may choose only to interpret formulas at leaf nodes, so the possible current states are $t_1, \ldots, t_8$, and q may know (from hearing 'heads') that the actual state belongs to $\{t_1, t_4, t_5, t_8\}$. The information about the possible states is reflected through constraints imposed on the choice of M, and the information about the actual current state is reflected by the set A in the definition of α_A. Namely, the current state belongs to A, and every possible current state belongs to M. We are interested in a lower bound on the confidence that φ holds when one considers all possible M consistent with our partial information.

Our previous definitions assume the following constraints on M: in forming M, the adversary must choose states s which are either in A or which have the property that they do not lie on any run which has a state in A. This constraint is equivalent to requiring that $M \cap A$ be a maximal independent subset of A. Thus, $\alpha_A(\varphi)$ is the greatest lower bound on the probability that a randomly generated (r, s) satisfies φ, given that $s \in A$ and that the adversary choice M is constrained as described above.

2.4 Examples

We consider two slightly more involved "coin-flipping" examples G_1 and G_2, which are illustrated in Figures 1 and 2. *Both G_1 and G_2 are synchronous*, meaning that we assume both agents can distinguish states on different levels of the trees. A minor variation of G_1 is extensively discussed in [FH88].

G_1: This game is played by two agents, p and q. p holds two seemingly identical coins, c_1 which is fair and c_2 which has a 0.8 bias towards "heads". p chooses non-deterministic-ally one of the coins and flips it. The coin falls either **heads** or **tails**.

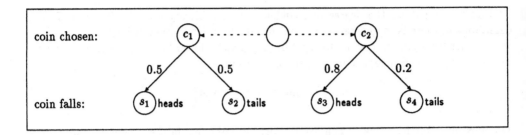

Figure 1: The system for game G_1.

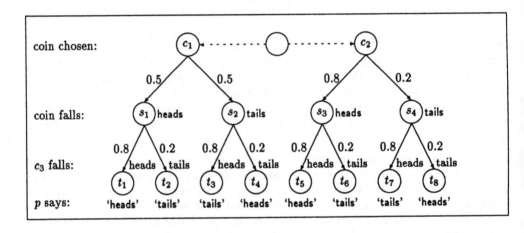

Figure 2: The system for game G_2.

G_2: This game is G_1 with an additional step: After p chooses a coin and flips it, p flips some coin c_3 that has a 0.8 bias to "heads". If c_3 falls heads, p tells q the result of the first coin flip. If c_3 falls tails, p lies to q about the result of the first coin flip.

In G_1 there are two trees (Markov processes), T_1 which is rooted at c_1, and T_2 which is rooted at c_2. The set of global states is

$$S = \{c_1, c_2, s_1, s_2, s_3, s_4\}.$$

The edges are labelled by the appropriate probabilities, e.g., the probability of reaching s_3 in one step from c_2 is 0.8.

Consider the set of basic facts $\{C1, C2, \text{heads}, \text{tails}\}$ where intuitively $C1$ (resp. $C2$) stands for "p chose c_1 (resp. c_2)", and heads (resp. tails) stands for "the coin fell 'heads' (resp. 'tails')". There, the evaluation I for G_1 is given by:

$$I(c_1) = \{C_1\}, \quad I(s_1) = \{C_1, \text{heads}\}, \quad I(s_2) = \{C_1, \text{tails}\}$$
$$I(c_2) = \{C_2\}, \quad I(s_3) = \{C_2, \text{heads}\}, \quad I(s_4) = \{C_2, \text{tails}\}.$$

The set of runs r of G_1 that pass through c_1 and for which the formula $\diamondsuit$tails is true at the point (r, c_1) is given by

$$r_{c_1}(\diamondsuit\text{tails}) = \{\langle c_1, s_2 \rangle\}.$$

Similarly, the runs r passing through c_2 and making $\diamondsuit$heads true at the point (r, c_2) is given by

$$r_{c_2}(\diamondsuit\text{heads}) = \{\langle c_2, s_3 \rangle\}.$$

Now consider G_2. Let PH stand for "p said 'heads'". PH holds in states $\{t_1, t_4, t_5, t_8\}$. Let $A = \{t_1, t_3\}$. A is independent, so by Observation 2,

$$\alpha_A(PH) = \alpha_{t_1}(PH) \cdot \frac{pr(\{t_1\})}{pr(\{t_1, t_3\})} + \alpha_{t_3}(PH) \cdot \frac{pr(\{t_3\})}{pr(\{t_1, t_3\})}$$

$$= 1 \cdot \frac{0.5 \cdot 0.8}{0.8} + 0 \cdot \frac{0.5 \cdot 0.2}{0.8} = 0.5$$

Let $A' = \{t_1, t_3, t_6, t_8\}$. A' is not independent but contains two maximal independent subsets, $\{t_1, t_3\}$ and $\{t_6, t_8\}$. Thus,

$$\alpha_{A'}(PH) = \inf\left\{\alpha_{\{t_1, t_3\}}(PH), \alpha_{\{t_6, t_8\}}(PH)\right\}$$

$$= \inf\{0.5, 0.2\} = 0.2.$$

Thus, if we know only that the current state is in A', the adversary can make the probability that p says 'heads' as low as 0.2 by always choosing tree T_2.

3 Belief

Consider the system G_1. If the coins look identical, then agent p, who chooses the coin and flips it, cannot distinguish between the states in each of the pairs $\{c_1, c_2\}$, $\{s_1, s_3\}$, and $\{s_2, s_4\}$. It can however distinguish between elements of different pairs. On the other hand, q can only distinguish between the sets $\{c_1, c_2\}$ and $\{s_1, \ldots, s_4\}$ but cannot distinguish between pairs of elements in the same set.

We assume that for each agent $i \in A$ the states of the system are partitioned by some equivalence relation $\sim_i$, where $s \sim_i s'$ if agent i cannot distinguish between s and s'. For every state s and agent i, we denote by $[s]_i$ the set of states that are indistinguishable from s by i, so $[s]_i = \{t \mid s \sim_i t\}$.

For example, in G_2, $\sim_p$ is the equivalence relation induced by the partition

$$\{\{c_1, c_2\}, \{s_1, s_3\}, \{s_2, s_4\}, \{t_1, t_5\}, \{t_2, t_6\}, \{t_3, t_7\}, \{t_4, t_8\}\},$$

and $\sim_q$ is the equivalence relation induced by

$$\{\{c_1, c_2\}, \{s_1, \ldots, s_4\}, \{t_1, t_4, t_5, t_8\}, \{t_2, t_3, t_6, t_7\}\}.$$

(Note that if G_2 were asynchronous then $\sim_q$ would include $\{c_1, c_2, s_1, \ldots, s_4\}$ as one partition.)

Consider now agent q when the system G_2 is in t_2, i.e., when c_1 was chosen, flipped and fell heads, and p told q 'tails'. q cannot tell whether the system is in t_2, t_3, t_6, or t_7. It knows however that if c_1 was chosen (i.e., the 'real' state is in S_{T_1}), then in 0.8 of the cases tails is true, and if c_2 was chosen, then in 0.5 of the cases tails is true. Similarly, if c_1 was chosen then in 0.2 of the cases heads is true, and if c_2 was chosen then in 0.5 of the cases heads is true. Therefore, q believes that no matter which coin is chosen, tails is true in at least 0.5 of the cases, and heads is true in at least 0.2 of the cases.

Let $B_q^\beta \varphi$ denote that "q believes, with degree of confidence at least β, that φ holds". Then, in t_2,

$$B_q^{0.5}\text{tails} \quad \text{and} \quad B_q^{0.2}\text{heads}.$$

Formally, we say that for every agent $i \in \mathcal{A}$, real number $\beta \in [0,1]$, and formula $\varphi \in \Phi$, $B_i^\beta \varphi$ holds at a point (r,s) iff the degree of confidence in φ at the set $[r(s)]_i$ is at least β, i.e.,

$$(r,s) \models B_i^\beta \varphi \quad \text{iff} \quad \alpha_{[r(s)]_i}(\varphi) \geq \beta$$

We next extend the set Φ by adding the belief operators B_i^β for every $i \in \mathcal{A}$ and $\beta \in [0,1]$ to the set of operators in Section 2 and closing it under the belief operator as well as under the old operators. We assume that all the previous semantic definitions hold for the extended set Φ.

If for some point (r,s), agent $i \in \mathcal{A}$, and formula $\varphi \in \Phi$, $(r,s) \models B_i^1 \varphi$, then we say that in (r,s) agent i *knows* φ, and abbreviate $(r,s) \models B_i^1 \varphi$ to $(r,s) \models K_i \varphi$. Note that $(r,s) \models K_i \varphi$ if $\alpha_{[r(s)]_i}(\varphi) = 1$, i.e., if φ is true with certainty in all the states that are indistinguishable to i from s. Our notion of knowledge coincides with the "classical" definitions of knowledge (see, e.g., [HM84,FI86]) in systems in which all the states are accessible from the initial state (i.e., states s such that $\mu(\pi_s) > 0$).

Let us return to G_1. At the beginning, the system is in either c_1 or c_2. Both p and q believe that the coin will fall heads with probability at least 0.5, and tails with probabililty at least 0.2. Indeed, we check that for every $i \in \{p,q\}$ and $c \in \{c_1,c_2\}$,

$$\alpha_{[c]_i}(\Diamond \text{heads}) = \inf_{T \in \{T_1,T_2\}} \alpha_{[c]_i \cap T}(\Diamond \text{heads})$$
$$= \inf\{0.5, 0.8\} = 0.5$$

and similarly that $\alpha_{[c]_i}(\Diamond \text{tails}) = 0.2$. Hence, for all runs r of G_1, $(r,c) \models B_i^{0.5}(\Diamond \text{heads})$ and $(r,c) \models B_i^{0.2}(\Diamond \text{tails})$.

However, after the coin has been flipped (i.e., in $s_1,\ldots,s_4$), p knows the result of the coin flip while q has gained no additional information about the result of the coin flip. Indeed, we can see that

$$\alpha_{[s_1]_p}(\text{heads}) = \alpha_{\{s_1,s_3\}}(\text{heads}) = 1 \quad \text{and} \quad \alpha_{[s_1]_p}(\text{tails}) = \alpha_{\{s_1,s_3\}}(\text{tails}) = 0,$$

whereas

$$\alpha_{[s_1]_q}(\text{heads}) = \alpha_{\{s_1,\ldots,s_4\}}(\text{heads}) = 0.5 \quad \text{and} \quad \alpha_{[s_1]_q}(\text{tails}) = \alpha_{\{s_1,\ldots,s_4\}}(\text{tails}) = 0.2.$$

Therefore, for all runs r, $(r,s_1) \models K_p \text{heads}$, whereas $(r,s_1) \models B_q^\beta \text{heads}$ is only true for $\beta \leq 0.5$. This corresponds to our intuition that p knows the outcome but q has learned nothing of it.

4   Applications

In the following sections, we show some classical examples of distributed systems where we believe that our formal notion of belief correctly captures what is happening.

4.1   Coordinated Attack and Average Belief

Consider the Coordinated Attack problem as stated in [HM84]:

> Two divisions of army are camped on two hilltops overlooking a common valley. In the valley awaits the enemy. It is clear that if both divisions attack the enemy simultaneously they will win the battle, whereas if only one division attacks it will be defeated. The divisions do not initially have plans for launching an attack on the enemy, and the commanding general of the first division wishes to coordinate a simultaneous attack (at some time the next day). ... The generals can only communicate by means of a messenger. Normally, it takes the messenger one hour to get from one encampment to the other. However, it is possible that he will get lost in the dark, or, worse yet, captured by the enemy. ... How long will it take to coordinate an attack?

A correct solution (protocol) should guarantee (among other things):

Safety: If either party attacks, then they both attack at the same time.

It is shown in [HM84], that no correct solution to the problem will ever result in a coordinated attack. The results of [HM84] apply even if we assume some fixed probability β of the messenger successfully delivering a message within one hour.[2]

Suppose however that we are given such a probability β, and we look for solutions that satisfy some weaker safety requirement. For example, consider the γ-*weak coordinated attack problem* in which we require:

γ-**Weak Safety:** The probability that both parties attack at the same time, given that some party attacks, is at least γ.

If $\gamma \leq \beta$ then the problem has a trivial solution: The first general (say p) sends a message to the other general (say q) with the attack time t, and then attacks at that time. If q receives the message, he also attacks at the designated time. Thus, p always attacks at time t, and since q receives p's message with probability β, q attacks at time t with probability β. Since $\beta \geq \gamma$, γ-weak safety is satisfied.

There are also solutions when $\gamma > \beta$. For example, if k is such that $(1 - \beta)^k \leq (1 - \gamma)$, then p can send k messengers to q carrying identical messages, and q attacks if it receives one or more messages. This occurs with probability at least $1 - (1 - \beta)^k \geq \gamma$.

Thus, we obtain:

---

[2]This observation is due to John Geanakoplos.

Theorem 1 *The γ-weak coordinated attack problem has a correct solution for any $\beta > 0$, where β is the probability of the messenger successfully delivering the message, providing at least $\lceil \log(1 - \gamma)/\log(1 - \beta) \rceil$ messengers are available.*

The crucial point in the [HM84] proof that the problem cannot be solved is that the parties need to obtain *common knowledge* about the attack time. (See the discussion there about common knowledge.) The system we set forth is much weaker, as it allows p to attack at time t when it only *believes* the other party will attack but is not certain.

Let C be some protocol for the γ-weak coordinated attack problem whose set of states is S_c. Let $S_p \subseteq S_c$ (resp. $S_q \subseteq S_c$) denote the set of states where p (resp. q) attacks at t. (Note that $S_p \cup S_q$ is an independent set of states.) An easy calculation gives:

Theorem 2 *If C solves the γ-weak coordinated attack problem, then*

$$\alpha_{S_p}(q \text{ attacks}) \geq \gamma \quad \text{and} \quad \alpha_{S_q}(p \text{ attacks}) \geq \gamma$$

As corollary to Theorem 2, we can show that:

Corollary 1 *Let C be a protocol that solves the γ-weak coordinated attack problem such that for every $s \in S_p$ (resp. $s \in S_q$), $[s]_p = S_p$ (resp. $[s]_q = S_q$). Then, for every point (r, s) where $s \in S_p$ (resp. $s \in S_q$), $(r, s) \models B_p^\gamma(q \text{ attacks})$, (resp. $(r, s) \models B_q^\gamma(p \text{ attacks})$).*

In other words, if p cannot tell apart the states in S_p, then in any γ-weak solution, p attacks only when $B_p^\gamma(q \text{ attacks})$. However, the states in S_p are not necessarily indistinguishable to p. This leads us to define the *average belief* of an agent:

Let $i \in A$, $\varphi \in \Phi$, and $S \subseteq S$. We say that *at a point (r, s), i has an average belief of φ with degree of confidence at least β over the set S*, and denote it by $(r, s) \models \overline{B}(S)_i^\beta \varphi$, if the following all hold:

1. For every $t \in S$, $[t]_i \subseteq S$.

2. $s \in S$.

3. $\alpha_S(\varphi) \geq \beta$.

We can now reformulate Theorem 2:

Theorem 3 *If C solves the γ-weak coordinated attack problem, then*

$$(r, s) \models \overline{B}(S_p)_p^\gamma(q \text{ attacks}) \quad (\text{resp.} \quad (r, s) \models \overline{B}(S_q)_q^\gamma(p \text{ attacks}))$$

for every point (r, s) such that $s \in S_p$ (resp. $s \in S_q$).

We can also prove a kind of converse to Theorem 2:

Theorem 4 *Let $\gamma \in [0, 1]$ and C be some protocol for the coordinated attack problem. If for every point (r, s) such that $s \in S_p$*

$$(r, s) \models \overline{B}(S_p)_p^\gamma q \text{ attacks},$$

and for every point (r, s) such that $s \in S_q$

$$(r, s) \models \overline{B}(S_q)_q^\gamma p \text{ attacks},$$

then C solves the γ'-weak coordinated attack problem for $\gamma' \geq \frac{\gamma}{2-\gamma}$.

4.2 Authenticated Byzantine Agreement

Authenticated Byzantine Agreement (ABA) is Byzantine agreement under the assumption of authentication. See [DS83] for a thorough discussion on the subject. It is said there that:

> "..., we assume a protocol that will prevent any processor from introducing a new value or message into the information exchange and claiming to have received it from another ..."

Indeed, all the Byzantine agreement protocols proposed there make heavy use of some ideal authentication scheme that guarantees the above.

For example, consider the simple protocol P for achieving ABA in [DS83]:

1. Initially, every processor p has a set of values $C_p = \emptyset$, and some default value v_d.

2. At step 1, the sender sends a signed message with its value to all the processors.

3. At every step $k = 2,\ldots,t + 1$, every processor p that received a properly signed message m in the previous step containing a value $v \notin C_p$, adds v to C_p, places his signature on m to obtain a new message m', and sends m' to all processors. A message received in step r is *properly signed* if it is signed by r distinct processors, the first of which is the sender and the last of which is the process from which the message was received.

4. At the end of step $t + 1$, every processor p for which $C_p = \{v\}$ for some v chooses that v, and every other processor p chooses the default value v_d.

Dolev and Strong [DS83] show that the above protocol indeed guarantees Byzantine agreement if the number of faulty processors is at most t. However, suppose that the signature scheme is not totally secure, so that under certain circumstances a faulty processor can forge the signature of a reliable one. Consider the case, for example, that the sender is nonfaulty and sent $v \neq v_d$ in step 1. At step $t + 1$, a faulty processor might send to some of the correct processors a message that contains another value v' together with the forged signature of the sender and (valid) signatures of the t faulty processors. Those correct processors receiving this bogus message will choose v_d, whereas the remaining correct processors will choose $v \neq v_d$, thereby violating Byzantine agreement.

If the sender is faulty, then it is sufficient for a faulty processor to forge a signature of any one correct processor. The argument proceeds along the same lines.

The scenarios described above might not be very likely; however, they have a positive probability of occurring when authentication is implemented through cryptographic techniques. For example, a signature might be forged simply through random coin flips; thus, forgery is always possible with probability at least 2^{-N}, where N bounds the message length. Thus, a real-life implementation of this protocol does *not* achieve Byzantine agreement since agreement sometimes fails to be reached.

What then is achieved? We define

γ-**Weak Agreement:** The probability that all correct processors choose the same value, given that all correct processors have chosen a value, is at least γ. Morevoer, if the sender is non-faulty, then the probability that all correct processors choose the sender's value, given that they have all chosen a value, is at least γ.

A protocol achieves *γ-weak Byzantine agreement* if it satisfies γ-weak agreement for any choice of faulty processors. We then have the following theorem.

Theorem 5 *If the probability of the faulty processors successfully forging the signature of a reliable processor is at most $1 - \gamma$, then protocol P achieves γ-weak Byzantine agreement.*

Similarly to the previous section, we let C denote a protocol for the Byzantine agreement protocol, and $S_{p,v}$ denote the set of global states reachable by an execution of C where the (correct) processor p has reached the decision v.

Dwork and Moses [DM86] introduce the notion of Simultaneous Byzantine Agreement (SBA), which is Byzantine agreement in which all processors choose values at the same step. They show that any protocol C that achieves SBA must satisfy

$$(r,s) \models \mathsf{K}_p(every\ correct\ q\ chooses\ v\ )$$

for every correct p and every point (r,s) such that $s \in S_{p,v}$. Protocol P, when run in an idealized environment with perfect authentication, achieves SBA, for all processors decide at the same step (cf. [DM86]).

A γ-weak Byzantine agreement protocol does not satisfy SBA since it does not even achieve agreement. We define a corresponding weak notion of SBA, termed γ-SBA, by adding to the condition of γ-weak agreement the requirement that all correct processors choose values at the same step.

We then have:

Theorem 6 *Let C be a γ-SBA protocol. Then, for every correct processor p and value v,*

$$(r,s) \models \overline{\mathsf{B}}(S_{p,v})_p^\gamma(every\ correct\ q\ decides\ v)$$

for every point (r,s) such that $s \in S_{p,v}$.

We can also prove the "SBA" version of Theorem 4:

Theorem 7 *Let $\gamma \in [0,1]$ and C be some SBA protocol in which all correct processors choose values at the same step. Assume for every value v and processor p,*

$$(r,s) \models \overline{\mathsf{B}}(S_{p,v})_p^\gamma(every\ correct\ q\ decides\ v),$$

for all point (r,s) such that $r(s) \in S_{p,v}$. Then C is a γ'-SBA protocol for $\gamma' \geq \frac{\gamma}{m(1-\gamma)+\gamma}$ where m denotes the number of correct processors.

5   Further Work

Real-world systems must make decisions based on uncertain information. We have shown how to model uncertainty in the framework of knowledge logics, and we have shown how allowing for uncertainty in two classical problems of distributed computing radically alters their properties. We believe this work is important not only for the formal machinery it provides but also to help clarify one's thinking in making subtle distinctions between probabilistic and non-deterministic choices.

In order to reason about cryptographic protocols, it is necessary to introduce *feasibility* into notions of knowledge and belief. One approach to the problem is given in [HMT88]. Our approach is to view computational complexity considerations like dark glasses over the eyes of an agent: Even though an agent's local view of two states is not the same, he may not be able to make any useful distinctions between them and thus should believe a fact with the same confidence as if the states were totally indistinguishable to him. (Note the similarity of this notion to that of average belief introduced in Section 4.) We further address this issue in [FZ87] in which we express what an accepting verifier believes *at the end* of an interactive proof of "knowledge" using concepts of relative knowledge and belief developed there. We are currently working to extend those concepts to the temporal logic framework presented here.

Acknowledgements

We would like to thank Sandeep Bhatt, Young-il Choo, and Joe Halpern for helpful and stimulating discussions, and David Greenberg for pointing out some errors in the final manuscript.

References

[DM86]   C. Dwork and Y. Moses, Knowledge and common knowledge in a Byzantine environment I: crash failures (extended abstract), *Theoretical Aspects of Reasoning about Knowledge: Proceedings of the 1986 Conference* (J. Y. Halpern, ed.), Morgan Kaufmann, 1986, pp. 149–170.

[DS83]   D. Dolev and H. R. Strong, Authenticated algorithms for Byzantine agreement, *SIAM Journal on Computing* 12:4, 1983, pp. 656–666.

[FH88]   R. Fagin and J. Y. Halpern, Reasoning about knowledge and probability: preliminary report, *Theoretical Aspects of Reasoning about Knowledge: Proceedings of the Second (1988) Conference* (M. Y. Vardi, ed.), Morgan Kaufmann, March 1988, pp. 277–293.

[FI86]   M. J. Fischer and N. Immerman, Foundations of knowledge for distributed systems, *Theoretical Aspects of Reasoning about Knowledge: Proceedings of the 1986 Conference* (J. Y. Halpern, ed.), Morgan Kaufmann, 1986, pp. 171–186.

[FZ87]   M. J. Fischer and L. D. Zuck, *Relative knowledge and beilief*, Technical Report YALE/DCS/TR 589, Yale University, 1987.

[GMR85]   S. Goldwasser, S. Micali, and C. Rackoff, The knowledge complexity of interactive proof-systems, *Proc. 17th ACM Symp. on Theory of Computing*, 1985, pp. 291–304.

[HM84]   J. Y. Halpern and Y. Moses, Knowledge and common knowledge in a distributed environment, *Proc. 3rd ACM Symp. on Principles of Distributed Computing*, 1984, pp. 50–61. A revised version appears as *IBM Research Report RJ 4421*, Aug., 1987.

[HMT88] J. Y. Halpern, Y. Moses, and M. Tuttle, A knowledge-based analysis of zero knowledge (preliminary report), *Proc. 20th ACM Symp. on Theory of Computing*, May 1988, pp. 132–147.

[Pnu83] A. Pnueli, On the extremely fair treatment of probabilistic algorithms, *Proc. 15th ACM Symp. on Theory of Computing*, 1983.

[PZ86] A. Pnueli and L. Zuck, Probabilistic verification by tableaux, *Proc. First IEEE Symp. on Logic in Computer Science*, 1986.

[TW87] M. Tompa and H. Woll, Random self-reducibility and zero knowledge interactive proofs of possession of information, *Proc. 28th IEEE Symp. on Foundations of Computer Science*, 1987, pp. 472–482.

[VW86] M. Y. Vardi and P. Wolper, An automata-theoretic approach to automatic program verification (preliminary report), *Proc. First IEEE Symp. on Logic in Computer Science*, 1986.

paradigms for real-time systems

Ron Koymans & Ruurd Kuiper

Vakgroep Theoretische Informatica
Technische Universiteit Eindhoven
POBox 513, NL-5600 MB Eindhoven

Erik Zijlstra

Foxboro Nederland NV
Koningsweg 30, NL-3762 EC Soest

introduction

Separation of concerns has been accepted generally as the key to successful software development. In particular it is important to separate the 'what' from the 'how', i.e. to distinguish between the goals accomplished by a programmed system and the means used to achieve the accomplishment. The 'what' is usually called 'specification', the 'how' 'implementation.' In a staged development process, an intermediate stage can be considered as implementation with respect to the preceding stages and as specification of the stages to follow.

Over the past decade formal specification methods have been subject of extensive research. The rationale behind this approach is that expressions stated with mathematical rigour rule out the problems of ambiguity that come with informal specification. Logical deductions can be made from formal expressions. Moreover, formal methods can be a foundation for automated development support tools which are required to master the size and complexity of large projects.

In the Descartes[*] project we adhere to the paradigm of staged, formal software development, the subject matter being embedded, real-time systems. These systems have special concerns, different from other systems or at least differently separated. For example, time and timing are of little or no concern to non-real-time systems. Consequently, programming and specification languages usually have no adequate capabilities to express requirements or properties related to these aspects.

In this report we present an analysis of real-time systems. We focus on the identification and clarification of aspects pertaining to the development of real-time systems. Two examples illustrate the analysis. They are taken from a collection of examples that have guided our work. The paper is concluded with a statement of capabilities required for the specification of real-time systems. Our goal for further research is to formalize these requirements and study the possibilities to enrich certain formal specification formalisms with these capabilities. Our list of candidates includes Statemate [St1] and Esterel [BMR83] on the operational side and special forms of Temporal Logic on the abstract side [KZ87]. It is also possible to screen a programming language like Ada against these requirements. It should be noted that our analysis is inspired equally by own experience, mathematical research in semantics and specification as well as by practical methods advocated for real-time systems.

---

[*]Esprit P-937: Debugging And Specification Of Ada Real-Time Embedded Systems.

2 real-time systems

In the present context the term *system* refers to signal- and data-processing hardware or software *environment* denotes the external sources and recipients of the data and signals processed. The environment may comprise other systems, but also physical processes and humans. A system is called *interactional*, if the system and its environment have a mutual influence upon one another during the operation of the system. An interactional system is typically *non-terminating*. We use the term *interactional* rather than *interactive*, as the latter term has a more restrictive interpretation through its connotation of mutual cooperation. The following characterization indicates, that we are interested in uncooperative interaction.

A *real-time* *system*, then, is a particular kind of interactional system: one that maintains an on-going relationship with an asynchronous environment, i.e. an environment that progresses irrespectively of the real-time system, in an uncooperative manner. Consequently, a real-time system is fully responsible for the proper synchronization of its operation with respect to its environment. In case real-time system fails to synchronize properly, there may still be a mutual influence, but the result will be erroneous, sometimes unpredictable or even disastrous, depending on the application. If the system is able to restore proper synchronization transparently, i.e. without external assistance and without loss of data or control, the system is called *soft-real-time*. If transparent recovery is not possible, the system is called *hard-real-time*.

In order to get a good perspective of the subject matter of real-time systems we present both classification and examples. Following the strategy of separation of concerns we distinguish between *behavioural* and *architectural* aspects. *Behaviour* refers to the causal relationships that are maintained by the system. These can be *functional,* i.e. relating to the values of signals and data exchanged with the environment, as well as *temporal,* i.e. relating to the ordering of activities with respect to the passage of time. By *architecture* we mean the structure that is implemented to realize the behaviour. As the origins of real-time behaviour are located in the environment of a real-time system, we start with an investigation of *real-time environments*.

2.1 real-time environments

For reasons of robustness and portability mutual, cooperative synchronization is to be preferred over real-time approach that allows the environment to progress asynchronously. Nevertheless, there are applications that require a real-time solution. Some environments are *inherently unable*, other environments are merely *not designed* to synchronize through mutual cooperation. Environments which are unable to synchronize are found in the following applications:

- *Data acquisition and control of physical processes.* A physical process is self-timed, its dynamic follows its own laws. It is virtually impossible to adapt a process to the data acquisition and control system (or at least very undesirable). The system should follow the process, not the other way around. This poses a hard-real-time problem. Error conditions in physical processes are often irreversible: transparent recovery is out of the question.

Applications with the *source independent from the recipient,* i.e. a one way flow of data and signals. This is often *inability by design,* e.g. in store-and-forward systems in data communication. If the source and the recipient of a system are separate entities, the source is completely unaware of the state of the system and there is no way to build mutual synchronization. By the same token this gives rise to a hard-real-time system.

Communication with imperfect equipment and over imperfect media. *Failure* is a peculiar form of inability to synchronize. Two systems may be designed to synchronize on a mutually cooperative basis, but if one of the two fails the other may be blocked indefinitely. If the transmission medium fails, both systems may be blocked. The requirement to recover from this situation, raises a soft-real-time problem: as the blocking would persist indefinitely there is no inherent constraint on the time of recovery.

In some situations a real-time approach is chosen as a result of design trade-off. There are various factors that may outweigh the advantages of a non-real-time approach.

Mutual synchronization may slow down the environment to an unacceptable degree.

Mutual synchronization requires additional signals to be exchanged. This may, in turn, require additional channels to be added to the interface, thereby increasing the hardware cost of the system.

This kind of design trade-offs are typically made during the decomposition of a large system into a number of sub-systems. Communication sub-systems are often organized in layers. Some low level layers are uni-directional channels and raise hard-real-time problems on this particular level. The next higher layer may correlate two uni-directional channels with opposite orientation and establish cooperative synchronization or permit error recovery. The upper layer, then, would be soft-real-time or even non-real-time. It is important to note that real-time problems may emerge as the result of a particular choice of decomposition, regardless of the function and environment of the system as a whole.

The next issue that we wish to discuss is demarcation line between the system and the environment: the *interface.* It consists of all points of influence in either direction and demarcates the scope of responsibility of the system. What is and what is not part of the interface depends on relationships that have to be maintained by the system. The interface is all the environment sees of the system and vice versa. The characteristics of the interface depend to a large extend on the environment. The elements of the interface consist of *state variables* or of *events.* This distinction is important for the behaviour of the system.

Essential is, that a state variable is *persistently present.* Throughout its existence a state variable has a value, representing *the state,* that changes with the progression of time. Some variables get their values from processes operating in the environment, other variables are set by the system. In interactive communication, some variables may be shared to the extent that both the system and its environment may set their values. State variables are *continuous,* or *discrete,* i.e. they vary respectively as continuous or discrete functions in time. 'Temperature' is an example of a continuous variable that characterizes the state of a reactor; 'Open' and 'close' are the discrete values of a variable that represents the state of a contact.

An event, on the other hand, is *intermittently present,* so we can speak about *occurrences.* Events may be generated by processes operating in the environment or by the system. In some environment events are virtually *instantaneous;* for instance, a bottle reaching the end of a conveyer belt. In other environments events may be *extended in time;* an example is the transmission of a message over communications link.

2.2 behaviour of real-time systems

The ingredients of the relationship between a real-time system and its environment are events, state variables and their evolution in time. The evolution of an event consists of its occurrences. The evolution of a state variable is made up of its variation of amplitude. On the one hand, we have event generated by the environment and state variables manipulated by the environment; on the other hand we have events produced by the system and state variables set by the system. The asymmetry between system and environment requires the actions of a system to depend on the dynamics of i environment. As far as the behaviour of the system is concerned, there is no causality in the other direction. Of course, each system is based on certain knowledge about the environment, but this is best an approximate model of a part of the environment. Any real-time system operates basically in feed-back mode; it is not possible to predict the future sufficiently precise. At any moment in time the system *knows* only the history of the evolution from the start of the system up to that moment. If the history is not in a desirable state, this *causes* the system to take some action so as to restore a desirable state. However, this happy state of affairs will not last for ever; new disturbances will occur and require the system to take further corrective action.

At this level of abstraction, real-time systems can be classified according to the role of time in the causal relationships maintained. Three classes of temporal relationships can be distinguished:

qualitative: expressing order in time. In general this is not enough for real-time.

relative: expressing not only order, but also distance in time. This permits, for instance, express how fast a system reacts to a cause. It cannot prevent the occurrence of drift.

absolute: relating events and values of state-variables to their moment of occurrence validity. This enables computations with time as a parameter.

A second, operational, view of real-time systems leads to another classification. An operational view capturing the notion of a *computation step,* can be based on the fact that the past cannot change, it can only be extended. In an operational view the past is reflected in the *(current) state of the system.* A extension of the input history gives rise to a certain extension of the output history, called *system response.* The system response depends on the particular extension of the input history as well as the state of the system. The extension of the input history may comprise occurrences of events changes of state variables and passage of time. The system response may consist of the generation events or some change of output state variables. This would be an *observable* response. Alternatively the system response may consist of a change of current state alone. Such a response would not immediately observable, but only through future responses. Ideally, a response is instantaneous, but reality there is always some latency that is inherent in the way systems work. Keeping the latency within tolerance, is part of the behaviour of a real-time system.

As a consequence of the same latency, a system has a discrete perception of the input history. This has implications for the relationships that can be maintained by a system between its input and output histories. These implications depend on whether the system responds to the occurrence of an event or to the evolution of a state variable. Consequently, two basic types of real-time behaviour can be distinguished: *event-processing* and *state-processing*.

The discrete perception of a state variable gives rise to a series of samples. In order to give a faithful picture of the environment, the samples must be taken sufficiently often; otherwise a stroboscopic phenomenon known as aliasing may occur. Operationally speaking, the system responds to the passage of time. The system takes a sample when it is time to do so. The required relationship between time and sampling depends on the environment. There is one general pattern that can be distinguished with respect to continuous applications: periodic sampling. The sampling of a continuous state variable is often done at regular intervals. This greatly simplifies the approximation algorithms. The time parameter reduces to a constant and does not need to be treated explicitly.

The discrete perception of a sequence of events leads to a partially ordered history. If the discrimination between sequentially ordered events is insufficient, the system may see one event instead of two or may not recognize the actual ordering of events in time. Operationally, this leads to non-determinacy with respect to events that occur close to one another. Under a discrete view, extended events are reduced to one or more significant instants in their progression. *Start* and *completion* are the most obvious candidates, provided they are distinguishable under the given granularity of time.

The classification in event-processing and state-processing behaviour is not new and can be found in the literature, be it under different names. Mellichamp [Mel83] distinguishes *clock-based* from *sensor-based* systems, the former being state-processing, the latter event-processing. We have chosen to use different names, as clocks and sensors are part of almost any real-time system. Moreover, they characterize the implementation rather than the behaviour. In his thesis, Mok uses the terms *sporadic* and *periodic* for event-processing and state-processing respectively [Mok83]. The word sporadic suggests that the behaviour is rare, whereas quite the opposite may be true. As indicated above, periodic behaviour is an important sub class of state-processing behaviour, including all clocks, samplers and sampled data controllers. On the other hand not all state-processing behaviour is purely periodic. We may cover a larger class of systems. The term *reactive* has been introduced by Harel and Pnueli for concurrent behaviour where the relationship between input and output is time-dependent rather than transformational [HP85]. The term seems to fit well with the operational view of real-time event-processing behaviour sketched above.

2.3 architecture of real-time systems

The *architecture* of a system is the structure designed to realize the required behaviour. Whereas the behaviour of a system is determined by the needs of the environment which it has to operate in, the architecture is determined by the developer of the system. It is impossible to discuss this subject exhaustively. With the purpose of formal specification and development in mind, we restrict ourselves to the four major issues that a developer faces:

System timing in relation to processing latency and self-timed execution, which are both inherent in micro-processor implementations.

- *Decomposition:* i.e. the behaviour of a system composed of the behaviour of its components.
- *Resource allocation:* the constraints that are imposed upon components as the result of a particular choice of resource allocation.
- *Reification of the interface,* i.e. the reconciliation of physical limitations with the need to exchange information with the environment.

2.3.1 system timing

A micro-processor system is *self-timed,* i.e. the execution of an instruction is automatically assumed as soon as all preceding instructions have been completed. We have adopted the notion of a self-timed system from Seitz [S80] who introduced the term for VLSI circuits as the opposite of *synchronous*. In synchronous system, each step is initiated by an external signal that may synchronize a number of parallel components in this manner. Within the resolution of the synchronization, one can tell exactly when an operation will be completed, by counting the number of steps. In a self-timed system there is no such direct coupling between the operation of the system and a global notion of time. We sketch the implications in relation to the operational view of real-time behaviour as described in section 2.2.

a. system response

An operation that generates a response can only be synchronized as for its beginning. The completion of the response takes some amount of time that depends not only on what steps have to be carried out but also on how fast they are performed. One of the main concerns in the development of a real-time system is to keep performance within promptness requirements. On the one hand, this is an algorithmic issue. On the other hand, it is also a matter of physical limitations of the underlying hardware. Moreover, in the case of programming the relationship between algorithm and actual performance varies with the programming language and with the compiler used. An analytical treatment of response timing will, in general, be restricted to safe estimates of maxima and minima, that have to be verified by measuring actual execution times.

b. event-processing

Taking it for granted that an event can trigger an operation, there are three aspects related to how often an event may occur. The first aspect concerns the discrimination of subsequent events. If the time needed to completely process an event is longer than the shortest temporal distance between two events, it is necessary to *decompose* the operation into two parts. The first part *detects* the event, i.e. records its occurrence in the state of the system. The second part produces the actual response and can be temporarily suspended when a new occurrence has to be recorded. The second aspect of the three, regards the maximal number of events that may have to be buffered in this manner. This depends on the maximal rate of occurrence on any finite time interval, the *maximal burst* of the event. Finally, we have to consider the maximal rate of occurrence on an infinite period of time, the *worst case average rate,* in order to determine the total load incurred on the system and verify that it does not exceed the capacity.

c. state-processing

The first point regarding state-processing is to ensure an adequate sampling rate. A cyclic self-timed operation is a perfectly adequate solution, provided no other relationship with the passage of time has to be maintained. As soon as a sample has to be associated with its moment of validity on an absolute time-line, one needs a *clock,* i.e. a self-timed component that is calibrated against a standard of time. There are two options. Either, the system operates in a cyclic, self-timed fashion and reads out the clock for an explicit time stamp with each sample. Or, the system behaves in a cyclic, periodic manner: starting each cycle at a sample time. This way, the moment of validity of a sample can be treated implicitly.

n important distinction between state- and event-processing becomes apparent. State-processing eals with amplitude variation. It is not an unreasonable assumption that the amount of work to rocess a sample is independent of the amplitude. If a choice is made for periodic sampling, the orkload pertaining to the processing of a state-variable is fixed. If the sampling frequency chosen is ased on false assumptions, this will, of course, affect the environment, but not the system itself. ontrol may be unstable, but the control algorithms are computed as required. Event-processing, on e contrary, deals with frequency variation. Assuming that the amount of work to be done for each ccurrence of an event is the same, the workload of the system varies with the frequency of ccurrence. If the system design is based on false assumptions regarding frequency distribution, this ay not only affect the environment, but also the system itself. The environment may see some events ot responded to, and the system may find its resources exhausted in time and space.

.3.2 decomposition

ecomposition is not exclusive for real-time systems, but there are a number of specific issues related) the decomposition of a real-time system. The general problem of decomposition is that the omponents behave jointly as required for the total system. In the early stages of development the goal f decomposition is separation of concerns so as to facilitate development and maintenance. This leads) the identification of a collection of sub-sytems.

 the abstract view, sketched in section 2.2, each sub-system maintains an on-going, causal elationship between events and state-variables at its interface. Part of the interface may relate to the nvironment of the total system and part of the interface to other sub-systems. All of the interface of e total system should be covered by the sub-systems and the interface between each pair of ub-systems should match, i.e. be the same on either side. A particular real-time aspect is that ecomposition should not create *temporal gaps* in the system; otherwise it would not be possible to erify the temporal properties of the whole on the basis of the behaviour of the components. As a onsequence, interfaces are transparent not only in a functional sense, but also in a temporal sense. ropagation of events and data should be handled by a sub-system, even though this is functionally ansparent. One could say, that decomposition into sub-systems reveals internal events and ate-variables of a system.

 later stages of the development, the objective of decomposition shifts to identification of nplementation entities. This brings us at the operational view of real-time systems. An implementa-)n entity is a self-timed operation that produces an observable response or changes the state of the 'stem. Each execution is initiated by some external or internal event. Internal events may include the king of a clock that signifies the passage of time. A special real-time aspect is that there is a ne-constraint on the duration of the operation. It is important to note that not all behaviour can be implemented in a single self-timed operation. For instance, in order to accommodate for a source and recipient with different timing characteristics, it is necessary to have at least two relayed operations; on adapted to the source and the other to the recipient.

2.3.3 resource allocation

With the identification of self-timed operations, the development process has reached the stage wher logical components can be associated with physical resources. In fact, one could assign resources abstract sub-systems at an earlier stage, but real-time aspects can only be analyzed at a more detaile level. There are two real-time issues: *performance* and *contention*.

The actual performance of a self-timed operation must stay within the behavioural requirements. Th basic problem of performance is that it depends ultimately on physical properties of matter which a outside control of the system developer. A developer of real-time software can only influenc algorithmic efficiency, but there are many factors beyond his control: e.g. programming languag compiler, hardware. Whereas these underlying levels give complete control over functional behaviou they do not permit full control over temporal aspects of behaviour. The main source of frustration the development of real-time systems is that implementation constraints may render a sequence decomposition steps unfeasible; even though the decomposition is logically sound.

The problem of contention arises when different operations share a resource. Contention phenomer are common for communication channels and storage units. For real-time programming the prima contention problem pertains to the sharing of a processor. In general a number of operations, dealir with independent events and state-variables, is assigned to the same processor. The developer ha two concerns. On the one hand, this constitutes a dynamic job-scheduling problem. On the oth hand, the total demand for processor usage has to stay within the capacity of the processor. Th scheduling problem is usually handled with simple heuristics, such as fixed priorities for event-proces ing and phase shifting for state-processing. More sophistic regimes like *earliest-deadline-first* shortest-slack-first* have been advocated by Mok [Mok83]. Others have studied the idea of *value-fun tions* that express the relationship between time and the contribution of an operation to the success the system. The scheduler should optimize the sum of all individual contributions. The drawback these more sophisticated approaches is the additional load incurred on the system if execute dynamically.

But even with the simple approaches, it is important to note that additional states and operations hav to be added to the system in order to keep track of the state of each individual operation. As a result processor sharing, self-timed operations may have to be interrupted so as to allow the system to hand another event or state-variable. This *context-switching* may take a considerable amount of process time. In order to guarantee correct behaviour it is no longer sufficient to require that a self-time operation can be executed with sufficient performance. On a shared processor, each operation shou be completed within its time-constraints *under the worst possible scenario of interrupts and conte switches*. In fact, allocation and scheduling lead to much stronger performance constraints than t original behavioural requirements. In this report our interest lies in temporal implementatic constraints, but similar problems emerge for other resources, e.g. memory space.

2.3.4 reification of the interface

In the early stages of development, the behaviour of a system is described in terms of events and state variables that are abstractions of physical reality, or data processing reality, as the case might be. This may hold true even for an operational view. At a certain stage, the abstractions have to be reified into concrete physical signals or program data. There is substantial literature on reification of stored data [J86]. We confine this paragraph to specific real-time issues.

The main point we wish to make is that the events and state variables mentioned in the behaviour of a system, may not exist in a discrete digital form or may not be capable of being exchanged in this form. The actual exchange of events may go through the exchange of state variables or vice versa. A couple of examples illustrate this:

abstraction		implementation	
state	temperature	state	electrical resistance
state	vehicle speed	event	axle rotation pulses
event	high pressure alarm	state	pressure state
event	message	event	last-byte-in

These are simple examples. In actual situations one may find more complicated translations; for instance, from a state and an event into an event. Furthermore, it should be noted that reification of the interface is often a multi-level issue. The ISO OSI reference model illustrates the idea of multi-level reification for data communication interfaces [Ta81]. In order to achieve a maximal degree of independence from the actual implementation of the interface, a system is decomposed into a *kernel system* and one or more *interface sub-systems*. The OSI standard is based on this principle. Also in data acquisition and control systems it is common to separate the control strategy from the instrumentation.

2.4 introduction of examples

In the following paragraphs we describe two examples of real-time systems. These examples have helped us to validate the analysis of real-time phenomena given in the previous sections. Within the Descartes project the examples serve as bench-marks for research in semantics, specification methods and development tools for real-time systems. The *Watch-dog timer* is the least pretentious and most simple of the examples. It has been specified in *Statemate* [St1], *me-too* [He86] and *Real-time Temporal Logic* [KKZ87]. Currently, the idea of *software protection by a watch-dog timer* is being tackled with a software development tool that analyses execution histories of Ada programs. Within the Descartes project we use more examples, e.g. the bitwise reception and transmission of characters on a serial link and a store-and-forward device connecting communication links with different line characteristics. However, none of the other examples have been treated successfully, so-far. This indicates that still a lot of work has to be done in this area.

More examples can be found in the literature on specification and development methods for real-time systems, notably Jackson [Ja83], Ward & Mellor [MW86/1,2,3] and Hatley & Pirbhai [HP87]. An

enjoyable reference with a strong orientation towards applications is the book by Foster [Fo81]. Th
book requires more imagination as it has not been written with the problems of specification in min
Rather, it focuses on the problems of implementation on micro-processor systems.

2.4.1 watch-dog timer

The purpose of a watch-dog timer is to monitor to a certain extent the healthy operation of a process
and the software executed by a micro-processor. Once a watch-dog timer has been enabled it has t
be reset periodically. If not reset timely, the timer expires and as a consequence the halt line of th
processor is activated. In addition a horn may be sounded to alert the operator. Actuators, if any, ma
be driven to a pre-defined 'fail safe' state.

Initially, through activation of the processor reset line, the watch-dog timer is awaiting to be enable
As one of the last system initialization steps the software enables the watch-dog timer. For diagnost
purposes the watch-dog can be permanently disabled by giving it a zero expiration time. Once enable
the timer cannot be disabled under software control. During normal operation software will reset th
timer periodically. Under certain faulty conditions the reset operation will not be performed, e.g.:

- the processor fails,
- the processor executes a halt instruction,
- the code has been modified,
- the processor traps to an endless loop with higher priority than the reset operation or
- the processor just has too much work to do before it reaches the reset operation.

Each of these cases signifies some fault, be it a hardware failure, a coding bug or a design flaw. Th
watch-dog timer detects the presence of a fault through the expiration of its timer and halts th
processor in order to minimize the damage which is caused by the failure. In a weird sense of the ter
this is a hard-real-time system: if the watch-dog fails to halt the processor if necessary or, perhap
worse, if the watch-dog halts the processor unnecessarily, the result will not be transparent
recoverable. The significant feature presented by this example is the concept of 'time-out'. Time-out
a generic name for a pseudo-event which is constituted by the absence of one or more other events f
some finite period of time. Time-outs are widely used in real time and distributed systems to safegua
one part of a system against malfunction of another part.

Because we are dealing with a hardware device, we are only interested in the behaviour of th
watch-dog timer and not in its architecture. The abstract behaviour of the timer is characterized t
relative time; only the distance between two subsequent reset-events counts. Operationally th
watch-dog timer is an event processing system, with operations associated with three external and o
internal event in the following way:

init	is the event that brings the watch-dog in the *wait-state*.
enable(t)	is the event that brings the watch-dog in the *enable-state* or *disable-state*, depending on the value of *t* and provided the timer is in the *wait-state*. This event will set *reset-time* and *time-to-halt* if *t* is positive
reset	is the event that sets *time-to-halt* equal to *reset-time* provided the watch-dog in the *enable-state*.

ime-out	is the (internal) event that will cause the *halt* event to be issued and the watch-dog to enter the *halt-state*.

The states mentioned have the following meaning.

ime-to-halt	denotes the state of a count-down timer that counts down in the applicable units of time and issues a *time-out* event when zero is reached.
eset-time	represents the time specified in the *enable(t)* event that brings the timer in the *enable-state*.
vait-state	is the state of the watch-dog after *init* and before *enable(t)* is received
nable-state	is the state entered from the *wait-state* when *enable(t)* with positive *t* is received.
disable-state	is the state entered from the *wait-state* when *enable(0)* is received.
alt-state	is the state entered from the *enable-state* when a *time-out* event occurs.

n the operational view the problems of self-timed execution become apparent. What happens when a *eset* is received after *time-out* but before the *halt* has been issued? Vice versa, What happens when a *ime-out* occurs after a *reset* has been received but before the count-down timer has been reset? How arge are these time windows? A good specification method will be capable to resolve these issues.

.4.2 starvation in fixed priority multitasking

his paragraph describes a multitask software architecture which has as one of its invaluable duties to eceive characters and store them into a video memory in order to make them visible for an operator. he importance of this task demands it to be protected by a watch-dog timer with an expiration time of s. The characters arrive on an asynchronous line. The source can be a keyboard, but also a data ommunication link. The system must be able to handle data transmission rates up to 19200 bits/s; ne character consisting of 10 bits.

he objective of this example is to illustrate multitasking based on fixed priorities: a common rchitecture of real time systems. The basic problem associated with fixed priority scheduling is tarvation. The possibility of starvation raises the need for protection, i.e. detection of starvation. The rotection required for the key function of the system is achieved by creating a special task with a lower riority that has to reset a hardware watch-dog timer. If the task with the higher priority starves, so will ne one with the lower priority and the watch-dog timer will expire. In addition this example raises the roblem of specifying system behaviour in the presence of errors.

he functional view of the system is quite simple. There is a reactive transaction, the 'keyboard andler', which is triggered by the arrival of a character. Its commitment is to store the character in the deo memory before the next one arrives. It operates under the assumption that characters arrive not ster than 1920 Hz. Furthermore there is an autonomous function, the 'watch-dog timer handler', hich initially enables the watch-dog timer with an expiration time of 3 s and which subsequently sets the timer with intervals shorter than 3 s.

The requirement to protect the character handling by means of a watch-dog timer is treated as an 'implementation directive' rather than a functional requirement. One is tempted to say that the watch-dog timer must not be reset under certain faulty conditions listed above. However, these errors exist only on the implementation level and then only in a wrong implementation (a program with a bug or a malfunctioning processor). The problem seems to be harder than the treatment of exceptions which are mere violations of assumptions and preconditions, e.g. division by zero. For such problems the assumptions and preconditions can be weakened and the specification can be extended to cover the exceptional cases. For these reasons the protection requirement cannot be reflected in the abstract functional view without enrichments of the descriptive framework that we have used so far. The enrichments required are not obvious and beyond the scope of this report. Thus we end up with the somewhat unsatisfactory implementation directive which is not expressible at the abstract level.

The implementation has a uni-processor multitask architecture. The implementation directive discussed above states that the keyboard handling is done by a task with higher priority than the watch-dog timer handler. The following Ada program characterizes the intended implementation. It is assumed that all hardware dependent constants are defined in the package Low_Level_IO. The function Store_to_Video_Memory (*) is supposed to be defined in the Video_Package. For the present discussion the only relevant property of this function is that it does not suspend execution of the calling task.

```
with Video_Package, Low_Level_IO;
use  Video_Package, Low_Level_IO;

task Keyboard_Handler is
      pragma PRIORITY (2); -- higher than Watchdog_Timer_Handler
      entry Keyboard_Interrupt;
      for Keyboard_Interrupt use at Keyboard_Interrupt_Vector;
      end Keyboard_Handler;

task Watchdog_Timer_Handler is
      pragma PRIORITY (1); -- lower priority than Keyboard_Handler
      end Watchdog_Timer_Handler;

task body Keyboard_Handler is
      Current_Char: CHARACTER;
      begin
      Send_Control(Keyboard_Control, Enable_Interrupts):
      loop
            accept Keyboard_Interrupt do
            Receive_Control(Keyboard_Data, Current_Char);
            end Keyboard_Interrupt;
            Store_to_Video_Memory(Current_Char);  -- (*)
      end loop;
      end Keyboard_Handler;

task body Watchdog_Timer_Handler is
      begin
      Send_Control(Watchdog_Timer_Enable, 3.0);
      loop
            delay 2.0;
```

```
        Send_Control(Watchdog_Timer_Reset,null);
  end loop;
  end Watchdog_Timer_Handler; }
```

his program suffices to demonstrate the protective working of the watch-dog timer against errors, bugs
nd failures. It does not show enough detail, though, to analyse more subtle timing problems. In order
o be able to treat the latter too, we descend one abstraction level.

ighest priority	rt clock interrupt servicer	protected levels
	keyboard interrupt servicer	
	timer task	
	keyboard_handler	
	watchdog_timer_handler	
	...	...
owest priority	idle task	unprotected levels

his table shows the two Ada tasks embedded in a minimal, yet typical arrangement. The physical time
 driven by a 100 Hz (hardware) real time clock. Every tenth interrupt the real time clock interrupt
ervicer resumes the timer task which maintains software timers for scheduling purposes, i.e. the
xecution management of delay statements. Every twentieth 10 Hz tick the watch-dog timer handler is
esumed, as its "delay 2.0" statement expires. At each keyboard interrupt an entry call is posted to the
eyboard handler by the keyboard interrupt servicer.

he execution of the tasks is managed by the 'scheduler', invisible in the table above but nonetheless
me consuming. For this example we adopt a simple three-state transition diagram for each task. At
ny moment there is a unique 'current' task nominated by the scheduler. This task is usually executing
xcept for temporary interrupts. If an interrupt servicer puts another task with higher priority than the
urrent task in the ready state, the current task is put back in the ready state and the other task
ecomes the new current. A task executing a delay or communication statement becomes suspended
ntil the delay expires or the communication has been established or completed. Every time a task
hanges state the scheduler verifies whether the current task still has higher priority than any other
ady task. If not or If the previous current task has suspended, the scheduler will select a new current
sk. There is an 'idle task' which never suspends; it is always ready or current.

 development method should be able to handle the following cases:

ealthy operation	everything goes as required
rogram with bug	e.g. an endless loop in a protected task should lead to starvation of the watch-dog timer handler.
PU overload	would also lead to starvation

requirements for specification of real-time systems

 specification has to describe the behaviour of a system without undue reference to the internal
ructure of the system. The internal structure of the system will usually be unknown at the time the
ecification is being written. The realization of the system is the very reason of writing the specification

in the first place. Any premature statement of the internal structure of the system under development pre-empts design trade-offs and results in inferior quality of implementation. It is necessary and sufficient to specify a system in terms of its behaviour at the interface with the environment.

With the description of real-time systems in section 2, it is now fairly simple to state the capabilities required for the specification of specific real-time aspects.

3.1 environment and interface

A specification has to state the interface between the system and its environment and the characteristics of the environment in as far as they are relevant for the operation of the system. We list the required specification elements for events and for state variables.

event | ownership (system, environment, both)
instantaneous or extended
pure or associated with data
    data range (if applicable)
expected or admissible
    resolution (minimal distance)
    number of events per time interval

state variable | ownership (system, environment, both)
continuous or discrete
    value range
required sampling pattern
expected or admissible
    rate of change (if continuous)
    rate of transition (if discrete)

If it is decided in advance to treat a state variable by periodic sampling, using a known control algorithm it is not necessary to consider the details of expected behaviour of state variables. In that case suffices to state the sampling rate required. If the dynamic behaviour of the system would depend on the value of a state variable as a function of time, it would indeed be necessary to analyse the time dependency in detail.

3.2 abstract behaviour

For the abstract specification of real-time behaviour one needs capabilities to express causal relationships between three elements:

environment | event histories
state variable histories (sampled)

passage of time | relative
absolute

system action | event generation
change of state variable

No system action can be instantaneous with its cause. An abstract view that allows instantaneous responses may be helpful as a first approximation of the behaviour of the system. For further development this view has to be discarded as no operational view can be consistent with it.

3 operational behaviour

For the operational specification of real-time behaviour one needs capabilities to express causal relationships between:

the *current* state of the system

the *current* values of the state variables

some trigger   this is one of:

> event generated by environment
> internal event generated by other operation
> passage of relative time (time-out)
> absolute time

some response   this is a combination of:

> the generation of an observable event
> the generation of an internal event
> the change of a state variable
> the change of system state

promptness   the maximal amount of time that may pass between the trigger and the response.

4 architecture

For the specification of the architecture of a real-time system, the following are required:

location   the static association between operations and processors.

performance   minimal and maximal execution times as a function of the static allocation.

scheduling   the resolution of contention between triggered operations allocated on the same processor.

the scheduling *overhead,* i.e. the time cost of scheduling operations.

clocks   the embodiment of absolute time.

timers   the embodiment of relative time.

references

BMR83   G. Berry, S. Moisan and J. P. Rigault, ESTEREL: Towards a synchronous and semantically sound high level language for Real Time applications, IEEE Real Time Systems, 1983.

Da82   B. Dasarathy, Timing Constraints of Real Time Systems: Constructs for Expressing Them, Methods for Validating Them, IEEE Real Time Systems 1982.

Fo81   C. C. Foster, Real Time Programming - Neglected Topics, Addison-Wesley series 'the Joy of Computing', 1981.

He86   P. Henderson, Functional Programming, Formal Specification and Rapid Prototyping, IEEE Transactions in Software Engineering 12, 1986.

Ho78   C. A. R. Hoare, Communicating Sequential Processes, Communications ACM, vol. 21 No 8, pp. 666-677, aug 1978.

HP85   D. Harel & A. Pnueli, On the Development of Reactive Systems, in: K. R. Apt (ed.) Logics and Models of Concurrent Systems, NATO ASI Series vol. F13, Springer 1985.

HP87   D. J. Hatley and I. A. Pirbhai, Strategies for Real-Time System Specification, Dorset House Publishing, 1987.

Ja83   M. A. Jackson, System Development, Prentice Hall International, 1983.

Jo86   C. B. Jones, Systematic Software Development Using VDM, Prentice Hall International, 1986.

KKZ87   R. Koymans, R. Kuiper and E. Zijlstra, Specifying Message Passing and Real-Time Systems with Real-Time Temporal Logic, in: ESPRIT'87 Achievements and Impact, North-Holland 1987.

La83   G. Le Lann, On Real-Time Distributed Computing, IFIP 1983.

Le80   D. W. Leinbaugh, Guaranteed Response Times in a Hard-Real-Time Environment, IEEE TSE, vol. 6, pp. 85-91, Jan 1980.

LY82   D. W. Leinbaugh and M. R. Yamini, Guaranteed Response Times in a Distributed Hard-Real-Time Environment, IEEE Real Time Systems 1982.

Mok83   A. K. Mok, Fundamental design problems of distributed systems for the hard-real-time environment, thesis, MIT 1983.

Mel83   D. Mellichamp, Real Time Computing with Applications to Data Acquisition and Control, Van Nostrand Reinhold 1983.

MW86/1 S. J. Mellor & P. T. Ward, Structured Development for Real-Time Systems, vol. 1: 'Introduction and Tools', Yourdon Press 1986.

MW86/2 S. J. Mellor & P. T. Ward, Structured Development for Real-Time Systems, vol. 2: 'Essential Modeling Techniques', Yourdon Press 1986.

MW86/3 S. J. Mellor & P. T. Ward, Structured Development for Real-Time Systems, vol. 3: 'Implementation Modeling Techniques', Yourdon Press 1986.

S80   C. Seitz, System Timing, in C. Mead & L. Conway, Introduction to VLSI Systems, Addison Wesley 1980.

Sh67   F. G. Shinskey, Process Control Systems, McGraw-Hill 1967.

St1   The Language of Statemate, AdCad Ltd, Rehovot Israel, 1987.

Ta81   A. S. Tanenbaum, Computer Networks, Prentice Hall International 1981.

W77   N. Wirth, Towards a Discipline of Real-Time Programming, C-ACM, vol. 20, No 8, aug 1977.

Towards a Theory of Replicated Processing

Luigi V. Mancini[1,2] and Giuseppe Pappalardo[1,3]

(1)   Computing Laboratory, University of Newcastle upon Tyne, UK
(2)   Dipartimento di Informatica, Università di Pisa, Italy
(3)   Università di Reggio Calabria, Italy

Abstract.

In the N-Modular Redundancy (NMR) approach, a computation is made reliable by executing it on several computers, and determining its results by a decision algorithm. This paper investigates a formal approach to the use of NMR in replicated distributed systems, for which it introduces a notion of correctness based on consistency with their non-replicated counterpart, and a local correctness criterion. We discuss how a replicated system component may be implemented by N base copies, a majority of which is non-faulty. The formal approach sheds light on the necessity of coordinating the copies and on the requirements they should satisfy; in particular the difficulty of replicating synchronous communication is pointed out. A practical approach is also briefly examined and shown to be consistent with the formal model.

> *Inside every replicated system there is a non-replicated system trying to get out.*

1.   Introduction

In their pursuit of fault-masking, real time systems designers have often employed N-Modular Redundancy (NMR) for the construction of reliable software. In this approach to fault-tolerance a computation is replicated in N copies which are executed by different processors, and reliable results are determined by performing a decision algorithm, e.g. majority voting, on the N outputs obtained.

Traditionally, the *base* object to which replication is applied has been a centralized computation [LV] [AK]. More recently, however, there has been considerable interest for the replication of distributed systems composed out of communicating processes. Distribution introduces some entirely new problems into NMR. Replicating processes is not enough - communication channels have to be replicated too, for a single channel would be a bottleneck for performance and a weak link for reliability. On the other hand, replicated communication, faults of arbitrary nature, and the nondeterminism inherent in distribution may cause copies of a process to receive input messages that are different or in a different order; yet, for non-faulty copies to remain consistent, they must process the same input sequences.

There is now a rich literature on replicated distributed systems (RDS). Techniques for their construction are proposed in [C] [G] [M] [MS] [MP1]; deadlock has been studied in [MK] [KM]. The starting point of the present paper is the definition of correct behaviour of an RDS - an issue to which insufficient attention has been paid so far. Our investigation is carried out in the formal setting provided by the CSP trace model, which is briefly presented in Section 2. In Section 3 we define an RDS to be correct with respect to, or to be a *replication* of, a base distributed system, if the behaviour of the latter may be inferred from that of the RDS (whence the aphorism that opens this paper). In Section 3 we also derive a local correctness criterion: for an RDS to be the replication of the base system it is sufficient that each replicated process in the RDS is the replication of the corresponding process in the base system. In Section 4 we adopt majority voting as a decision algorithm, and address the problem of implementing a replication PN of a base process P by assembling N copies of P, under the usual NMR fault assumption that a majority of copies is non-faulty. We show that non-faulty copies of P should be coordinated so that they all receive every input message of which PN has received a majority, and so that they all process the same input message sequence. These results are similar to those given in [S2] [L1] for a distributed system containing a single replicated process, which does not therefore receive replicated input like ours. In Section 5 the design approach of [M] is shown to be consistent with our formal model. Finally, by way of conclusions, we discuss whether there are limitations on the class of base distributed systems that can be replicated. In particular we point out some difficulties in replicating synchronous communication.

2. The trace model of CSP

CSP [H] is a language for the description of concurrency. Informally, a CSP process P can be regarded as a black box characterized by a set aP called the *alphabet* of P. P may engage in interaction with its environment. Atomic instances of this interaction are called *actions* and must be elements of aP.

A *trace* of a process P is a sequence of actions that P can be observed to engage in. The set of the traces of P is denoted by tP. Traces provide information about the interactions a process may accept. They are suitable for reasoning about partial correctness: assuming a process does produce some traces, these may be shown to satisfy some required property. However, albeit partially correct, a process may refuse to do anything, i.e. may deadlock. Thus, for the purpose of verifying total correctness, the description of a process should include, together with its traces, information about its *refusals*.

As deadlock in replicated distributed systems has already been studied successfully in [KM] and [MK], this paper will concentrate on partial correctness and can therefore adopt the so-called trace model of CSP [H]. In this model a process P is identified with a pair (A,T), satisfying the laws **P1-P4** below. In accordance with intuition, **P3** stipulates that the empty trace $<>$ is a trace of every P, and **P4** that any prefix of a trace of P is also a trace of P.

P1 A is a non-empty, countable set; it is defined to be aP.

P2 T is a subset of A^*; it is defined to be tP.

P3 $<> \in T$.

P4   If $t \in T$ and $t1$ is a prefix of t, then $t1 \in T$.

Thus CSP language operators are defined in terms of how they return a process, i.e. an alphabet-traces pair, by combining operands, which may be processes themselves. However, for our purposes, neither the syntax nor the semantics of CSP need be described in detail. In fact, essential to our treatment are only the identification of a process with its interaction traces, and the ability to compose processes. Accordingly, these are the only aspects of CSP that will be introduced in the next two subsections.

2.1   Actions and traces

Actions and channels

Actions may be denoted simply by identifiers. However it is convenient to introduce also structured actions of the form $c!v$, where v is a value and c a *channel*; $c!v$ is said to *occur* at c and to cause v to be *exchanged*. We associate with each process P a set of channels χP, and stipulate that if $c \in \chi P$ then the action $c!v$ is in the alphabet aP. Indeed, we shall deal with processes whose alphabet contains only actions of the form $c!v$, i.e. for such a process P:

$$aP = \{c!v \mid c \in \chi P\}$$

As a consequence, we shall be able to identify P with the pair $(\chi P, tP)$ in lieu of (aP, tP).

Traces

The following notation is similar to that of [H] (t and u range over traces):

-   $<>$ is the empty trace, $<a_1,...,a_n>$ is the trace whose i-th element is action a_i;
-   the trace $a\char94 t$ is obtained by prefixing action a to t; the trace $t\char94 u$ by appending u to t;

- $t \leq u$ holds true if t is a prefix of u; $t \leq^n u$ holds true if t is a prefix of u and their lengths differ by n or less.

$t\lceil C$, where C is a set of channels, is the trace obtained by *projecting* t on C, i.e. by deleting from t all the actions that do not occur at channels in C. A trace can also be filtered by a predicate p containing a free variable x that ranges on trace elements [B]; $t\lceil p$ is obtained from t by deleting all the elements x for which $p(x)$ is false. E.g.:

$$<c!1,d!2,c!3,e!6>\lceil\{c,e\} = <c!1,c!3,e!6>$$

$$<c!1,d!2,c!3,e!6>\lceil\{c,e\}\lceil(x\neq 3) = <c!1,e!6>$$

2.2   Composing processes

Parallel composition

Parallel composition models synchronous communication between processes. The process $P\|Q$ is obtained by connecting processes P and Q in such a way that: (i) each of them is free to engage independently in any action that is not in the other's alphabet, but (ii) they have to engage simultaneously in all the actions that are in both their alphabets. Therefore $P\|Q$ engages in $c!v$ iff: (i) $c\in\chi P$-χQ and P engages in $c!v$ or $c\in\chi Q$-χP and Q engages in $c!v$, or (ii) $c\in\chi P\cap\chi Q$ and both P and Q engage in $c!v$. It follows that if a trace of $P\|Q$ is projected on χP the result should be a trace of P, and likewise for Q. This justifies the formal definition:

$$\chi(P\|Q) = \chi P\cup\chi Q$$
$$\tau(P\|Q) = \{t \mid t\lceil\chi P\in\tau P \wedge t\lceil\chi Q\in\tau Q\}$$

Parallel composition is commutative and associative.

Concealment

Let P be a process and C a set of channels; then $P\backslash C$ is a process that behaves like P with the actions occurring at C made invisible. Formally:

$$\chi(P\backslash C) = \chi P\text{-}C$$
$$\tau P\backslash C = \{t\lceil(\chi P\text{-}C)\mid t\in\tau P\}$$

Concealment is associative in that $(P\backslash C)\backslash D = P\backslash(C\cup D)$. It is often used to conceal the interaction that takes place at the channels shared by processes combined by $\|$. It should be noted that in a more general scope than that of this paper the introduction of concealment would suggest the adoption of a failure-based model [H].

2.3 Specifications for CSP

It is possible to introduce a logic language having the set of traces as its intended model, and regard its formulae as specifications of CSP processes. Let ψ be a formula containing the variable t free; then we say that a process P satisfies the specification ψ, and write

P **sat** ψ

if and only if ($\Rightarrow$ is used to denote logical implication):

$\forall t.\ t \in traces(P) \Rightarrow \psi(t)$

3. Modelling replicated distributed systems

3.1 The notion of N-replication

This section deals with the formalization of the notion of *N-replication* ($N > 1$). Intuitively the *N*-replication of a *base* process P is a *replicated* process PN which has N copies of each channel of P (Fig. 3.1), and behaves consistently with P (in a sense to be made precise later). The requirement on the channels may be formalized by:

R1 $\chi PN = \chi P \times \{1,...,N\}$

As a notational convenience $(c,n) \in \chi PN$ is written $c[n]$; $c[n]$ is also termed a replicated channel or a *version* or *copy* of the *base* channel c. We shall also write c^N for $\{c[1],...,c[N]\}$ and C^N, where $C = \{c,d,...\}$, for $c^N \cup d^N \cup ...$

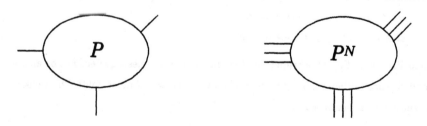

Fig. 3.1 - A base system P and its N-replication PN

We now consider the notion of consistency between PN and P. Ideally, PN should behave as though it contained N copies of P, so that each trace of PN should be one of P with the generic action $c!v$ replaced by a permutation of $\{c[1]!v,...,c[N]!v\}$. In general, however, this may be impossible to obtain in the presence of faults, the tolerance of which on the other hand is exactly the motivation for replicating P. Thus we adopt a less demanding view: if PN is an N-replication of P and t^N is a trace of PN, it should be possible to extract from t^N a trace of P. Thus we assume the existence of a relation *extract* such that:

R2 $\quad t^N \in \tau PN \wedge extract(t^N,t) \Rightarrow t \in \tau P$

and

E1 $\quad \forall t^N. \, \exists t. \, extract(t^N,t)$

A practical way of implementing an extraction function is to add identifiers to messages, as we shall call values exchanged by processes. In particular, messages exchanged by a base process via a given channel are assumed to carry distinct identifiers. So we assume that there exist two sets *Msgs* and *Idents*, and a function $id: Msgs \rightarrow Idents$, such that:

R3 $\quad aP = \{c!m \mid c \in \chi P \wedge m \in Msgs\}$
$\quad\quad aPN = \{c[n]!m \mid c \in \chi P \wedge 1 \leq n \leq N \wedge m \in Msgs\}$
$\quad\quad t \in \tau P \wedge t = \; <...c!m1,...,c!m2,...> \; \Rightarrow id(m1) \neq id(m2)$

Consider now the trace $t^N \ulcorner c^N \ulcorner (id(x)=i)$ obtained from a trace t^N of PN by including only those actions that occur at a copy of the base channel c and exchange a message of identifier i. We assume that if t is extracted from t^N, then each action $c!m$ of t is *elected* from the trace $t^N \ulcorner c^N \ulcorner (id(x)=i)$, where $i = id(m)$. For this purpose we assume the existence of a function *elect* such that:

E2 $\quad elect(t^N \ulcorner c^N \ulcorner (id(x)=i)) = c!m \; \wedge \; id(m)=i$
$\quad\quad \vee \; elect(t^N \ulcorner c^N \ulcorner (id(x)=i)) = NIL$

E3 $\quad extract(t^N,t) \; \wedge \; e = elect(t^N \ulcorner c^N \ulcorner (id(x)=i)) \; \Rightarrow$
$\quad\quad\quad \textbf{if } e = NIL \textbf{ then } t \ulcorner c \ulcorner (id(x)=i) = \; < >$
$\quad\quad\quad \textbf{else } t \ulcorner c \ulcorner (id(x)=i) = \; <e> \; \vee \; t \ulcorner c \ulcorner (id(x)=i) = \; < >$

The second disjunct of **E3**'s else branch implies that an elected message need not be an element of the extracted trace (although, by the first disjunct, the converse must hold). The reason for this will be made clear in Section 4.1.

It seems reasonable to require that extraction should be context-independent, in the sense that if t is extracted from t^N, the contribution of $t^N \ulcorner C^N$ to t should be independent of the actions deleted from t^N by $\ulcorner C^N$.

E4 $\quad extract(t^N,t) \Rightarrow extract(t^N \ulcorner C^N, t \ulcorner C)$
E5 $\quad extract(s^N \ulcorner C^N, t) \Rightarrow \exists u. \, (u \ulcorner C = t \wedge extract(s^N,u))$

At this point it may be helpful to summarize the definition of N-replication. Given a relation *extract* and a function *elect* that satisfy **E1-E5**, PN is said to be an N-replication of P with respect to *elect* and *extract* if and only if **R1-R3** hold true.

An important consequence of **R2** is that if the base system satisfies a specification, so does the N-replication once its traces have been filtered by *extract*. Hence the **sat** inference rule:

> If P **sat** ψ
> then PN **sat** $\forall u.(extract(t^N, u)) \Rightarrow \psi(u)$

In view of this result, we shall say that PN is *correct* with respect to P if PN is an N-replication of P. Since this definition abstracts from the internal structure of P and PN, it may be viewed as a global correctness criterion.

3.2   A local correctness criterion for replicated distributed systems

The property of being an N-replication of a base process distributes (in the algebraic sense) through parallel composition and concealment. Before proving these results as Theorems 3.1 and 3.2, it is interesting to discuss their implications.

A *distributed system* is defined as a set of *component* processes connected at their shared channels, which may or may not be concealed to the environment. Thus, in the formalism of CSP a distributed system DS takes the form:

$$DS = (P \| Q \| \dots)\backslash C$$

A *replicated distributed system* DS^N is obtained from the distributed system DS by replacing each component process $P, Q,\dots$ by an N-replication $PN, QN,\dots$ and concealing the channel set C^N:

$$DS^N = (PN \| QN \| \dots)\backslash C^N$$

The following theorems ensure that DS^N is effectively an N-replication of DS, i.e. is correct with respect to DS. This yields a local correctness criterion for distributed systems: DS^N is correct if its components $PN, QN,\dots$ are correct.

Theorem 3.1   If PN and QN are N-replications of P and Q respectively, then $PN\|QN$ is an N-replication of $P\|Q$.

Proof. Showing that **R1** and **R3** hold valid is routine. To verify **R2** we must show that

$$t^N \in \tau(PN\|QN) \wedge extract(t^N, t) \Rightarrow t \in \tau(P\|Q).$$

The assumption $t^N \in \tau(PN\|QN)$ implies, by the definition of parallel composition, that $t^N\lceil\chi PN \in \tau PN$ and $t^N\lceil\chi QN \in \tau QN$. By **E4**, from $extract(t^N, t)$ we may infer

$$extract(t^N\lceil\chi PN, t\lceil\chi P) \quad \text{and} \quad extract(t^N\lceil\chi QN, t\lceil\chi Q)$$

which, owing to the hypothesis that PN and QN are N-replications of P and Q respectively, imply that $t\lceil\chi P\in\tau P$ and $t\lceil\chi Q\in\tau Q$. Hence, by the definition of parallel composition, $t\in\tau(P\|Q)$. $\square$

Theorem 3.2   If PN is an N-replication of P, then $PN\backslash CN$ is an N-replication of $P\backslash C$.

Proof. The proof that **R1** and **R3** are valid under the proviso is routine. To verify **R2** we must show that

$$t^N\in\tau(PN\backslash CN)\wedge extract(t^N,t)\ \Rightarrow\ t\in\tau(P\backslash C)$$

The assumption $t^N\in\tau(PN\backslash CN)$ implies, by the definition of concealment:

(*) $\exists s^N.\ t^N=s^N\lceil(\chi PN\text{-}CN)\wedge s^N\in\tau PN$

Hence, the assumption $extract(t^N,t)$ may be rewritten as $extract(s^N\lceil(\chi PN\text{-}CN),t)$. Thus by **E5**:

(**) $\exists u.\ u\lceil(\chi P\text{-}C)=t\wedge extract(s^N,u)$

From (*) and (**) we infer $s^N\in\tau PN$ and $extract(s^N,u)$, which, owing to the hypothesis that PN is an N-replication of P, imply $u\in\tau P$. So, since $u\lceil(\chi P\text{-}C)=t$ by (**), the definition of concealment implies $t\in\tau(P\backslash C)$. $\square$

3.3   I/O distributed systems

The notion of *I/O process* generalizes that of pipe [H]. P is termed an I/O process if its channel set χP can be partitioned into a set of input channels ιP and one of output channels ωP, and for some f:

PS P **sat** $t\lceil\omega P\le f(t\lceil\iota P)$

i.e. the output message sequence is a prefix of a function of the input message sequence. Note that P may be an I/O process by conforming to a stronger specification, e.g.

$$P\ \textbf{sat}\ t\lceil\omega P\le^1 f(t\lceil\iota P)$$

which implies **PS**; however the unavoidable delays between input and output entail the fact that

$$P\ \textbf{sat}\ t\lceil\omega P=f(t\lceil\iota P)$$

is impossible unless $\iota P=<\,>$. An example of an I/O process is provided by a buffer, i.e. a process B that satisfies:

$$\iota B=\{in\}\qquad\qquad\omega B=\{out\}\qquad\qquad B\ \textbf{sat}\ t\lceil out\le(t\lceil in)[out/in]$$

where $[out/in]$ denotes renaming of channel out to in.

$DS=(P\|Q\|\dots)\backslash C$ is termed an *I/O distributed system* if (i) the components $P,Q,\dots$ are I/O processes, and (ii) whenever a channel c is shared among a subset D_c of components it is an output for only one of them; thus we can model both unicasting ($|D_c|=2$: c is shared by two components only) and multicasting ($|D_c|>2$: c is shared by more than two components). In the sequel we restrict our attention to replicated I/O distributed systems; this is not essential to ensure that replication is possible, but makes clearer the intuition underlying the formal treatment, by ruling out the complex multi-party interactions permitted in CSP.

4.   Implementing replication

Section 3 has shown that an I/O distributed system may be replicated by replicating its component I/O processes. This section addresses the problem of assembling N copies of a base I/O process P to implement an N-replication P^N of P despite given fault assumptions.

An important issue is determining the class of I/O processes for which an N-replication may be implemented from N base copies. Rather than indicating this class a priori, we prefer to let it emerge during the formal treatment.

4.1   Extraction by majority voting

Another important issue in the design of an N-replication P^N of a base process P is the interplay between the fault assumptions and the extraction strategy in terms of which P^N replicates P. However we shall restrict our treatment to the extraction which is nearly always used in practice: *majority voting*; the design goal then becomes the classical NMR one: to tolerate a minority of faulty copies. We use $\lfloor N \rfloor$ to denote the majority out of N votes, i.e. we let:

$$\lfloor 2p+1 \rfloor = \lfloor 2p \rfloor = p+1$$

Majority voting consists, in our approach, in defining the function *elect* as follows. To compute

$$elect(<c[n_1]!m_1,...c[n_K]!m_K>)$$

(where the messages m_k have all the same identifier) the trace argument is scanned from head to tail; the result is $c!m$ if m is the first value to occur $\lfloor N \rfloor$ times, *NIL* if there is no such m.

We further assume that the set *Idents* of message identifiers is totally ordered, and that the projection of an extracted trace on a given channel is ordered by message identifiers, without gaps:

E6 $extract(t^N,t) \Rightarrow no\_gaps(t)$ where $no\_gaps(t) \Leftrightarrow \forall c.\ no\_gap(t \lceil c)$

$no\_gap(u)$ is defined to be true if whenever $u = <...c!m1,c!m2,...>$, $id(m2)$ is the immediate successor of $id(m1)$ in the ordering defined over *Idents*. Finally, we require that all extracted traces should be maximal, in the sense that if $c!m$ can be elected it should be included in the extracted trace, provided that **E6** is not thereby violated. It follows that :

E7 $extract(t^N,t) \wedge extract(t^N,t1) \Rightarrow \forall c.\ t \lceil c = t1 \lceil c$

We conclude this section by an example in which **E3**'s second disjunct applies, i.e. in which an elected message does not enter in the extracted trace:

$$extract(t^N,t) \land elect(t^N \lceil c^N \lceil (id(x)=i)) \neq NIL \land t \lceil c \lceil (id(x)=i) = <>$$

Assume that $N=3$ so that $\lfloor N \rfloor = 2$, that m^a denotes a message of identifier $id(m^a)=a$, that $t^N = <c[1]!m^a, c[2]!m^a, c[1]!m^\beta, c[2]!m^\beta, c[1]!m^\gamma, c[1]!m^\delta, c[3]!m^\delta>$, and that $a<\beta<\gamma<\delta$; then:

$$elect(t^N \lceil c^N \lceil (id(x)=a)) = c!m^a \qquad elect(t^N \lceil c^N \lceil (id(x)=\beta)) = c!m^\beta$$
$$elect(t^N \lceil c^N \lceil (id(x)=\gamma)) = NIL \qquad elect(t^N \lceil c^N \lceil (id(x)=\delta)) = c!m^\delta$$

Thus, if t and t^N are such that $extract(t^N,t)$ holds, then t cannot contain a message of identifier γ, for $elect(t^N \lceil c^N \lceil (id(x)=\gamma)) = NIL$; therefore t cannot contain the elected $c!m^\delta$ either, or otherwise *no_gaps* would be violated; formally:

$$t \lceil c \lceil (id(x)=\delta) = <>$$

4.2   The implementation

In this section we show how to build an N-replication P^N of an I/O process P by feeding N copies of P through a *coordinator COORD*.

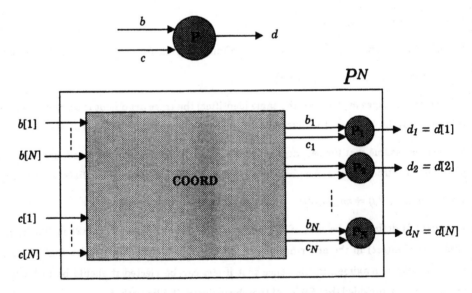

Fig. 4.1 - An architecture for a N-replication of the base process P

The architecture of P^N is shown in Fig. 4.1. The inputs to *COORD* coincide with the inputs to P^N:

$$\iota COORD = \iota P^N = \{c[1],...,c[N] \mid c \in \iota P\}$$

The N copies of P are denoted as $P_1,...,P_N$; accordingly, the channels of P_n $(1 \leq n \leq N)$ are named by subscripting the channels of P:

$$\iota P_n = \{c_n \mid c \in \iota P\} \qquad \omega P_n = \{d_n \mid d \in \omega P\} \qquad \text{for } 1 \leq n \leq N$$

Since the outputs of P^N are the union of those of $P_1,...,P_N$, we assume that if d is an output channel of P, then the outputs d_n of P_n and $d[n]$ of P^N coincide:

$$d_n = d[n] \quad \text{for all } d \in \omega P \text{ and } 1 \leq n \leq N$$

The copies $P_1,...,P_N$ are fed by the coordinator, so the outputs of the latter are divided into N groups of $|\iota P|$ channels, and each group coincides with the input channel set of some P_n. Finally, we introduce a useful convention: t and $t1$ range over the traces of P, t_n ranges over the traces of P_n and t^N over those of P^N. We shall often have to rename a trace t_n of P_n as a trace of P; this is accomplished by the substitution $t_n[\chi P/\chi P_n]$.

We now define the behaviour of the coordinator and of the copies of P. It is assumed that a predicate *non-faulty*(n) holds true for n if both P_n and its input from the coordinator are non-faulty. The coordinator specification is:

CS $COORD$ sat $\exists j.\ extract(u \lceil \iota COORD, j)$

$$\wedge \quad (\forall n.\ non\text{-}faulty(n) \Rightarrow (u \lceil \iota P_n)[\chi P/\chi P_n] \leq j)$$

CS imposes two requirements on the generic trace u of $COORD$: (i) the non-faulty outputs of $COORD$ (viz. $u \lceil \iota P_n$) must be, up to channel renaming, prefixes of the same trace j, which (ii) must be extracted from the replicated input to $COORD$ (viz. $u \lceil \iota COORD$). Often, the former requirement has been assumed to be sufficient for replicated systems correctness; in fact it only guarantees that the states of the copies of P remain consistent, but the latter requirement is necessary as well for the input/output behaviour of P^N to be correct.

Non-faulty copies of the I/O process P behave like P up to channel renaming:

PB $\forall n.\ non\text{-}faulty(n) \Rightarrow (t_n \in \iota P_n \Leftrightarrow t_n[\chi P/\chi P_n] \in \iota P)$

Thus the specification **PS** of Section 3.3 can be adapted to give, for all n:

P_nS P_n sat $non\text{-}faulty(n) \Rightarrow (t_n \lceil \omega P_n)[\chi P/\chi P_n] \leq f((t_n \lceil \iota P_n)[\chi P/\chi P_n])$

We begin the proof that P^N is an N-replication of P by showing that under the additional assumption that f is monotonic, i.e.

A1 $x \leq y \Rightarrow f(x) \leq f(y)$

it turns out that the outputs from the non-faulty copies of P are all prefixes of the same trace. As explained in Section 6, monotonicity can be interpreted as meaning that P is deterministic.

Lemma 4.1   If $t^N \in \iota PN$, there exists a j such that if *non-faulty*(n) then $t^N \ulcorner \omega P_n[\chi P/\chi P_n] \leq f(j)$.

Proof. If $t^N \in \iota PN$, the structure of PN implies that there exist a trace $u \in \iota COORD$ and, for each n, a trace $t_n \in \iota P_n$ such that:

$$(*) \qquad u \ulcorner \iota P_n = t_n \ulcorner \iota P_n \qquad\qquad t_n \ulcorner \omega P_n = t^N \ulcorner \omega P_n$$

We may therefore apply **CS** to u and infer that there exists a j such that, if *non-faulty*(n),

$$(u \ulcorner \iota P_n)[\chi P/\chi P_n] \leq j$$

whence, by the first equality (*):

$$(t_n \ulcorner \iota P_n)[\chi P/\chi P_n] \leq j$$

Since f is monotonic, we may apply it to both sides, and use **P_nS**, transitivity and the second equality (*) to infer:

$$(t^N \ulcorner \omega P_n)[\chi P/\chi P_n] \leq f(j) \qquad\qquad\qquad \square$$

Assume that a majority of the traces $t^N \ulcorner \omega P_n$ $(1 \leq n \leq N)$ that make up $t^N \ulcorner \omega PN$ are prefixes of a trace satisfying *no_gaps*; then it is possible to show that there exists a k such that, up to renaming, the projection on an output channel d of any trace extracted from $t^N \ulcorner \omega PN$ is a prefix of the projection on $d[k]$ of t^N.

Lemma 4.2   If *extract*$(t^N \ulcorner \omega PN, v_{ext})$, and there exists a v_{max} such that *no_gaps*(v_{max}) and the set

$$S = \{n \mid (t^N \ulcorner \omega P_n)[\chi P/\chi P_n] \leq v_{max}\}$$

has cardinality $|S| \geq \llcorner LN \lrcorner$, then for some $k \in S$:

$$\forall d.\ d \in \omega P \Rightarrow v_{ext} \ulcorner d \leq (t^N \ulcorner d[k])[\chi P/\chi P_n]$$

Proof. Let k be the index in $S = \{n \mid (t^N \ulcorner \omega P_n)[\chi P/\chi P_n] \leq v_{max}\}$ for which the trace $t^N \ulcorner \omega P_k[\chi P/\chi P_k]$ is the longest. If an action $d!m$ is in v_{ext}, by **E3** $d!m$ must have been elected, so the set

$$S_m = \{n \mid d[n]!m \text{ is in } t^N \ulcorner \omega P_n\}$$

must have cardinality $|S_m| \geq \llcorner LN \lrcorner$. Thus the hypothesis $|S| \geq \llcorner LN \lrcorner$ implies $S \cap S_m \neq \{\}$. It follows that $k \in S_m$ must hold, or if $h \in S \cap S_m$ the trace $(t^N \ulcorner \omega P_k)[\chi P/\chi P_k]$ could not be longer than $(t^N \ulcorner \omega P_h)[\chi P/\chi P_h]$. Thus the elements of v_{ext} must also be in $(t^N \ulcorner \omega P_k)[\chi P/\chi P_k]$, and, as a result, the elements of $v_{ext} \ulcorner d$ must also be in $(t^N \ulcorner d[k])[\chi P/\chi P_k]$ for $d \in \omega P$. That $v_{ext} \ulcorner d \leq (t^N \ulcorner d[k])[\chi P/\chi P_k]$ follows from the fact that both v_{ext} and $t^N \ulcorner \omega P_k$ satisfy *no_gaps*: v_{ext} by **E6** and $t^N \ulcorner \omega P_k$ by the hypothesis on v_{max}. $\qquad\qquad \square$

Lemma 4.2 could be coupled in the obvious way to Lemma 4.1, if $f(j)$ returned a trace satisfying *no_gaps*. So we make the assumption:

A2 $\forall j.\ no\_gaps(f(j))$

This allows us to prove:

Lemma 4.3   If $t^N \in \iota PN$ and $|\{n \mid non\text{-}faulty(n)\}| \geq \lfloor N \rfloor$, there exist a $t1 \in \iota P$, a j and a v such that:

$$extract(t^N \lceil \iota PN, j) \wedge extract(t^N \lceil \omega PN, v)$$
$$\wedge \quad t1 \lceil \iota P \leq j \wedge \forall d. \, d \in \omega P \Rightarrow v \lceil d \leq t1 \lceil d$$

Proof. Owing to the structure of PN, if $t^N \in \iota PN$ there exist $u \in \iota COORD$ and, for each n, $t_n \in \iota P_n$ such that:

(*) $t^N \lceil \iota PN = u \lceil \iota COORD$ $u \lceil \iota P_n = t_n \lceil \iota P_n$ $\forall d. \, d \in \omega P \Rightarrow t_n \lceil d_n = t^N \lceil d[n]$

Thus **CS** ensures that there exists a j such that $extract(t^N \lceil \iota PN, j)$ and, if n is non-faulty,

(**) $(u \lceil \iota P_n)[\chi P / \chi P_n] = (t_n \lceil \iota P_n)[\chi P / \chi P_n] \leq j$

By **E1**, Section 3.1, there must exist a v such that $extract(t^N \lceil \omega PN, v)$. By Lemma 4.1, all non faulty copies, which are a majority by hypothesis, issue an output trace which is a prefix of $f(j)$, and it has been assumed that $no\_gaps(f(j))$. Hence, letting $v_{max} = f(j)$ and $v_{ext} = v$, we may invoke Lemma 4.2 to infer that there exists a k such that $non\text{-}faulty(k)$ and:

$$\forall d. \, d \in \omega P \Rightarrow v \lceil d \leq (t^N \lceil d[k])[\chi P / \chi P_k]$$

whence, by applying the last formula of (*):

(***) $\forall d. \, d \in \omega P \Rightarrow v \lceil d \leq (t_k \lceil d_k)[\chi P / \chi P_k]$

Finally, as $t_k \in \iota P_k$ and k is non-faulty, **PB** implies that $t1 = t_k [\chi P / \chi P_k]$ is a trace of ιP. Thus (**) (taking $n = k$) and (***) may be rewritten as:

$$t1 \lceil \iota P \leq j \qquad \text{and} \qquad \forall d. \, d \in \omega P \Rightarrow v \lceil d \leq t1 \lceil d \qquad \qquad \square$$

We need one more assumption (whose intuitive meaning will be explained in Section 6) concerning the traces of the I/O process P:

A3 $(t1 \in \iota P \wedge \forall c. \, (c \in \iota P \Rightarrow t1 \lceil c \leq t \lceil c) \wedge \forall d. \, (d \in \omega P \Rightarrow t \lceil d \leq t1 \lceil d)) \Rightarrow t \in \iota P$

We are now sufficiently well equipped to prove the main result of this section.

Theorem 4.4   If a majority of copies of P are non-faulty, then PN is an N-replication of P.

Proof. We need to show that **R1**, **R2** and **R3** (Section 3.1) hold. **R1** and **R3** are trivial to prove, so we concentrate on **R2**, viz.:

$$t^N \in \iota PN \wedge extract(t^N, t) \Rightarrow t \in \iota P.$$

Assume $t^N \in \iota PN$ and $extract(t^N, t)$. By **E4**, Section 3.1:

(*) $extract(t^N \lceil \iota PN, t \lceil \iota P)$ and $extract(t^N \lceil \omega PN, t \lceil \omega P)$

By Lemma 4.3, there exist j and v such that:

$$extract(t^N \lceil \iota PN, j) \qquad \text{and} \qquad extract(t^N \lceil \omega PN, v)$$

whence, by (*) and **E7**, Section 4.1:

(**) $\forall c. \, c \in \iota P \Rightarrow t \lceil c = j \lceil c$ and $\forall d. \, d \in \omega P \Rightarrow t \lceil d = v \lceil d$

Lemma 4.3 also guarantees the existence of $t1 \in \iota P$ such that:

$$t1 \lceil \iota P \leq j \qquad \text{and} \qquad \forall d. \, d \in \omega P \Rightarrow v \lceil d \leq t1 \lceil d$$

Thus, by (**) and transitivity:

$$\forall c.\, c \in \iota P \Rightarrow t1\lceil c \leq t\lceil c \qquad \text{and} \qquad \forall d.\, d \in \omega P \Rightarrow t\lceil d \leq t1\lceil d$$

whence, by **A3**, we may conclude that $t \in \iota P$. □

5. An example: the Join algorithm

In this section we consider an example implementation of replication. Fig. 5.1, which should be

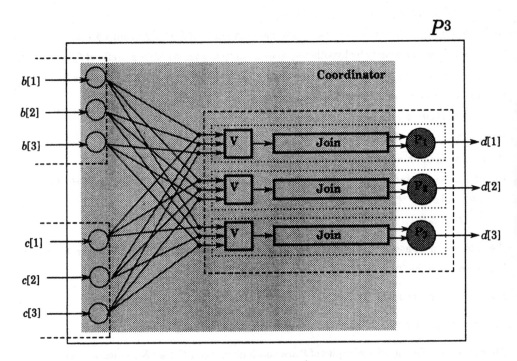

Fig. 5.1. The 3-replication of P according to *Join*

compared to Fig 4.1, shows the coordinator proposed in [M]. This coordinator is composed out of $N*|\iota P|$ distributors and N modules. Each distributor is fed through a replicated input channel and is connected via a link to every module. The modules contain a majority voter **V** and a *Join* unit. It is assumed that distributors and links may fail in any fashion that does not violate the property **DELIVER**: if a message enters the coordinator in a majority of copies, it will be delivered to every voter in a majority of copies. Periodically, the *Join* units perform a byzantine agreement [LSP] to agree on the voted messages that will be passed to the copies of the base process P. In [MP2,MP3] we give a formal proof that the coordinator satisfies the specification **CS** of Section 4.2 regardless of how many modules are faulty.

In a real implementation, the components inside the dashed borders in Fig. 5.1 are located at the same site, and those inside the dotted borders probably run on the same processor. If links are conventionally attributed to the distributors' site, the assumption that a minority of processors per site may fail ensures that (i) **DELIVER** is respected and (ii) non-faulty outputs of the coordinator feed non-faulty copies of P and must be a majority. As stated above, (i) guarantees that the coordinator satisfies its specification; therefore (ii), as shown in Section 4.2, guarantees that P^N implements an N-replication of P.

6.   Concluding remarks

By way of conclusions we discuss the properties **A1-A3** introduced in Section 4.2. There we have presented a technique by which an I/O process P that satisfies:

$$P \text{ sat } t\lceil\omega P \leq f(t\lceil\iota P)$$

can be replicated provided that:

A1 f is monotonic, i.e. $x \leq y \Rightarrow f(x) \leq f(y)$;

A2 (messages in a trace carry identifiers and) for all traces j and channels c the identifiers of $f(j)\lceil c$ are ordered without gaps;

A3 $(t1 \in \iota P \wedge \forall c. (c \in \iota P \Rightarrow t1\lceil c \leq t\lceil c) \wedge \forall d. (d \in \omega P \Rightarrow t\lceil d \leq t1\lceil d)) \Rightarrow t \in \iota P$.

The intended meaning of **A1** is that the base system P should be deterministic - a term which is unfortunately quite overloaded (see e.g. [H]). In this context it is employed to mean that in any state P may offer to engage in at most one output action (this property may be shown to be equivalent to f being monotonic). Indeed, if different non-faulty copies of P can transform the same input into different outputs, it is hard to see how to ensure the correctness of P^N. We deem therefore that **A1** is a requirement of a fundamental nature, though it may take different forms in different treatments. E.g., Cooper reached similar conclusions in his design and implementation of a distributed replicated system [C], (although he also allows for relaxing determinism at the cost of transparency).

A2 is a requirement which most real systems satisfy by using sequence numbers for messages. Sequence numbers are unnecessary if physical channels do not reorder input messages; in this case, however, messages should be considered to be implicitly numbered in accordance with the arrival order. (As an aside, note that CSP channels are synchronous, so that physical channels that may reorder messages or be otherwise faulty have to be modelled inside the coordinator.) Other systems make use of increasing timestamps [L1] [L2]. There will in general be gaps between the timestamps of consecutive messages; however, since the fulfillment of the input stability condition [S1] ensures that messages are processed in the order they were sent, we may still consider messages to be implicitly numbered. Thus timestamp-based systems too may be regarded - at a convenient abstraction level - as satisfying **A2**.

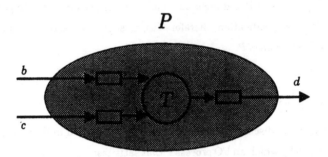

Fig. 6.1. A process satisfying **A3**

A3 implies that P behaves as though it contained a processing I/O element T communicating with the environment via unbounded buffers (Fig. 6.1). Indeed if $t1$ is known to be a trace of P and t is obtained from $t1$ as specified in **A3**, then t must also be a trace of P, for the added input messages and the missing output messages may be lingering inside the queues. Intuitively, the need for **A3** may be understood as follows: as the coordinator cannot help introducing some buffering, its effect can be ignored only if communication between components of the distributed system takes place through unbounded buffers anyway. This may be seen as a limitation on the class of distributed systems that can be implemented by replication. This rather strong view may be perhaps mitigated by weakening the notion of implementation, so as to allow a target distributed system with bounded buffers to be implemented by one with the same components and larger buffers. Either view should be reflected in extant NMR designs by a corresponding assumption, which is instead generally omitted.

At this point the reader may wonder how fundamentally **A3** limits the class of distributed systems that can be implemented - in a strict sense - by replication. Actually, two solutions do come to mind to replicate the synchronous, unbuffered communication advocated in [H]: (1) timing message exchanges at regular intervals, large enough to guarantee that all the N-replications involved are ready; (2) introducing some form of replicated, reliable acknowledgements. None of these however seems particularly appealing. Rather than embedding synchronous message passing in replication mechanisms, it is probably best to implement it on top of the abstraction of reliable buffered processes offered by the kind of replication discussed here.

Acknowledgements

The authors are grateful to Prof. B. Randell and Prof. S.K. Shrivastava for their comments and suggestions. This work was supported by the Royal Signals and Radar Establishment of the U.K. Ministry of Defence.

References

[AK]   Avizienis, A., Kelly, J.K.J., "Fault tolerance by design diversity: concepts and experiments", *IEEE Computer*, vol. 17, no. 8, pp. 67-80, Aug. 1984.

[B]   Bird, R. S., "The promotion and accumulation strategies in transformational programming", *ACM Transactions on Programming Languages and Systems*, vol. 6, no. 4, Oct. 1984.

[C]   Cooper, E, "Replicated distributed programs", *Proc. of the 10th ACM Sym. on Operating Systems Principles*, pp. 63-78, Washington, Dic. 1985.

[G]   Goldberg, J., "SIFT: A provable fault-tolerant computer for aircraft flight control", *Inform. Processing 80 Proc. IFIP Congr.*, pp. 151-156, Tokyo, Japan, Oct. 1980.

[H]   Hoare, C.A.R., "Communicating sequential processes", *Prentice Hall International*, 1985.

[KM]   Koutny, M., and Mancini, L., "Synchronizing events in replicated computations", Technical Report TR/237, Computing Laboratory, University of Newcastle upon Tyne, June 1987 (to appear in *The Journal of Systems and Software*).

[L1]   Lamport, L., "The implementation of reliable distributed multiprocess sustems", *Computer Networks*, pp. 95-114, vol. 2, no. 2, May 1978.

[L2]   Lamport, L., "Time, clocks and the ordering of events in a distributed system", *Comm. ACM*, vol. 21, no. 7, pp. 558-565, July 1978.

[LSP] Lamport, L., Shostak, R., Pease, M., "The Byzantine Generals problem", *ACM Transactions on Programming Languages and Systems*, pp. 382-401, vol. 4, no. 3, July 1982.

[LV]   Lyons, R.E., Vanderkulk, W., "The use of triple-modular redundancy to improve computer reliability", *IBM Journal of Research and Development*, pp. 200-209, vol. 6, no. 2, Apr. 1962.

[M]   Mancini, L., "Modular redundancy in a message passing system", *IEEE Trans. Software Eng.*, pp. 79-86, vol. SE-12, no. 1, Jan. 1986.

[MK]   Mancini, L., Koutny, M., "Formal specification of N-modular redundancy", *1986 ACM Computer Science Conference*, pp. 199-204, Cincinnati, Ohio, Feb. 1986.

[MP1] Mancini, L., Pappalardo, G., "The *Join* algorithm: ordering messages in replicated systems", *Safecomp 86*, pp. 51-55, Sarlat, France, Oct. 1986.

[MP2] Mancini, L., Pappalardo G., "On resolving nondeterminism in replicated distributed systems", *IFIP Conf. on Distributed Processing*, Amsterdam, The Netherlands, Oct. 1987.

[MP3] Mancini, L., Pappalardo G., "Proving correctness properties of a replicated synchronous program", to appear in *The Computer Journal*.

[MS]   Mancini, L., Shrivastava, S.K., "Exception handling in replicated systems with voting", *16th Int. Conf. on Fault Tolerant Computing*, pp. 384-389, Vienna, Austria, July 1986.

[MSS]   Melliar-Smith, P.M., Schwartz, R., "Formal specification and mechanical verification of SIFT: a fault-tolerant flight control system", *IEEE Trans. on Computers*, vol. C-31, no. 7, pp. 616-630, July 1982.

[S1]   Schneider, F.B., "Synchronization in distributed programs", *ACM Transactions on Programming Languages and Systems*, vol. 4, no. 2, pp. 125-148, Apr. 1982.

[S2]   Schneider, F.B., "The state machine approach", in Paul, M., and Siegert, H.J. (eds.), *Distributed systems - methods and tools for specification, an advanced course*, LNCS vol. 190, pp. 444-454, Springer-Verlag, 1985.

Reasoning About Atomic Objects

Maurice P. Herlihy and Jeannette M. Wing
Computer Science Department
Carnegie Mellon University
Pittsburgh, Pennsylvania 15213-3890
U.S.A.[1]

Abstract

Atomic transactions are a widely-accepted technique for organizing activities in reliable distributed systems. In most languages and systems based on transactions, atomicity is implemented through atomic objects, which are typed data objects that provide their own synchronization and recovery. This paper describes new linguistic mechanisms for constructing atomic objects from non-atomic components, and it formulates proof techniques that allow programmers to verify the correctness of such implementations.

1. Introduction

A *distributed system* consists of multiple computers (called nodes) that communicate through a network. Programs written for distributed systems, such as airline reservations, electronic banking, or process control, must be designed to cope with failures and concurrency. Concurrency arises because each process executes simultaneously with those at other nodes as well as those at the same node, while failures arise because distributed systems consist of many independently-failing components. Typical failures include node crashes, network partitions, and lost messages.

A widely-accepted technique for preserving consistency in the presence of failures and concurrency is to organize computations as sequential processes called *transactions*. Transactions are *atomic*, that is, serializable and recoverable. *Serializability* [26] means that transactions appear to execute sequentially, and *recoverability* means that a transaction either succeeds completely or has no effect. A transaction's effects become permanent when it *commits*, its effects are discarded if it *aborts*, and a transaction that has neither committed or aborted is *active*.

---

[1]This research was sponsored by the Defense Advanced Research Projects Agency (DOD), ARPA Order No. 4976, monitored by the Air Force Avionics Laboratory Under Contract F33615-84-K-1520. The views and conclusions contained in this document are those of the authors and should not be interpreted as representing the official policies, either expressed or implied, of the Defense Advanced Research Projects Agency or the US Government.

In most languages and systems based on transactions, atomicity is implemented through *atomic objects*, which are typed data objects that provide their own synchronization and recovery. Languages such as Argus [19], Avalon [12], and Aeolus [32] provide a collection of primitive atomic data types, together with constructs for programmers to define their own atomic types. The most straightforward way to define a new atomic type is to use an existing atomic data type as a representation, but objects constructed in this way often support inadequate levels of concurrency [31]. Instead, it is often necessary to implement new atomic objects by carefully combining atomic and non-atomic components, and it is the responsibility of the programmer to ensure that the implementation is indeed atomic at the "right" level of abstraction.

In this paper,

- We describe new linguistic mechanisms for constructing atomic objects from non-atomic components. These mechanisms are currently being implemented as part of the Avalon [12] project at Carnegie Mellon.

- We formulate proof techniques that allow programmers to verify the correctness of atomic objects implemented using our mechanisms.

Although language and system constructs for implementing atomic objects have received considerable attention in the distributed systems community, the problem of verifying the correctness of programs that use those constructs has received surprisingly little attention. Techniques for reasoning about concurrent programs are well-known [1, 13, 18, 25], but are not adequate for reasoning about atomicity. They typically address issues such as mutual exclusion or the atomicity of individual operations; they do not address the more difficult problems of ensuring the serializability of arbitrary sequences of operations, nor do they address recoverability. Reasoning about atomicity is inherently more difficult than reasoning about concurrency alone.

We view the development of new linguistic mechanisms and proof techniques as complementary tasks. Verification techniques can serve not only as aids for reasoning about atomic objects, and hence about transaction-based distributed systems, but also as the foundation of a methodology for their design and implementation. This notion is analogous to Gries's contention that loop invariants and termination functions facilitate the development of programs-in-the-small [9], and Liskov and Guttag's similar contention that representation invariants and abstraction functions facilitate the development of programs-in-the-large [20].

This paper is organized as follows. In Section 2, we present our model and basic definitions, and in Section 3, we introduce and motivate the relevant language primitives provided by Avalon. In Section 4, we describe our verification techniques, which are illustrated by an extended example in Section 5. Section 6 concludes with a discussion and a brief overview of related work.

2. Model

The basic containers for data are called *objects*. Each object has a *type*, which defines a set of possible *values* and a set of primitive *operations* that provide the only means to create and manipulate objects of that type. For example, a file might provide Read and Write operations, and a FIFO queue might provide Enq and Deq operations.

A computation is modeled by a *history*, which is a finite sequence of *events*. An *invocation* event is written as $x\ op(args^*)\ A$, where x is an object name, op an operation name, $args^*$ a sequence of arguments, and A a transaction name. A *response* event is written as $x\ term(res^*)\ A$, where *term* is a termination condition, and res^* a sequence of results. We use "Ok" for normal termination. A *commit* or *abort* event is written $x\ Commit\ A$ or $x\ Abort\ A$, and it indicates that the object x has learned that transaction A has committed or aborted[2]. A response *matches* an earlier invocation if their object names agree and their transaction names agree. An invocation is *pending* if it has no matching response. An *operation* in a history is a pair consisting of matching invocation and response events. An operation p_0 *lies within* p_1 in H if the invocation event for p_1 precedes that of p_0 in H, and the response event for p_1 follows that of p_0.

A *transaction subhistory*, $H \mid A$ (H at A), of a history H is the subsequence of events in H whose transaction names are A. $H \mid S$ and $H \mid x$ are defined similarly, where S is a set of transactions and x is an object. A history is *complete* if every invocation has a matching response. Let *complete(H)* denote the longest complete subhistory of H. Histories H and G are *equivalent* if $complete(H) \mid A = complete(G) \mid A$ for all transactions A.

A history H is *well-formed* is it satisfies the following conditions for all transactions A:
1. The first event of $H \mid A$ is an invocation.
2. Each invocation in $H \mid A$, except possibly the last, is immediately followed by a matching response or by an abort event.
3. Each response in $H \mid A$ is immediately preceded by a matching invocation, or by an abort event.
4. If $H \mid A$ includes a commit or abort event, it must be the last event.

A well-formed history H is *sequential* if:
1. Transactions are not interleaved. I.e., if any event of transaction A precedes any event of B, then all events of A precede all events of B.
2. All transactions, except possibly the last, have committed.

Each object has a *sequential specification* that defines a set of *legal* sequential histories for that object. This set is defined indirectly by using conventional specification techniques, e.g., the axiomatic style of Larch [10], that describe an object's values and pre- and postconditions on its operations. For example, the sequential specification for a FIFO queue object includes all and only histories in which items are enqueued and dequeued in FIFO order. A sequential history H involving multiple objects is *legal* if it is legal at each object, i.e., each subhistory $H \mid x$ belongs to the sequential specification for x.

H is *atomic* if $H \mid committed(H)$, the subhistory associated with committed transactions, is equivalent to some legal sequential history. We focus here on "pessimistic" atomicity mechanisms, in which an active transaction with no pending invocations is always allowed to commit. H is *on-line atomic* if every well-

---

[2]Although Avalon permits transactions to be nested [24, 27], this paper considers only single-level transactions.

formed history *H'* constructed by appending *commit* events to *H* is atomic. Any sequential history equivalent to *H'* | *committed(H')* is called a *serialization* of H. *H* is on-line atomic if every one of its serializations is legal.

The only practical way to ensure atomicity in a decentralized distributed system is to have each object perform its own synchronization and recovery. Nevertheless, *H* is not necessarily atomic just because *H* | *x* is atomic for each object *x*. To ensure that all objects choose compatible serialization orders, it is necessary to impose certain additional restrictions on the behavior of atomic objects. Atomic objects in Avalon are subject to the restriction that transactions must appear to execute sequentially in the order they commit, a property that Weihl [30] has called *hybrid atomicity*. Hybrid atomicity is a local property, meaning that if each object is hybrid atomic, a system composed of hybrid atomic objects is itself hybrid atomic. Thus, under this restriction, it suffices to consider only object subhistories.

To capture this restriction, we make the following adjustments to our model. When a transaction commits, it is assigned a logical timestamp [17], which appears as an argument to that transaction's commit events. These timestamps determine the transactions' serialization order. Commit timestamps are subject to the following well-formedness constraint, which reflects the behavior of logical clocks: if *B* executes a response event after *A* commits, then *B* must receive a later commit timestamp. Henceforth a history is atomic if its transactions are serializable in commit timestamp order, and it is on-line atomic if the result of appending commit events with well-formed commit timestamps is atomic.

q Enq(x) A	q Enq(x) A
q Enq(y) B	q Enq(y) B
q Ok() B	q Ok() B
q Ok() A	q Ok() A
q Commit(1:30) A	q Commit(1:15) B
q Commit(1:15) B	q Deq() C
q Deq() C	q Ok(y) C
q Ok(y) C	

Figure 2-1: H₁ (left) is on-line atomic, but H₂ (right) is not.

For example, consider the two histories H_1 and H_2 for a FIFO queue *q* shown in Figure 2-1. H_1 is on-line atomic. It has two serializations: one in which *B* precedes *A*, and one in which *B* precedes *A* and *A* precedes *C*, and it is easily verified that both are legal. H_2, however, is atomic but not on-line atomic since the history $H'_2 = H_2 \bullet q$ *Commit(1:00) A* • *q Commit(1:30) C* is not equivalent to any legal sequential queue history (*y* is dequeued out of order).

The use of commit-time serialization distinguishes Avalon from other transaction-based languages, which are typically based on some form of strict two-phase locking [5]. We chose to support commit-time serialization because it permits more concurrency than two-phase locking [30], as well as better availability for replicated data [11]. Because commit-time serialization is compatible with strict two-phase locking, applications that use locking can still be implemented in Avalon.

3. Language Constructs

Avalon is currently being implemented as extensions to C++ [29]. The basic language construct for implementing atomicity in Avalon is the *tid* (transaction identifier) data type. Tids are a partially ordered set of values. The two most important operations provided by tids are creation and comparison. The *creation* operation, written:

```
tid t = *(new tid);
```

creates a new tid value, and the *comparison* operation, written:

```
t1 < t2;
```

returns information about the order in which its arguments were created. If the comparison evaluates to *true*, then (1) every serialization that includes the creation of *t1* will also include the creation of *t2*, and (2) the creation of *t1* precedes the creation of *t2*. If *t1* and *t2* were created by distinct transactions *T1* and *T2*, then a successful comparison implies that *T1* is committed and serialized before *T2*, while if *t1* and *t2* were created by the same transaction, then *t1* was created first. If the comparison evaluates to *false*, then the tids may have the reverse ordering, or their ordering may be unknown. Comparison induces a partial order on tids that "strengthens" over time: if *t1* and *t2* are created by concurrent active transactions, they will remain incomparable until one or more of their creators commits. If a transaction aborts, its tids will not become comparable to any new tids.

Atomic objects in Avalon provide *Commit* and *Abort* operations that are called by the system as transactions commit or abort. Commit typically discards recovery information for the committing transaction, and Abort typically discards the tentative changes made by the aborting transaction. Both Commit and Abort have a tid argument, which is used as follows. If *t* is the argument to Commit, then any tid *t'* satisfying the predicate:

```
isDesc(t',t)
```

was created by the committed transaction *t*.

The argument for Abort is defined analogously. Intuitively, Commit and Abort operations in Avalon are expected to affect liveness, but not safety. For example, delaying a Commit or Abort operation may delay other transactions (e.g., by failing to release locks) or reduce efficiency (e.g., by failing to discard unneeded recovery information), but it should never cause a transaction to observe an erroneous state[3].

An atomic object in Avalon is defined by a C++ class that inherits from the Avalon built-in class *atomic* (see [12]). Syntactically, a class is defined by a collection of *members*, which are the components of the object's representation, and a collection of operation implementations. With occasional minor variations, implementations of operations of atomic objects in Avalon have the following form:

```
tid t = *(new tid);
when(TEST)
  pinning()
    BODY;
```

---

[3]We do not address liveness properties in this paper, though certain ones are clearly of great interest. We rely on the extensive work on temporal logic, e.g., [23], for reasoning about liveness.

The **new** statement generates a new tid which is used to "tag" the current operation. The **when** statement is a conditional critical region: the statement enclosed by the **when** is executed when **TEST** evaluates to *true*. **TEST** is typically an expression comparing the operation's newly created tid to other tids embedded in the object's representation. When **TEST** evaluates to *true*, the operation can be executed without violating atomicity. To ensure proper crash recovery, as distinct from transaction recovery, an object may be modified only within statements of the form: **pinning()** **BODY**. The **pinning** statement is included here for completeness; we do not address crash recovery in this paper. **BODY** computes a result and updates the object's state.

4. Verification

This section outlines a verification methodology for implementations of atomic objects.

An *implementation* is a set of histories in which events of two objects, a *representation* (rep) object r of type Rep and an *abstract* object a of type Abs, are interleaved in a constrained way: for each history H in the implementation, (1) the subhistories H | r and H | a satisfy the usual well-formedness conditions; and (2) for each transaction A, each representation operation in H | A lies within an abstract operation. Informally, an abstract operation is implemented by the sequence of rep operations that occur within it.

Our correctness criterion for the implementation of an atomic object a is as follows: The object is atomic if for every history in its implementation, H | a is atomic. We typically do not require H | r to be atomic.

To show the correctness of an atomic object implementation, we must generalize techniques from the sequential domain. Let *Rep* be the implementation object's set of values, *Abs* the set of values of the (sequential) data type being implemented, and OP the sequential object's set of operations. The subset of *Rep* values that are legal values is characterized by a predicate called the *rep invariant*, $I: Rep \rightarrow bool$. The meaning of a legal representation is given by an *abstraction function*, $A: Rep \rightarrow 2^{OP^*}$, defined only for values that satisfy the invariant. Unlike abstraction functions for sequential objects [15] that map the rep value to a single abstract value, our abstraction functions map the rep value to a set of sequential histories of abstract operations.

Our basic verification technique is to show inductively that the following properties are invariant. Let r be an object state after accepting the history H, and let $Ser(H)$ denote the set of serializations of H.

1. $\forall\ S$ in $A(r)$, S is a legal sequential history, and
2. $Ser(H) \subseteq A(r)$.

These two properties ensure that every serialization of H is a legal sequential history, and hence that H is on-line atomic. Note that if we were to replace the second property with the stronger requirement that $Ser(H) = A(r)$, then we could not verify certain correct implementations that keep track of equivalence classes of serializations. In the inductive step of our proof technique, we show the invariance of these two properties across a history's events, e.g., as encoded as statements in program text.

5. An Example: A Highly Concurrent FIFO Queue

In this section, we illustrate our verification technique by applying it to a highly concurrent atomic FIFO queue implementation. Our implementation is interesting for two reasons. First, it supports more concurrency than commutativity-based concurrency control schemes such as two-phase locking. For example, it permits concurrent Enq operations, even though Enq's do not commute. Second, it supports more concurrency than any locking-based protocol, because it takes advantage of state information. For example, it permits concurrent Enq and Deq operations while the queue is non-empty.

5.1. The Representation

Information about Enq and Deq invocations is recorded in the following data structures:

```
struct enq_rec {
  item* what;                       // item enqueued
  tid enqr;                         // who enqueued it
  enq_rec(tid t, item* x)           // constructor
    {enqr = t; what = x;};
};
struct deq_rec {
  item* what;                       // item dequeued
  tid enqr;                         // who enqueued it
  tid deqr;                         // who dequeued it
  deq_rec(tid d, tid e, item* x)    // constructor
    {deqr = d;
     enqr = e;
     what = x;
    };
};
```

The *enqr* component is a tid generated by the enqueuing transaction, *deqr* is a tid generated by the dequeuing transaction, *what* is a pointer to the enqueued item, and the last component defines a constructor operation for initializing the struct.

The queue is represented as follows:

```
class queue: public atomic {
  deq_stack deqd;                   // Stack of dequeued items
  enq_heap enqd;                    // Heap of enqueued items
public:
  queue();                          // Create empty queue
  void enq(item*);                  // Enqueue an item
  item* deq();                      // Dequeue an item
  void commit(tid);                 // Called on commit
  void abort(tid);                  // Called on abort
};
```

The *enqd* component is a *partially ordered queue* (or heap) of *enq_rec*'s, ordered by their *enqr* fields. The *deqd* component is a stack of *deq_rec*'s used to undo aborted Deq operations.

5.2. The Operations

If B is an active transaction, then we say A is *committed with respect to* B if A is committed, or if A and B are the same transaction. Enq and Deq must satisfy the following (informally stated) synchronization constraints to ensure atomicity. Transaction A may dequeue an item if (1) the most recent transaction to execute a Deq is committed with respect to A, and (2) there exists a unique oldest element in the queue whose enqueuing transaction is committed with respect to A. A may enqueue an item if the last item dequeued was enqueued by a transaction committed with respect to A.

Given these conditions, Enq and Deq are implemented as follows:

```
void queue::enq(item* x) {
  tid who = *(new tid);                       // Caller's tid
  when (deqd.empty() || deqd.top().enqr < who)
    pinning()                                 // Making update
      enqd.insert(enq_rec(who,x));            // Record enqueue
}

item* queue::deq() {
  tid who = *(new tid);                       // Caller's tid
  when ((deqd.empty() || deqd.top().deqr < who) &&
        enqd.top_exists() && enqd.top().enqr < who)
    pinning(){                                // Making update
      enq_rec e = enqd.remove();              // Move from enqueued heap..
      deqd.push(deq_rec(who,e.enqr,e.what));  // to dequeued stack.
      return e.what;
    }
}
```

Enq enters its critical region when the item most recently dequeued was enqueued by a transaction committed with respect to A. The enqueuer's tid and the new item are inserted in *enqd*. Deq enters its critical region when the most recent dequeuing transaction has committed with respect to the caller, and *enqd* has a unique oldest item. It removes the item from *enqd* and records it in *deqd*.

In addition to Enq and Deq operations, the queue provides Commit and Abort operations that are applied to the queue as transactions commit or abort:

```
void queue::commit(tid who) {
  when(true)                          // Always ok to commit.
    pinning()                         // Making update.
      // Discard any deq records.
      if (!deqd.empty() && deqd.top().deqr < who) deqd.reset();
}

void queue::abort(tid who) {
  when(true)                          // Always ok to abort.
    pinning(){                        // Making update.
      while (!deqd.empty()) {         // Undo aborted dequeues.
        deq_rec d = deqd.top();
        if (isDesc(d.deqr,who)) {//   // Dequeued by aborting transaction?
          enqd.insert(enq_rec(d.enqr,d.what)); // Put it back ...
          d = deqd.pop();}            // and discard deq record.
        else break;                   // No more dequeues to undo.
      }
      enqd.discard(who);              // Undo aborted enqueues.
```

}

}

The commit operation discards deq records for committed transactions, and the abort operation discards enq and deq records for aborted operations.

5.3. Representation Invariant, Abstraction Function, and Proof Sketch

We start with a lemma about sequential queue histories. Let Q be a sequential queue history (not necessarily legal). Define the auxiliary functions $ENQ(Q)$ and $DEQ(Q)$ to yield the sequences of items enqueued and dequeued in Q:

$DEQ(\Lambda) = \text{emp}$ $ENQ(\Lambda) = \text{emp}$
$DEQ(Q \bullet Deq(x)) = DEQ(Q) \bullet x$ $ENQ(Q \bullet Enq(x)) = ENQ(Q) \bullet x$
$DEQ(Q \bullet Enq(x)) = DEQ(Q)$ $ENQ(Q \bullet Deq(x)) = ENQ(Q)$

Here, "Enq(x)" and "Deq(x)" are shorthand for Enq and Deq operations, "$\bullet$" denotes concatenation, "emp" the empty sequence of items, and "Λ" the empty history.

When reasoning about serializations, we need a way to recognize when it is legal to insert an operation in the *middle* of a legal sequential history.

Lemma 1: Let $Q = Q_1 \bullet Q_2$ be a legal sequential queue history, and let p be a queue operation. The sequential history $Q' = Q_1 \bullet p \bullet Q_2$ is legal if $DEQ(Q')$ is a prefix of $ENQ(Q')$.

This lemma indirectly characterizes the conditions under which queue operations may execute concurrently; an analogous lemma would be needed for any other data type to be verified.

5.3.1. Representation Invariant

The queue operations preserve the following representation invariant.[4] For all rep values r:

1. No item is present in both the *deqd* and *enqd* components:

   $(\forall d: deq\_rec) \, (\forall e: enq\_rec) \, (d \in r.\text{deqd} \wedge e \in r.\text{enqd} \Rightarrow e.\text{what} \neq d.\text{what})$

2. Items are ordered in *deqd* by their enqueuing and dequeuing tids:

   $(\forall d1, d2: deq\_rec) \, d1 <_d d2 \Rightarrow (d1.\text{enqr} < d2.\text{enqr} \wedge d1.\text{deqr} < d2.\text{deqr})$

   where $<_d$ is the total ordering on *deq_rec*'s imposed by the *deqd* stack.

3. Any dequeued item must previously have been enqueued:

   $(\forall d: deq\_rec) \, d \in r.\text{deqd} \Rightarrow d.\text{enqr} < d.\text{deqr}$.

Our proof technique requires that we show the representation invariant is preserved across the implementation of each abstract operation. It is conjoined to the pre- and postconditions of each of the operations' specifications.

---

[4]For brevity, we assume items in the queue are distinct, an assumption that could easily be relaxed by tagging each item in the queue with a timestamp.

5.3.2. Abstraction Function

Let P be a set of tids. P is a *prefix set* if, for all tids t and t', if $t \in P \wedge t' < t$, then $t' \in P$.

Lemma 2: If H is an on-line atomic history for a set of tids and S is a serialization of H, then the tids whose creation operations appear in S form a prefix set.

Define the auxiliary function $OPS(r, P)$ to yield the partially ordered set of operations tagged by tids in P. The elements of $OPS(r, P)$ are given by:

$$\{\text{Enq}(x) \mid (\exists\, e{:}enq\_rec \in r.\text{enqd})\; e.\text{what} = x \wedge e.\text{enqr} \in P \,\vee$$
$$(\exists\, d{:}deq\_rec \in r.\text{deqd})\; d.\text{what} = x \wedge d.\text{enqr} \in P \} \cup$$
$$\{\text{Deq}(y) \mid (\exists\, d{:}deq\_rec \in r.\text{deqd})\; d.\text{what} = y \wedge d.\text{deqr} \in P\}$$

Each operation is "tagged" with a tid ($e.\text{enqr}$, $d.\text{enqr}$, or $d.\text{deqr}$). These tids induce a partial order on the elements of $OPS(r, P)$.

Let S be a partially ordered set of operations, and S' a sequence of operations. S' is a *linearization* of S if $elements(S) = elements(S')$ and $order(S) \subseteq order(S')$.

$$A'(r, P) = \{Q \mid Q \text{ is a linearization of } OPS(r, P)\}$$

The abstraction function $A(r)$ is defined as the union of $A'(r, P)$ over all prefix sets P. Note that $A(r)$ typically includes more histories than $Ser(H)$.

5.3.3. Proof Sketch

The queue implementation is verified by showing inductively that every sequential history in $Ser(H)$ lies in $A(r)$ and that every sequential history in $A(r)$ is legal. For brevity, we give an informal summary of our arguments here; the formal proofs for the Enq and Deq operations are in the next section.

Suppose the object completes an operation Enq(x) with tid t, carrying the accepted history H to H', and the representation r to r'. It is immediate from Lemma 2 that $Ser(H') \subseteq A(r')$. To show that every history in $A(r')$ is legal, let $Q' \in A(r')$. If Q' fails to satisfy the prefix property of Lemma 1, there must exist y in $DEQ(Q')$ such that x precedes y in $ENQ(Q')$, implying that the Enq of x is serialized before the Enq of y. Let t' be the enqueuing tid for the item at the top of the *deqd* stack, and let t'' be the enqueuing tid for y. The **when** condition for Enq ensures that $t' < t$, and the rep invariant ensures that $t'' \leq t'$, hence that $t'' < t$, which is impossible if the Enq of x is serialized first.

Similarly, suppose the object completes an operation Deq(x) with tid t, carrying the representation r to r'. Let $Q = Q_1 \bullet Q_2 \in A(r)$ and $Q' = Q_1 \bullet \text{Deq}(x) \bullet Q_2 \in A(r')$. The rep invariant and the first conjunct of the **when** condition for Deq ensure that x is not an element of $DEQ(Q)$, and the second conjunct then ensures that x is the first element of $ENQ(Q) - DEQ(Q)$. Together, they imply that $DEQ(Q') = DEQ(Q) \bullet x$ is a prefix of $ENQ(Q') = ENQ(Q)$, hence that Q is legal by Lemma 1.

If a commit or abort event carries the accepted history H to H', and the corresponding commit or abort operation carries r to r', we must show that (1) $A(r') \subseteq A(r)$, and (2) that no history in $A(r) - A(r')$ is in $Ser(H')$. Property 1 ensures that every sequential history in $A(r')$ is legal, and Property 2 ensures that no valid serializations are "thrown away." For Commit, we check that every discarded history is missing a operation of a committed transaction, and for Abort, we check that every discarded history includes an operation of an aborted transaction; either condition ensures that the discarded history is not an element of $Ser(H')$.

Naturally, this verification relies on properties of sequential queues. To verify an implementation of another data type, one would have to rely on a different set of properties, but the arguments would follow a similar pattern. The basic synchronization conditions are captured by a type-specific analog to Lemma 1, characterizing the conditions under which an operation can be inserted in the middle of a sequential history. The rep invariant and abstraction function define how the set of possible serializations is encoded in the representation, and an inductive argument is used to show that no operation, commit, or abort event can violate atomicity.

5.4. Proof of Correctness for Enqueue and Dequeue

We will show that if the prefix property (1) holds of all serializations $h \in A(r)$ at the invocation of the enqueue operation, it holds of all serializations $H' \in A(r')$ at the point of return. In the following, for $H \in A(r)$, $H' \in A(r')$, let $H = H_1 \bullet H_2$ and $H' = H_1 \bullet op \bullet H_2$ such that $\forall p \in H_1 \neg(who < tid(p)) \wedge \forall p \in H_2 \neg(tid(p) < who)$, where op is the enqueue or dequeue operation, as the case may be.

5.4.1. Enqueue

We decorate the enqueue operation with two assertions, one after the when condition, and one at the point of return.

```
void queue::enq(item* x) {
    tid who = *(new tid);              // Caller's tid.
    when (deqd.empty() || deqd.top().enqr < who)
```
$$WHEN: \{\forall y \; y \in elements(DEQ(h)) \Rightarrow tid(Enq(y)) < who\}$$
```
        pinning()                      // Making update.
          enqd.insert(enq_rec(who,x)); // Record enq.
```
$$POST: \{DEQ(h') = DEQ(h)\}$$
```
}
```

Proof: Case 1: The queue is empty. Trivial since the antecedent of WHEN is false.

Case 2: The queue is nonempty. Then let y be an item dequeued in H, which implies that the tid of the enqueue operation of y is ordered before who by the WHEN assertion. The enqueue operation must be in H_1 since (1) the tids of all enqueue operations of dequeued items are all ordered before that of deqd.top().enqr (by the rep invariant), which is ordered before who (by the when condition); and (2) who is not ordered before any operation in H_1 (by the definition of $H = H_1 \bullet H_2$). Since the enqueue operations of all dequeued items are in H_1,

$$DEQ(H) \text{ prefix } ENQ(H_1) \tag{*}$$

At the point of return, let $e = Enq(x)/Ok()$. From POST we have that:

$DEQ(H') = DEQ(H)$, which by (*)
$\Rightarrow DEQ(H') \text{ prefix } ENQ(H_1)$
$\Rightarrow DEQ(H') \text{ prefix } ENQ(H_1 \bullet e \bullet H_2)$
$\Rightarrow DEQ(H') \text{ prefix of } ENQ(H')$.

5.4.2. Dequeue

Here is the annotated Deq operation:

```
item* queue::deq() {
   tid who = *(new tid);           // Caller's tid.
   when ((deqd.empty() || deqd.top().deqr < who) && // Check for conflict
         enqd.top_exists() && enqd.top().enqr < who)
```

$\{WHEN: \forall \text{ Deq operations } d \text{ in } h \text{ (tid(d) < who} \Rightarrow d \text{ in } H_1)\}$

```
   pinning(){                      // Making update.
     enq_rec e = enqd.remove();// Transfer from enqueued heap...
     deqd.push(deq_rec(who,e.enqr,e.what)); // to dequeued stack.
     return e.what;
   }
```

$\{POST: DEQ(h') = DEQ(h) \bullet x \wedge ENQ(h') = ENQ(H_1) \bullet ENQ(H_2)\}$

```
}
```

and the proof:

Proof: From the first conjunct of the **when** condition and the second clause of the rep invariant, we know that $DEQ(H) = DEQ(H_1)$. The second conjunct implies that there exists some $x = first(ENQ(H) - DEQ(H))$, the first item in the sequence of enqueued items that have not yet been dequeued. The third conjunct implies that this item, x, is in H_1. Thus, by properties on sequences, there exists some $x = first(ENQ(H_1) - DEQ(H_1))$.

At the point of return, let $d = Deq()/Ok(x)$. POST implies that

$DEQ(H_1 \bullet d) \text{ prefix } ENQ(H_1 \bullet d)$

$\Rightarrow DEQ(H') \text{ prefix } ENQ(H_1 \bullet d)$

$\Rightarrow DEQ(H') \text{ prefix } ENQ(H_1 \bullet d \bullet H_2)$

$\Rightarrow DEQ(H') \text{ prefix } ENQ(H').$

6. Discussion and Related Work

Atomicity has long been recognized as a basic correctness property within the database community [2]. More recently, several research projects have chosen atomicity as a useful foundation for general purpose distributed systems, including Avalon [12], Argus [19], Aeolus [32], and TABS [28][5]. Of these projects, however, only Avalon and Argus provide linguistic support for programmers to design and implement user-defined atomic data types, which Weihl and Liskov [31] argue is necessary for building large, realistic systems. To our knowledge, Avalon is the only language project to address the issue of verifying implementations of atomic objects.

Part of the Avalon design philosophy is that verification is facilitated by making constructs for synchronization and recovery as explicit as possible. For example, the tid data type makes the set of serializations directly observable to programs, and our example verification relies heavily on the properties of this built-in data type. Similarly, explicit user-defined commit and abort operations provide direct control over transaction recovery. By contrast, Argus relies on the programmer to encode

---

[5]EXODUS [6] and Dixon and Shrivastava's language [4], like Avalon, extend C++ to support recoverability, but neither give programmers control over serializability.

information about the set of serializations in "atomic variants," treating commit and abort processing as a side-effect of normal operations. For a more detailed evaluation of the implicit approach in Argus, see Greif et al. [8].

The axiomatic approach for program verification is particularly well-suited for "syntax-directed" verification of sequential and concurrent programs. Axiomatic proof techniques originated with Hoare's axioms [14] for sequential program statements and were later extended for abstract data types by introducing abstraction functions [15], representation invariants, and data type induction rules. The axiomatic approach was also extended to shared-memory models of concurrent programs [25], and to message-passing models of distributed programs [1, 16]. One of the principal conclusions of our work is that such "pure" syntax-directed axiomatic methods seem poorly suited for reasoning about atomicity. In the sequential and concurrent domains, an object's state can be given by a single value, and each new operation simply transforms one value to another as prescribed by the appropriate axiom. Auxiliary variables are used to keep track of history information and the states (e.g., program counters) of concurrent processes. In the transactional domain, however, an atomic object's state must be given by a *set* of possible serializations, and each new operation is inserted somewhere "in the middle" of certain serializations (see Lemma 1). This distinction between physical and logical ordering is easily expressed in terms of reordering histories, but seems awkward to express axiomatically, i.e., using assertions expressed in terms of program text alone. Of course, the proofs in this paper could be axiomatized simply by encoding the set of serializations as auxiliary data, but we have found the resulting proofs complex and unnatural.

Best and Randell [3], Weihl [30], and Lynch and Merritt [22] have proposed formal models for transactions and atomic objects. Best and Randell use *occurrence graphs* to define the notion of atomicity, to characterize interference freedom, and to model error recovery. Their model does not exploit the semantics of data, focusing instead on event dependencies. Weihl's model is similar to ours: atomic objects are defined in terms of state machines and computations are modeled as histories. Lynch and Merritt model nested transactions and atomic objects in terms of *I/O automata*, which have been used to prove correctness of general algorithms for synchronization and recovery [7, 21]. None of these models were intended for reasoning about individual programs.

Our technique lies between "pure" syntax-directed axiomatic approaches and model-oriented operational ones. Because we wish to reason about specific programs, not abstract algorithms, our approach relies on annotating program text with assertions. Our assertion language, however, refers to operations, histories, and sets of histories directly, making it richer and more expressive than the usual first-order logic-based assertion languages. We have found our approach more natural for reasoning about transaction-based distributed systems where serializability and recoverability cannot be treated as independent properties.

References

[1]   K.R. Apt, N. Francez, and W.P. DeRoever.
        A Proof System for Communicating Sequential Processes.
        ACM Transactions on Programming Languages and Systems 2(3):359-385, July, 1980.

[2]   P.A. Bernstein and N. Goodman.
        A survey of techniques for synchronization and recovery in decentralized computer systems.
        ACM Computing Surveys 13(2):185-222, June, 1981.

[3]   E. Best and B. Randell.
        A Formal Model of Atomicity in Asynchronous Systems.
        Acta Informatica 16(1):93-124, 1981.

[4]   G. Dixon and S.K. Shrivastava.
        Exploiting Type Inheritance Facilities to Implement Recoverability in Object Based Systems.
        In *Proceedings of the 6th Symposium in Reliability in Distributed Software and Database Systems.*
            March, 1987.

[5]   K.P. Eswaran, J.N. Gray, R.A. Lorie, and I.L. Traiger.
        The Notion of Consistency and Predicate Locks in a Database System.
        Communications ACM 19(11):624-633, November, 1976.

[6]   J.E. Richardson and M.J. Carey.
        Programming Constructs for Database System Implementation in EXODUS.
        In *ACM SIGMOD 1987 Annual Conference*, pages 208-219. May, 1987.

[7]   M.P. Herlihy, N.A. Lynch, M. Merritt, and W.E. Weihl.
        On the correctness of orphan elimination algorithms.
        In *17th Symposium on Fault-Tolerant Computer Systems.* July, 1987.
        Abbreviated version of MIT/LCS/TM-329.

[8]   I. Greif, R. Seliger, and W.E. Weihl.
        Atomic Data Abstractions in a Distributed Collaborative Editing System.
        In *Proceedings of the 13th Annual ACM SIGACT-SIGPLAN Symposium on Principles of
            Programming Languages*, pages 160-172. January, 1986.

[9]   D. Gries.
        The Science of Programming.
        Spinger-Verlag, New York, 1981.

[10]   J.V. Guttag, J.J. Horning, and J.M. Wing.
        The Larch Family of Specification Languages.
        IEEE Software 2(5):24-36, September, 1985.

[11]   M.P. Herlihy.
        A quorum-consensus replication method for abstract data types.
        ACM Transactions on Computer Systems 4(1), February, 1986.

[12]   M.P. Herlihy and J.M. Wing.
        Avalon: Language Support for Reliable Distributed Systems.
        In *The Seventeenth International Symposium on Fault-Tolerant Computing*, pages 89-94. July,
            1987.
        Also available as CMU-CS-TR-86-167.

[13]   M.P. Herlihy and J.M. Wing.
        Axioms for concurrent objects.
        In *Fourteenth ACM Symposium on Principles of Programming Languages*, pages 13-26. January
            1987.

[14]   C.A.R. Hoare.
         An Axiomatic Basis for Computer Programming.
         Communications of the ACM 12(10):576-583, October, 1969.

[15]   C.A.R. Hoare.
         Proof of Correctness of Data Representations.
         Acta Informatica 1(1):271-281, 1972.

[16]   J. Hooman and W.-P. de Roever.
         The Quest Goes On: A Survey of Proof Systems For Partial Correctness of CSP.
         Lecture Notes in Computer Science 224: Current Trends in Concurrency.
         Springer-Verlag, 1986, pages 343-395.

[17]   L. Lamport.
         Time, clocks, and the ordering of events in a distributed system.
         Communications of the ACM 21(7):558-565, July, 1978.

[18]   L. Lamport.
         Specifying Concurrent Program Modules.
         ACM Transactions on Programming Languages and Systems 5(2):190-222, April, 1983.

[19]   B.H. Liskov, and R. Scheifler.
         Guardians and actions: linguistic support for robust, distributed programs.
         Transactions on Programming Languages and Systems 5(3):381-404, July, 1983.

[20]   B.H. Liskov and J.V. Guttag.
         Abstraction and Specification in Program Development.
         The MIT Press, 1986.

[21]   N. Lynch.
         A Concurrency Control For Resilient Nested Transactions.
         Technical Report MIT/LCS/TR-285, Laboratory for Computer Science, 1985.

[22]   N. Lynch and M. Merritt.
         Introduction to the Theory of Nested Transactions.
         In *Proceedings of the International Conference on Database Theory.* Rome, Italy, September, 1986.
         Sponsored by EATCS and IEEE.

[23]   Z. Manna and A. Pnueli.
         Verification of concurrent Programs, Part I: The Temporal Framework.
         Technical Report STAN-CS-81-836, Dept. of Computer Science, Stanford University, June, 1981.

[24]   J.E.B. Moss.
         Nested Transactions: An Approach to Reliable Distributed Computing.
         Technical Report MIT/LCS/TR-260, Laboratory for Computer Science, April, 1981.

[25]   S. Owicki and D. Gries.
         Verifying Properties of Parallel Programs: An Axiomatic Approach.
         Communications of the ACM 19(5):279-285, May, 1976.

[26]   C.H. Papadimitriou.
         The serializability of concurrent database updates.
         Journal of the ACM 26(4):631-653, October, 1979.

[27]   D.P. Reed.
         Implementing atomic actions on decentralized data.
         ACM Transactions on Computer Systems 1(1):3-23, February, 1983.

[28]   A.Z. Spector, J. Butcher, D.S. Daniels, D.J. Duchamp, J.L. Eppinger, C.E. Fineman, A. Heddaya, and P.M. Schwarz.
Support for Distributed Transactions in the TABS prototype.
IEEE Transactions on Software Engineering 11(6):520-530, June, 1985.

[29]   B. Stroustrup.
The C++ Programming Language.
Addison Wesley, 1986.

[30]   W.E. Weihl.
Specification and implementation of atomic data types.
Technical Report TR-314, Massachusetts Institute of Technology Laboratory for Computer Science, March, 1984.

[31]   W.E. Weihl, and B.H. Liskov.
Implementation of resilient, atomic data types.
ACM Transactions on Programming Languages and Systems 7(2):244-270, April, 1985.

[32]   C.T. Wilkes and R.J. LeBlanc.
Rationale for the design of Aeolus: a systems programming language for an action/object system.
Technical Report GIT-ICS-86/12, Georgia Inst. of Tech. School of Information and Computer Science, Dec, 1986.

A formal treatment of interference in remote procedure calls

Giuseppe Pappalardo[1,2] and Santosh K. Shrivastava[1]

(1) Computing Laboratory, The University of Newcastle upon Tyne, UK
(2) Università di Reggio Calabria, Italy

ABSTRACT

Remote procedure calls (rpcs) are a distributed programming facility enabling a client program to call a procedure that will be executed by a server computation running on a remote machine. It would be desirable that remote and local procedure calls could be treated uniformly, so as to make distribution transparent to the programmer. But transparency may be impaired if, because of communication or machine failures, computations serving the rpc of a client are allowed to interfere with computations serving later rpcs of that client. This paper gives a formal treatment of interference in rpcs. The formalism used is that of occurrence graphs. The main result obtained is a sufficient condition for rpcs to be interference-free. The practical significance of this condition is highlighted by relating it to interference prevention techniques often adopted in the design of rpc mechanisms.

1. Introduction

Remote procedure calls (rpcs) are a widely used language facility for distributed programming. They provide a *client* program with the ability to call procedures whose code and parameters may reside on a remote machine. After invoking an rpc the client blocks, while an underlying mechanism, the *rpc protocol*, takes care of: (i) sending a *call message* to the remote machine, (ii) starting on it a *server computation* which executes the called procedure, and (iii) transmitting the computation results back to the client's machine. Eventually the client returns from the call - either *successfully*, with some results received from the remote machine, or *abnormally*, with an *exception* signalling that some problem has occurred. Within this fundamental scheme many variations can be considered, concerning mainly the mapping of computations onto processes, and the adoption of reliability measures to cope with machine or communication failures.

The above description implies that rpcs afford some degree of abstraction from distribution and the related message passing. But in the sequel we shall require that abstraction from distribution, or *transparency*, should be as complete as possible. This is because, ideally, the programmer should be able to treat remote and local procedure calls (lpcs) uniformly. Transparency issues are discussed at length in [Nel]; among them we focus on the notions of *call semantics*, *nested rpcs*, *orphans* and *interference*.

Exactly-once semantics. When a lpc returns, the called procedure is known to have been executed exactly once if the return from it is successful, or partially - up to the point when an exception was raised - if the return is abnormal. Transparency requires that the same should apply to rpcs.

Nested rpcs. Like lpcs, rpcs should be allowed to nest: a computation serving an rpc should be able to invoke rpcs itself. It is therefore natural to associate with each computation a chain of ancestor rpcs.

Orphans. The execution of the procedure called by a lpc cannot continue after the lpc has return-ed (because the return of a lpc is always the consequence of the callee terminating), nor can it survive a crash that disrupts the process executing the caller program (because caller and callee are executed by the same process). For transparency's sake (and to avoid wasting resources) such *orphan* executions must not arise in the remote case either: no server computation should continue after any of its ancestor rpcs has returned successfully, returned abnormally, or has been disrupted by a crash of the calling client. Unfortunately, in the last two circumstances the requirement is not an easy one to meet, for client and server are on different machines connected by a communication medium, and each of these may fail independently. Consider e.g. the difficulties arising if the rpc protocol causes rpcs to return abnormally, should no reply be received within a given interval: when this happens, the remote server computation may well be still executing, and will become an orphan unless appropriate measures are taken. Likewise, measures are needed to deal with computations that become orphans because a crash disrupts the client they are serving.

Interference. The loss of transparency due to orphans makes the programmer's burden heavier, by forcing him to worry about *interference* between orphans and legitimate computations. As an example, suppose that a client obtains a lock on a remote terminal and issues two rpcs *display(file1)*, *display(file2)*. If *display(file1)* returns abnormally and leaves an orphan which is allowed to interfere with the computation for *display(file2)*, then the lines of the two files may freely mix on the terminal screen! As the problem would not arise were the terminal local, the example illustrates the inconvenience of non-transparency. Even subtler problems may arise with nested rpcs; e.g. even a call that returns successfully may leave orphans that will interfere with computations for subsequent calls. This is illustrated in Fig. 1.1: the client p_1 on site A makes an rpc c_1 to site B and the server computation p_2 on B makes an rpc c_2 to site C; c_2 returns abnormally, leaving an orphan p_3 on C, but p_2 on B completes and causes c_1 to return successfully. A subsequent rpc c_1' made by p_1 to C may now produce at C a computation p_3' that will interfere with p_3.

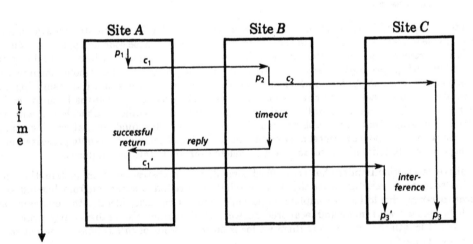

Fig. 1.1 - Interference in a nested call

At-least-once semantics. For particular applications one might settle for a non-transparent semantics allowing more than one computation to take place on behalf of a single rpc [LaB]. Even for such applications, however, it is unlikely that the ban on interference may be lifted. Rather, the designer who adopts at-least-once semantics will have to watch out also for interference between the multiple executions serving a call.

At-most-once semantics. Under this semantics, adopted e.g. in [LS], an rpc returns successfully iff it has given rise to one execution, abnormally iff it has had no effects. Nelson [Nel] argues - and we share his view - that at-most-once semantics is "pleasant", but is not required for transparency. At-most-once rpcs enjoy the property which is sometimes called "atomicity with respect to failure", but we shall use the term atomicity to mean "atomicity with respect to concurrency", in the sense introduced in Section 2.

This paper gives a mathematical treatment of interference in remote procedure calls. The formalism used, occurrence graphs [BR], is briefly introduced in Section 2. Sections 3 and 4 informally describe the assumed rpc execution model (a sort of common core of all rpc protocols), and orphans and interference. These concepts are formalized in Section 4 and 5. Although the formalization is of interest in itself, the main result of the paper, to be found in Section 6, is the formulation of a sufficient condition for rpcs to be interference-free in the presence of orphans; basically, the condition says that, if a call c precedes a call c', then on each node any work for c should precede any work for c'. Section 7 discusses how this condition can be ensured by extermination, expiration and crashcounts - three interference prevention techniques often adopted in the design of rpc protocols [Nel], [PS].

2.   A brief overview of occurrence graphs

Occurrence graphs were introduced in [BR] as a means of studying atomicity and interference in concurrent systems. In this section we briefly review some definitions and concepts of that paper.

Definition 2.1   An *occurrence graph* (og) is a pair $(Act, \rightarrow)$, where Act is a set and $\rightarrow$ is an irreflexive binary relation over Act.   □

Ogs are intended as a formal means of describing computations (i.e. schedules) performed by parallel programs, whereby members of Act are interpreted as primitive program actions, hereafter termed *simple actions*, and the relation $\rightarrow$ as an ordering over them. Let $\Rightarrow$ denote the transitive closure of $\rightarrow$, then we give the

Definition 2.2   Given an og $(Act, \rightarrow)$, and two distinct simple actions a and b:
- if $a \Rightarrow b$, we say that a *happens before* or *precedes* b;
- if neither $a \Rightarrow b$ nor $b \Rightarrow a$, we write $a \| b$ and say that a and b are *concurrent*.   □

Note that, if an og is acyclic, the relation $\Rightarrow$ is irreflexive and therefore a (strict) partial order; in this case it coincides with the the time ordering of [LaL].

As it is $\Rightarrow$ rather than $\rightarrow$ that conveys the desired meaning of a temporal ordering, we will not distinguish between ogs that have the same $\Rightarrow$. Given a computation of a program, we require the relation $\Rightarrow$ of the computation's og to contain the pair $a \Rightarrow b$ whenever:

PO (program ordering): a and b occur in the program within some construct that constrains a to precede b; or, if **PO** does not apply:

DO (data ordering): a and b access the same data object†, and a is performed before b in the computation considered.

This definition means that, even though a may be performed before b in a computation, if a and b are unconstrained by **PO** and are not mutually exclusive, i.e. if they are potentially concurrent, then $a \| b$ will hold in the og describing the computation. The motivation for this approach is that it permits the formulation of the atomicity criterion expounded below.

---

†   In fact, it would be sufficient to require $a \Rightarrow b$ only when a and b access the same object and either of them is a write.

Consider a concurrent program P containing the fragments $A_1,...,A_n$, which will be momentarily assumed disjoint. Traditionally, $A_1,...,A_n$ have been said to be *atomic actions* in a given computation of P if this computation is *serializable*, i.e. has the same effect as one in which the executions of the A_is do not interleave. Best and Randell [BR] formalize these concepts through the use of ogs. They consider the A_is to be atomic if the computation og becomes an acyclic graph when the actions of each A_i are "collapsed" into a single node. Otherwise, if the collapsed og contains a cycle $A_i \Rightarrow A_j \Rightarrow A_i$, A_i will be said to be interfered with by A_j. These definitions can be understood as follows. Suppose that A_i accesses a subset s_i of the program state. In a computation whose collapsed og is acyclic, no A_i can be interleaved with any extraneous simple actions on s_i, or by **DO** the og would not be acyclic. Thus the program state is transformed by each A_i as though A_i were executed in isolation. We may conclude that if the computation og is acyclic, the A_is are atomic actions.

[BR] generalize their atomicity criterion to nested actions as detailed below.

Definition 2.3   An *abstraction hierarchy* over a set *Act* is a tree having subsets of *Act* as nodes and satisfying the following:
- *Act* is its root;
- if $a \in Act$, then $\{a\}$ (still termed a simple action, with slight licence) is a leaf;
- if A is an internal node and $\{A_1, A_2,...,A_n\}$ is the set of its children, then $\cup_i A_i = A$ and $\cap_i A_i = \{\}$ hold; A is termed an *activity* or *compound action* and $A_1, ..., A_n$ its *subactivities*. $\square$

Note that the left-to-right ordering of hierarchy tree nodes is irrelevant to the hierarchy defined.

Definition 2.4   A *structured occurrence graph* (sog) is a triple $(Act, \rightarrow, AbsH)$ such that $(Act, \rightarrow)$ is an og and $AbsH$ an abstraction hierarchy over *Act*. $\square$

Definition 2.5   An *abstraction level* of an abstraction hierarchy over *Act* is the set of (simple or compound) actions left immediately below by a "cut" intercepting the edges of the abstraction hierarchy tree. *Act* (viz. the hierarchy tree root) is called the *most abstract* level. The set of the hierarchy tree leaves is called the *least abstract* level. $\square$

It can be easily proved that an abstraction level L satisfies to: $\cup \{A | A \in L\} = Act$, and $\cap \{A | A \in L\} = \{\}$. This is consistent with the idea that defining abstraction levels is a way of structuring actions by proceeding bottom-up, so that no simple actions can be "missed out" or "counted twice".

Definition 2.6   Let L be an abstraction level and $A \in L$. The *expansion* of L with respect to A, denoted by L/A, is the set $(L-A) \cup \{A_i | A_i$ is a subactivity of $A\}$. $\square$

It is easily proved that L/A is an abstraction level itself.

Definition 2.7   Let $G = (Act, \rightarrow, AbsH)$ be a sog and L an abstraction level of $AbsH$. The *view* of G at L, denoted by $G@L$, is the og $(L, \rightarrow_L)$, where the relation $\rightarrow_L$ is defined by:

$$A \rightarrow_L B \text{ iff } A, B \in L, A \neq B \text{ and } a \rightarrow b \text{ for some } a \in A \text{ and } b \in B \qquad \square$$

(often the subscript L is omitted). Note that $G@L$ is indeed an og, in that $\rightarrow_L$ is, as required by Definition 2.1, irreflexive. Intuitively, $G@L$ is obtained from the og $(Act, \rightarrow)$ by collapsing the simple actions of each activity $A \in L$ into the node A of $G@L$, and simplifying any redundant edges resulting. Likewise, $G@(L/A)$ is the view obtained from $G@L$ by "opening up" A.

Definition 2.8   A sog is said to *satisfy atomicity* if none of its views contains a cycle. $\square$

[BR] also gives the formal definitions - which we omit - of *interference* between activities and of *atomic occurrence* of an activity. Intuitively, B interferes with A if B occurs strictly after part of A and strictly before another part of A; conversely, A occurs atomically if it is not interfered with by any other activity. The atomicity of a sog and the atomicity of its activities are related by the

Theorem 2.1   A sog satisfies atomicity if and only if all of its activities occur atomically. $\square$

Example 2.1 An og *G1* is shown in Fig. 2.1 (left), together with a possible abstraction hierarchy and three abstraction levels, *L1 L2* and *L3* (centre). *G1* and the abstraction hierarchy define a sog *G* which satisfies atomicity; accordingly, none of the views shown on the right is cyclic.

An extra link in *G1*, however, can make *G* a sog that does not satisfy atomicity (Fig. 2.2). Notice that the view *G@L2* contains now a cycle $A \Rightarrow B \Rightarrow A$, which implies that *B* interferes with *A*.

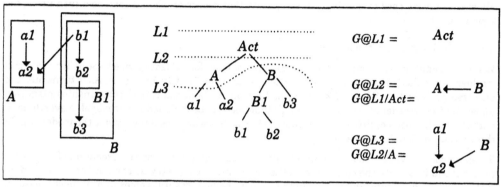

Fig. 2.1 - A structured occurrence graph that satisfies atomicity

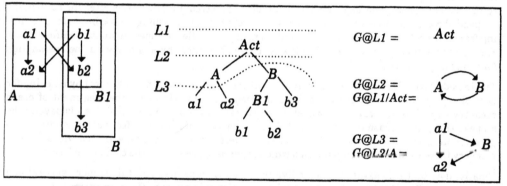

Fig. 2.2 - A structured occurrence graph that does not satisfy atomicity

3.   A general execution model

This section informally introduces an rpc "execution model" as the basis for the formalization given later. Rather then an rpc protocol, the execution model is a set of properties (tagged in bold for further reference) that are general enough to be true for every conceivable rpc protocol. Also for the sake of generality, we assume an at-least-once rather than exactly-once semantics (cf. **S2** below), for the treatment of the former easily specializes to the latter but not conversely.

From a physical point of view, an rpc system is composed out of *sites*. (**S1**) Sites perform *computations* made up of actions with a local effect and of rpcs. (**S2**) An rpc may result in more than one server computations being activated on the site to which it is made. (**A1**) On the site on which it is invoked, an rpc actually consists of two distinct actions: an invocation and a return; the latter may be *normal*, *abnormal* or *crashed*. About the order in which computation actions occur, three assumptions are made. The first applies within a site: **(PO1)** computations are sequential, and the return from an rpc is the next (local) action a computation performs after the invocation of that rpc. The second two apply across sites: **(PO2)** the invocation of an rpc precedes any remote computation serving it, and **(PO3)** the normal return of an rpc is the result of the completion of one of the remote computations that serve the rpc.

As required by transparency (cf. *Nested rpcs*, Introduction), computations serving an rpc are allowed to invoke rpcs themselves; this suggests that recursion should somehow turn up in the formalization.

3.1   Peeking under the model

We have sought to make our model "general" so that the formalization need not be fraught with irrelevant details. Moreover, we have omitted to state our fault assumptions. As it turns out, the universe described by S1 and S2, the classification A1, and the causal relationships disguised under the **PO** precedence constraints are all that needs to be included in our model. Nevertheless, part of what has been omitted may be inferred by - so to speak - "peeking" under the model, and in this section we shall do so as a help to intuition.

When an rpc is invoked, the rpc protocol causes a message requesting the execution of the called procedure to be sent to the called site. If the caller site uses a retry mechanism or the communication system duplicates data, the called site may receive several copies of a request message. This explains how an rpc may give rise to multiple server computations (cf. S2).

A computation that issues an rpc is suspended until the rpc returns (cf. **PO1**). A normal return may be thought of as the consequence of a reply from the remote site (cf. **PO3**), and an abnormal return as that of a timeout expiring before a reply is received; in either case, after the return, the suspended computation is resumed. It is also possible that after issuing an rpc but before returning from it the computation is disrupted and then, after a while, resumed (in an unspecified state). Such a resumption is considered to follow a "crashed" return, by analogy with the resumption following a return proper.

The introduction of crashed returns only aims at making the model more general by catering for possible rpc protocols that use some form of crash recovery. However, the treatment of crash recovery - which is generally performed in the context of at-most-once semantics - is beyond the scope of this paper. Crash recovery need only concern us insofar as, by effectively extending computation lives beyond crashes, it may give rise to interference with orphans. Indeed without crash recovery there would be no computations which orphans of pre-crash calls could interfere with.

Finally, note that it is assumed that individual computations may fail: this is more general and yet not more difficult to treat than the usual assumption that a crash affects an entire site.

4.   Extended activation trees and interference

4.1   Basic definitions

The first step of our formalization is to assume three sets: S, the sites, P, the computations, and C, the rpcs. We further presuppose the functions *onsite*: $P \rightarrow S$, *tosite*: $C \rightarrow S$, *rcalls*: $P \rightarrow C^*$, *caller*: $C \rightarrow P$ and a relation *serves* $\subseteq P \times C$. Below we introduce their intended meanings and the constraints such meanings entail.

The local part of computation p is performed at the site *onsite*(p). The rpc c is made to the remote site *tosite*(c).

If computation p sequentially invokes the rpcs $c_1, ..., c_n$ ($n \geq 0$), then we let *rcalls*$(p) = <c_1, ..., c_n>$ and *caller*$(c_i) = p$ ($0 \leq i \leq n$). The function *caller* is well-defined, for an rpc can be invoked by one computation only. If *rcalls*$(p) = <>$ ($<>$ is the empty string), p is said to be a *bottom* (i.e. completely local) computation.

p serves c means that computation *p* has been activated as a result of rpc *c*; hence the requirement that if *p serves c*, then *onsite(p)* = *tosite(c)*. For a given *c*, under the at-least-once semantics assumed, there may be zero, one or more *p*s such that *p serves c*; in the former case *c* is said to be *barren*. On the other hand, for a given *p* there can be either one or no *c* such that *p serves c*; in the latter case *p* is referred to as a *top* computation. The properties of *serves* are illustrated in fig. 4.1.

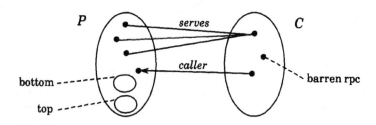

Fig. 4.1 - Relation *serves* and function *caller*

4.2   Extended activation trees

The above functions provide some information concerning a computation (although not its full characterization). As a means of portraying this information, we now introduce the notion of extended activation tree (eact) of a computation. The eact $T[p]$ of a computation *p* has root *p* and, from left to right, a child $T[c]$ for each rpc *c* in *rcalls(p)*; $T[c]$ has root *c* and a child $T[q]$ for each computation *q* such that *q serves c*, where $T[q]$ is the eact for *q*. It is required - this is in fact an additional constraint on *serves* and *rcalls* - that all nodes of an eact should be distinct. Note that eact leaves are either bottom computations or barren rpcs.

Thus, the definition of eact is, as expected, recursive and entails that only top eacts, i.e. eacts of top computations, are not subtrees of any other eact. Note that eacts are partially ordered trees: a left-to-right order has only been defined among the children of a computation node *p*, so as to reflect the order in which *p* makes its rpcs, but not among the children of an rpc *c*; this is consistent with the choice of introducing *rcalls* as a string-valued function and *serves* as a relation.

Example 4.1 The eact in fig. 4.2 describes top computation p_1, which runs on site *A* and sequentially performs the rpcs c_1, c_2 and c_3 to site *B*; of these, c_3 is barren (e.g. because of a message loss), whereas c_2 and c_1 are served on *B* by p_4 and by p_2 and p_3 respectively; p_4 performs an rpc c_4 back to site *A*, where p_5 is activated as a result.

4.3   Local vs. remote procedure calls

Eacts obviously aim at extending the well-known concept of activation tree (act) for local, conventional procedure calls (lpc) [ASU]; thus, a comparison between eacts and acts may be useful to highlight the differences between rpcs and lpcs. The discussion below is rather informal: the reader is referred to Section 2 for the definitions of atomicity and interference freeness, and to Section 5 for the formal treatment.

4.3.1   Lpcs

In the absence of crashes, a lpc *c* gives rise to exactly one (entirely local) computation p_c and returns only on termination of p_c, which does not therefore survive the return of its originating call. As pointed out in [Nel], the same can be assumed even in the presence of crashes, for the crash sweeps away both p_c and the caller of *c*. Two consequences follow. First, computations need not be represented explicitly in an act, except for the main program at the root (corresponding to the top computations of an eact). Second, lpcs give rise to a single thread of control. In more detail, at any time instant there is an *activated call path*, starting at the root of the act, such that the only

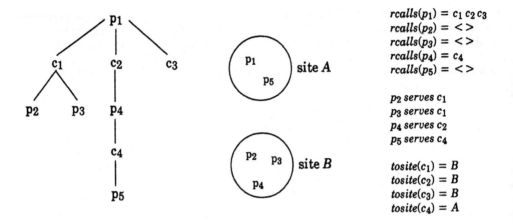

Fig. 4.2 - An extended activation tree

computation being executed serves the last call in the path. Meanwhile (NI1) each computation for a call higher up in the path is waiting for the next call in the path to return, and (NI2) each call lying to the left of the path has returned and the computation for it has terminated. (The activated path is in practice recorded in the call stack).

4.3.2 Rpcs

Let us now turn to rpcs and eacts. According to assumption S2, an rpc may have multiple server computations, which so far nothing in our model prevents from being concurrent. It is also possible that a computation p returns from an rpc c to site A and proceeds, while a computation p' set up on A to serve c still survives thus becoming an orphan. In practice this may happen under two circumstances: (i) when c's return is abnormal or crashed, or (ii) - provided that c has multiple server computations - when c's normal return is due to the termination of a server p'' other than p'. Therefore an rpc may give rise to several threads of control: at any time a top eact, unlike an act, may have several paths with rpcs awaiting return and several (sub)computations executing.

However, for the sake of transparency, we stipulate that a top computation is acceptable only in the following two cases.

(i) If, like its local counterpart, it gives rise to a single thread of control, viz., more specifically, if it satisfies NI1 and NI2, and moreover (NI3) the additional threads due to the at-least-once assumption are not concurrent.

(ii) If it produces the same results as some top computation satisfying (i), i.e. if any subcomputations carried out concurrently, within different threads of control, have the same effect as though they were not concurrent.

Intuition suggests that concurrent subcomputations are harmless so long as they do not reach the same site, where they might access the same data objects in such a way that interference arises.

(ii) may be rephrased in the light of the concepts introduced in Section 2: a top computation is acceptable if its structured occurrence graph satisfies atomicity or, equivalently (Theorem 2.1), if its subcomputations do not interfere with each other. Hence a methodology for a formal treatment: define the sog of the top computation, and devise correctness criteria that ensure that it satisfies atomicity. We shall accomplish these two tasks in Section 5 and 6 respectively.

4.4 A classification of interference

Given a top computation with its eact, suppose that two (sub)computations p_1 and p_2 interfere. We may distinguish three cases, depending on which of the NI requirements is violated.

I1 Closed inter-call interference: p_1 and p_2 lie on the same eact path. Assume that p_1 is an ancestor of p_2 (otherwise the dual reasoning applies): for p_1 and p_2 to be concurrent, p_1 must have returned from the call that gave rise to p_2, so p_2 is obviously an orphan.

I2 Open inter-call interference: p_1 and p_2 have a computation node p as least common ancestor in the eact. Owing to the meaning of the left-to-right position of the children of a computation node, the orphan among p_1 and p_2 is the one that has the leftmost path to p, for it originates from a less recent rpc of p.

I3 Intra-call interference: p_1 and p_2 have a call node as least common ancestor in the eact.

These definitions and the concepts previously introduced are illustrated in the

Example 4.2 The computation of Example 4.1 might follow this scenario (before c_3 is invoked): p_1 makes rpc c_1 to site A, where p_2 and p_3 are started; because of a timeout expiry c_1 returns abnormally and p_1 proceeds by making rpc c_2 to site B, thus activating p_4; the latter makes c_4 to A, where p_5 is activated, but shortly after c_4 returns abnormally and p_4 resumes; meanwhile c_2 has also returned abnormally and p_1 has resumed. At this point p_1, p_2, p_3, p_4 and p_5 might well be executing simultaneously, thus producing several interference patterns, as summarized in Table 4.1. The scenario is described in Fig. 4.3 by the computation eact (from Fig. 4.2) and a temporal diagram (dashed lines indicate waiting for return, T an abnormal return).

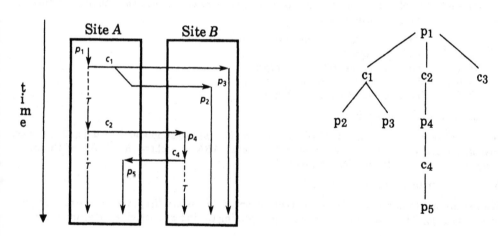

Fig. 4.3 - Interference scenario

5. A formal treatment of rpc atomicity: histories

5.1 Preliminaries

As noted in Section 4, in order to study rpc atomicity we need to characterize a top computation p_t by a structured occurrence graph, which we shall term the *history* of p_t and denote by $H[p_t]$. Being a structured occurrence graph, $H[p_t]$ must consist of a set of simple actions $Act[p_t]$ endowed with an abstraction hierarchy and an irreflexive precedence relation $\rightarrow$. These are defined in the next

Interference type	Interfering computations	
intra-call	(p_2,p_3)	
open inter-call	(p_2,p_4)	p_2 is an orphan
	(p_3,p_4)	p_3 is an orphan
closed inter-call	(p_1,p_5)	p_5 is an orphan

Table 4.1 - Interference patterns

three subsections and then illustrated by Example 5.1. To convince himself that our formalization is indeed adequate, the reader need only compare it to our informal execution model (the correspondence between informal notions introduced in Sections 3.1 and formal definitions is emphasized by labelling both with the tags **A**, **S** and **PO**).

5.1.1 The set of simple actions

Given a top computation p_t, for each computation p in the eact $T[p_t]$ we assume a finite non-empty set of simple actions $s\_actions[p]$. $Act[p_t]$, the set of simple actions of $H[p_t]$, is defined as the union of the sets $s\_actions[p]$.

Since $s\_actions[p]$ is finite, it is countable; thus, when convenient (cf. Figs. 5.1, 5.2 and 5.3), its elements can be represented as $w[p,n]$ for $1 \leq n \leq |s\_actions[p]|$. Each $a \in s\_actions[p]$ is intended to represent a simple action of computation p, and is therefore associated with an attribute $a.t$, which can take one of the following values:

LOC	if a is an action whose effect is local to *onsite(p)*;
CALL	if a is the invocation of an rpc;
NORM	if a is the normal return of an rpc;
ABN	if a is the abnormal return of an rpc;
CRSH	if a is the crashed return of an rpc.

We further assume the requirement:

A1   For each rpc c in $rcalls(p)$, there are in $s\_actions[p]$ two simple actions $i[c]$ and $r[c]$, such that $i[c].t = CALL$ and either $r[c].t = NORM$ or $r[c].t = ABN$ or $r[c].t = CRSH$. All of the other elements of $s\_actions[p]$ have attribute *LOC*.

5.1.2   Structuring the action set

We now proceed to introducing the second component of the history $H[p_t]$, viz. an abstraction hierarchy on $Act[p_t]$. This is achieved by recursively defining the indexed activities $w[p]$ and $rpc[c]$:

S1

$$w[p] = \{a \in s\_actions[p] \mid a.t = LOC\} \cup \bigcup_{c \in rcalls(p)} rpc[c]$$

S2

$$rpc[c] = \{i[c], r[c]\} \cup \bigcup_{p \; serves \; c} w[p]$$

According to these definitions, $w[p]$ comprises all the simple actions - both local and remote - performed by computation p; $rpc[c]$ comprises the invocation and return of remote call c together with the simple actions performed by the computations serving c.

Thus, the hierarchy tree of a history $H[p_t]$ can be obtained from the eact $T[p_t]$ by the rules:

H1 each computation node p is renamed $w[p]$; each call node c is renamed $rpc[c]$;

H2 for each $a \in s\_actions[p]$, a leaf a is attached to $w[p]$ if $a.t = LOC$, to $rpc[c]$ if $a = i[c]$ or $a = r[c]$; we convene that $i[c]$ shall be the leftmost child of $rpc[c]$ and $r[c]$ the rightmost.

Example 5.1 The temporal diagram in Fig. 5.1 on the left depicts the behaviour of top computation p_0. After some local activity, p_0 makes the remote call c_1, which gives rise on the called site to computation p_1. Immediately after returning successfully from c_1, p_0 makes the remote call c_2, which gives rise on the called site to computation p_2. Finally, p_0 returns successfully from c_2 and, after some local activity, terminates. The eact $T[p_0]$ is shown in Fig. 5.1, centre. The hierarchy tree of the history $H[p_0]$, which is shown in Fig. 5.1 on the right, is obtained from $T[p_0]$ by applying the above rules **H1** and **H2**, and assuming that each vertical line in the temporal diagram corresponds to a single simple action.

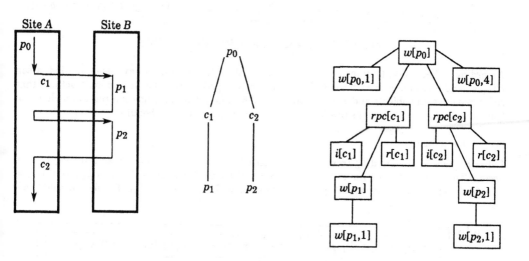

Fig. 5.1 - A computation scenario, the eact and the hierarchy tree

5.1.3   The precedence relation

As noted in Section 2, the relation $\Rightarrow$ of the sog $H[p_t]$ should be determined by **PO**, the set of precedence constraints entailed by the rpc protocol, and **DO**, the particular schedule that p_t enforces on simple actions accessing the same data objects.

As for **PO**, a set of precedence constraints that any rpc protocol should imply has already been identified as part of our informal execution model. The formalization is:

PO1 (i) The restriction of $\Rightarrow$ to the set $s\_actions[p]$ is a total order.
     (ii) If $p = caller(c)$, then $i[c] \Rightarrow r[c]$ and there is no $a \in s\_actions[p]$ such that $i[c] \Rightarrow a \Rightarrow r[c]$.

PO2 If p serves c, then $i[c] \Rightarrow a$ for all $a \in w[p]$.

PO3 If $r[c].t = NORM$, then there is a p such that p serves c and $a \Rightarrow r[c]$ for all $a \in s\_actions[p]$.

For each set $s\_actions[p]$ it is assumed that the total order postulated by **PO1** agrees with the numbering $w[p,n]$.

It is worth while to note that **PO1** implies that $\Rightarrow$ is an asymmetric relation. The proof is by contradiction: if for some a and b both $a \Rightarrow b$ and $b \Rightarrow a$ held, $a \Rightarrow a$ would follow, owing to the transitivity of $\Rightarrow$ and contradicting **PO1** (i). Thus, **PO1** forbids cycles to occur in histories (but not in their views, see next section).

Fig. 5.2 depicts the precedence constraints entailed by **PO1-PO3**, and the position of the constrained simple actions in the hierarchy tree. Note how triangles are used to represent hierarchy (sub)trees - e.g. the triangle with vertex $rpc[c]$ is the hierarchy subtree with root $rpc[c]$. Dashed lines represent paths in the hierarchy tree.

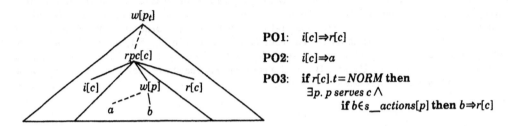

PO1: $i[c] \Rightarrow r[c]$

PO2: $i[c] \Rightarrow a$

PO3: **if** $r[c].t = NORM$ **then**
$\exists p. \, p \text{ serves } c \land$
if $b \in s\_actions[p]$ **then** $b \Rightarrow r[c]$

Fig. 5.2 - Precedences due to **PO1**, **PO2** and **PO3**

According to Section 2, to determine $\Rightarrow$ fully, after the **PO** constraints have been applied, a sog $H[p_t]$ should be completed with the **DO** precedences,viz. precedences between simple actions that reference the same objects and are not constrained by **PO**. Note that this requires a knowledge of the semantics of simple actions in addition to the knowledge of their schedule.

5.2   Interference

Let $H[p_t]$ be a history and L_p (resp. L_c) an abstraction level containing the activity $w[p]$ (resp. $rpc[c]$). The **PO** conditions imply that in the view $H[p_t]@L_p/w[p]$ (resp. $H[p_t]@L_c/rpc[c]$), where $w[p]$ ($rpc[c]$) has been "opened up", precedences such as those shown in Fig. 5.3 should hold. This

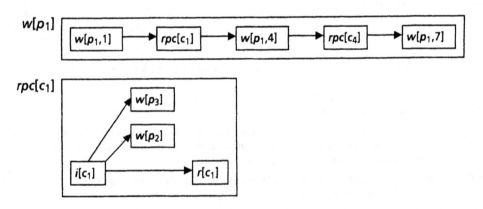

Fig. 5.3 - Precedences within views of a history

matches well the intuition behind the model of Section 3.1. Histories containing only precedences of this kind might be shown to satisfy atomicity. However, the question must be raised whether the graph edges introduced by the neglected **DO** precedences may jeopardize the atomicity of histories by introducing cycles in views like those of Fig. 5.3. We expect this to be possible, given that so far the formalization, faithful to the informal execution model, has omitted taking into account **DO**. The following example shows a history that satisfies **PO1-PO3** and yet, because of the **DO** precedences, does not satisfy atomicity.

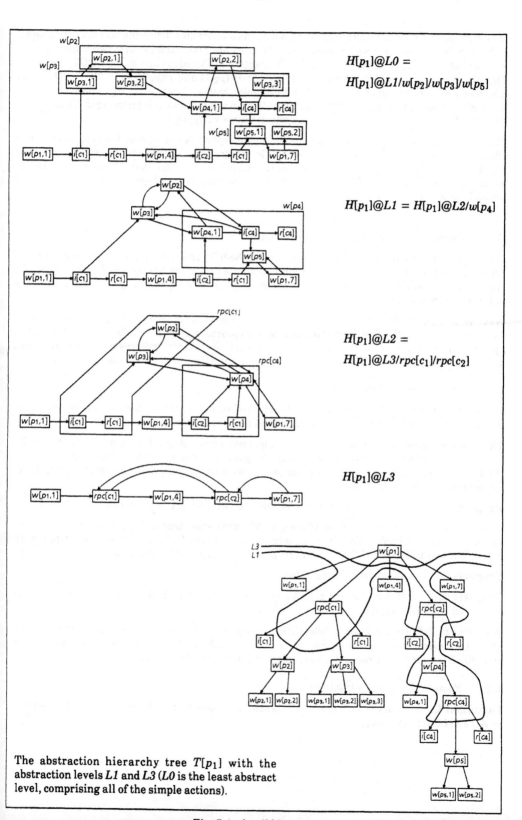

$H[p_1]@L0 =$
$H[p_1]@L1/w[p_2]/w[p_3]/w[p_5]$

$H[p_1]@L1 = H[p_1]@L2/w[p_4]$

$H[p_1]@L2 =$
$H[p_1]@L3/rpc[c_1]/rpc[c_2]$

$H[p_1]@L3$

The abstraction hierarchy tree $T[p_1]$ with the abstraction levels $L1$ and $L3$ ($L0$ is the least abstract level, comprising all of the simple actions).

Example 5.2   The history $H[p_1]$ in Fig. 5.4 describes in greater detail the scenario of Example 4.2. (Note the correspondence between the abstraction hierarchy and the first two subtrees of the eact in Fig. 4.2). It has been assumed that in addition to the edges due to **PO1-PO3**, the graph $H[p_1]@L0$ contains edges due to **DO**, e.g. $w[p_3,1] \rightarrow w[p_2,1]$ and $w[p_2,1] \rightarrow w[p_3,2]$. All the more abstract views shown below $H[p_1]@L0$ contain cycles, thus - as expected - $H[p_1]$ does not satisfy atomicity; in particular, whenever two computations p_i and p_j listed as interfering in Table 4.1 are present at level L, they are contained in a cycle in the view $H[p_1]@L$.

Histories would enable us to formalize the concept of orphan, and the three kinds of interference identified in Section 4.4. However, as this would require some of the definitions omitted in our short overview on ogs, we have chosen not do so. Suffice it to say that, if a history satisfies atomicity, then, by virtue of Theorem 2.1, all of its activities $w[p]$ and $rpc[c]$ occur atomically and do not interfere with each other.

6.   Correctness criteria for rpc atomicity

We begin this section by introducing the "lies-to-the-left" relation over the hierarchy trees of structured occurrence graphs. This relation is then used to define the notion of *monotonicity* for sogs, and monotonicity is shown to be a sufficient condition for a sog to satisfy atomicity, i.e. for its activities to be interference-free.

Next we strengthen the condition **PO1** of Section 5.1.3 so as to constrain rpc histories to be monotonic and, consequently, free from interference. This provides us with a sufficient condition for an rpc protocol to be correct with respect to interference: if the protocol enforces the new **PO1**, it will produce interference-free rpc histories. Finally, we discuss the practical significance of **PO1**.

6.1   The lies-to-the-left relation

Consider a generic sog G. Since simple and compound actions of G are nodes of its hierarchy tree, we may speak of *path* (from the root), *ancestor* and *descendant* of an action.

The relative position of any two (simple or compound) actions A and B as nodes of the hierarchy tree must fall into one of three cases: either the path to A lies to the left of that to B (denoted $A \gg B$), or viceversa ($B \gg A$), or A and B are on the same path. The following properties are direct consequences of the definition of $\gg$.

Property 6.1   The restriction of $\gg$ to an abstraction level is a total relation.

Proof. Let L be an abstraction level of a sog G. We must show that if $A \in L$, $B \in L$ and $A \neq B$, then either $A \gg B$ or $B \gg A$ holds. This immediately follows from the Definition 2.5 of abstraction level: a cut of the hierarchy tree of G cannot intercept nodes that lie on the same path.   □

Property 6.2 $\gg$ is a transitive relation.   □

Property 6.3   If A and B are activities of a hierarchy tree, then $A \gg B$ implies $a \gg b$ for all simple actions $a \in A$ and $b \in B$.   □

According to Definition 2.3, the $\gg$ relation over a sog hierarchy tree, i.e. the left-to-right ordering of the tree nodes, is irrelevant in that it does not affect the abstraction hierarchy defined by the tree. However, for our purposes it is convenient to link the relations $\gg$ and $\Rightarrow$.

6.2   Monotonicity and atomicity

Definition 6.1   A sog $G = (Act, \rightarrow, AbsH)$ is said to be *monotonic* if, for every two simple actions $a \in Act$ and $b \in Act$, $a \gg b$ implies $\neg(b \Rightarrow a)$.   □

Theorem 6.4   A monotonic sog satisfies atomicity.

Proof. We must prove that if G is monotonic, then for no abstraction level L the og $G@L$ is cyclic. By contradiction, assume that $G@L$ is cyclic; then it must contain a cycle $A \Rightarrow B \Rightarrow A$ with $A \neq B$, for if all its cycles were of the form $A \Rightarrow A$, the og $G@L$ would have to contain a self-loop $A \rightarrow_L A$, which contradicts the irreflexivity postulated by Definition 2.1. By the Definition 2.7 of view, this implies that for some $a1 \in A$, $b1 \in B$, $b2 \in B$ and $a2 \in A$, $a1 \Rightarrow b1$ and $b2 \Rightarrow a2$ hold. On the other hand, since $A \in L$ and $B \in L$, by Property 6.1 either $A \gg B$ or $B \gg A$ must hold, whence either $a2 \gg b2$ or $b1 \gg a1$ must hold, by Property 6.3. In either case the monotonicity hypothesis is contradicted: by $b2 \Rightarrow a2$ if $a2 \gg b2$, by $a1 \Rightarrow b1$ if $b1 \gg a1$.   □

6.3   Implementing monotonicity

Hereafter it will be assumed that the rpc protocol is capable of enforcing a stronger version of the condition PO1 given in Section 5.1.3.:

PO1   If $onsite(p1) = onsite(p2)$, $a1 \in s\_actions[p1]$, $a2 \in s\_actions[p2]$, and $a1 \gg a2$, then $a1 \Rightarrow a2$.

According to Section 2, $\Rightarrow$ should be the transitive relation satisfying PO1-PO3 and, in addition, as required by DO, containing either (a,b) or (b,a) for each pair of simple actions a and b that reference the same object. However, as any such a and b must occur on the same site, the new PO1 suffices to ensure what required by DO. Thus, in contrast with the conclusions of Section 5.1.3, PO1-PO3 are now enough to determine $\Rightarrow$ completely. In the sequel $\Rightarrow$ will be assumed to be the smallest transitive relation satisfying PO1, PO2, and PO3.

6.3.1   Well-definedness

In this subsection we show that the new $\Rightarrow$ is well-defined, in that it satisfies the old PO1 of Section 5.1.3 and is therefore in accordance with the intended execution model of Section 3. We show first the

Lemma 6.5   If $H[p_t] = (Act[p_t], \rightarrow, AbsH)$ is a history, $a1 \in Act[p_t]$, $a2 \in Act[p_t]$, and $a1 \neq a2$, then $a1 \Rightarrow a2$ implies $a1 \gg a2$.

Proof. the hypothesis $a1 \Rightarrow a2$ means that there exists a chain $a1 = a_0 \Rightarrow a_1 \Rightarrow \ldots a_n = a2$ such that each $a_i \Rightarrow a_{i+1}$ ($1 \leq i < n$) directly follows from the application of one of PO1-PO3. The proof that, given such a chain, $a1 \gg a2$ holds is by induction on n.

Basis. Assume $n = 1$. If $a1 \Rightarrow a2$ is implied by PO1, it is PO1 itself that entails $a1 \gg a2$. If $a1 \rightarrow a2$ is implied by PO2 or PO3, $a1 \gg a2$ follows from the rule H2, Section 5.1.2, for constructing the hierarchy tree. The reader may refer to Fig. 5.2 to satisfy himself that if $a1 \Rightarrow a2$ follows from PO2 or PO3, then $a1 \gg a2$ holds (take $a1 = i[c]$ and $a2 = a$ for PO2, and $a1 = b$ and $a2 = r[c]$ for PO3).

Induction. Easily follows from Property 6.2 (transitivity of $\gg$).   □

We may now prove that histories satisfy the condition PO1 of Section 5.1.3.

Theorem 6.6   Let $H[p_t]$ be a history and p one of its computations. Then the restriction of $\Rightarrow$ to the set $s\_actions[p]$ is a total order. Moreover, if $p = caller(c)$, then $i[c] \Rightarrow r[c]$ holds, while $i[c] \Rightarrow a \Rightarrow r[c]$, with $a \in s\_actions[p]$, does not.

Proof. First we prove that the restriction of $\Rightarrow$ to $s\_actions[p]$ is a total order. Let $a \in s\_actions[p]$, $b \in s\_actions[p]$ and $a \neq b$. If $a \gg b$, then $a \Rightarrow b$ and $\neg(b \Rightarrow a)$ must follow - $a \Rightarrow b$ from $a \gg b$ by PO1, $\neg(b \Rightarrow a)$ because by Lemma 6.5 $b \Rightarrow a$ would imply $b \gg a$, but by Property 6.1 $a \gg b$ and $b \gg a$ cannot be both valid. Likewise, if $b \gg a$, then $b \Rightarrow a$ and $\neg(a \Rightarrow b)$ must hold. In conclusion either $a \Rightarrow b$ or $b \Rightarrow a$ holds.

As for the second part of the thesis, rule H2, Section 5.1.2, for constructing the hierarchy tree entails that $i[c] \gg r[c]$ holds and $i[c] \gg a \gg r[c]$, with $a \in s\_actions[p]$, does not. Thus $i[c] \Rightarrow r[c]$ follows from $i[c] \gg r[c]$ by **PO1**; $i[c] \Rightarrow a \Rightarrow r[c]$, with $a \in s\_actions[p]$, cannot hold or, by Lemma 6.5, $i[c] \gg a \gg r[c]$ would also hold. □

6.3.2 Correctness

The histories considered in this section can be proved to be monotonic and hence, by Theorem 6.4, to satisfy atomicity. This is tantamount to proving correct any rpc protocol satisfying **PO1** (in the revised version), **PO2** and **PO3**.

Theorem 6.7   Histories are monotonic.

Proof. By contradiction, assume that a history $H[p_t]$ is not monotonic, i.e. that for two simple actions a and b both $a \gg b$ and $b \Rightarrow a$ hold. Then, by Lemma 6.5, also $b \gg a$ should hold, contradicting Property 6.1, which requires that the restriction of $\gg$ to simple actions (the least abstract level) should be a total relation. □

6.4   The intuitive meaning of PO1

Although the new form given to **PO1** is elegant and permits concise proofs, its practical implications may be obscure. The intuitive meaning of **PO1** can be best appreciated from the three properties below, which may replace it as correctness criteria.

POI1   If $onsite(p1) = onsite(p2)$ and $...w[p1]\, rpc[c2]\, ...\, w[p2]$ is the path to $w[p2]$, then $a2 \Rightarrow r[c2]$ holds for all $a2 \in s\_actions[p2]$.

POI2   If $onsite(p1) = onsite(p2)$, $w[p1] \gg w[p2]$ and the least common ancestor of $w[p1]$ and $w[p2]$ is $w[p]$, then $a_1 \Rightarrow a_2$ for all $a_1 \in s\_actions[p1]$ and $a_2 \in s\_actions[p2]$.

POI3   If $onsite(p1) = onsite(p2)$, $w[p1] \gg w[p2]$ and the least common ancestor of $w[p1]$ and $w[p2]$ is $rpc[c]$, then $a_1 \Rightarrow a_2$ for all $a_1 \in s\_actions[p1]$ and $a_2 \in s\_actions[p2]$.

The above labels and formulations emphasize that **POI1-POI3** orderly correspond and cope with the interference patterns I1-I3 identified in Section 4.4. The following formulations should be even more intuitive.

POI1   Any work performed on behalf of an rpc on the site where the rpc has been invoked must precede the rpc return (whether normal, abnormal or crashed).

POI2   If a client invokes rpc *c1* before rpc *c2*, any work made on a site on behalf of *c1* must precede any work made on the same site on behalf of *c2*.

POI3   If computations *p1* and *p2* serve the same rpc, either any work that is part of *p1* precedes any work that is part of *p2* on every site, or viceversa.

The reader should recall the convention stipulated in Section 4.2 for eacts and therefore extended to hierarchy trees: the children of a computation node are its remote calls, arranged from left to right in the order in which they are invoked. This explains how the two variants of **POI2** are related. Note also that the first variant of **POI3** provides an interpretation of the left-to-right position of the children of a call node: if $w[p1]$ and $w[p2]$ are children of $rpc[c]$ and $w[p1] \gg w[p2]$, then any work that is part of *p1* will precede any work that is part of *p2* on every site.

7.   The implementation of interference prevention

Crashcounts, *extermination* and *expiration* are three of the best-known strategies for interference prevention through orphan-killing. Their relative merits are compared in [Nel], where they were proposed for the *Emissary* rpc protocol. Expiration and crashcounts have also been adopted for the *Rajdoot* [PS] rpc protocol.

Restricting ourselves to exactly-once semantics, the one supported by the noted rpc protocols, we shall discuss how the above techniques can be employed to ensure **POI1** and **POI2**. Specifically, extermination and crashcounts cope with orphans left behind by crashes, expiration with orphans of calls that have returned abnormally because of a timeout expiration. Note that, in accordance with [Nel] and [PS], in this section we make the assumption that a crash affects an entire site rather than individual computations.

7.1 Crashcounts

A site's crashcount records the number of times the site has crashed. Let c be a generic rpc with eact path $p_t c_1 p_1...c_n p_n c$; in [PS] the *rpc-path* of c is defined as the list $<(s_t,\kappa_t),(s_1,\kappa_1),...,(s_n,\kappa_n)>$, where $s_i = onsite(p_i)$ and κ_i is the crashcount of s_i. The rpc protocol of [PS] employs crashcounts as follows. The message requesting a computation to be started on behalf of a call contains the rpc-path of the call. Each site uses the rpc-paths received to maintain a table recording the highest known crashcount of the other sites in the network; whenever the crashcount for site s has to be updated, any outstanding computation for a call whose rpc-path contained s is aborted. When a request message is received, a computation is started only if no site in the rpc-path has a crashcount lower than that known locally.

The two eacts of Fig. 7.1 illustrate the position of the computations $p1$ and $p2$ in terms of which POI1 and POI2 are formulated.

With reference to Fig. 7.1.a, assume that the site s of $p1$ and $p2$ crashes before $p1$ has returned from $c2$, and that $p1$ is later restarted by the crash recovery procedure. Owing to the crashcount mechanism, no action of $p2$ can take place after the recovery: if the request message that would give rise to $p2$ on s is received after s recovers, it will be ignored because it carries an obsolete crashcount for s.† This ensures that if $r[c2]$ is crashed, $a2 \Rightarrow r[c2]$ holds for all $a2 \in s\_actions[p2]$, as required by POI1.

As for POI2, with reference to Fig. 7.1.b, assume that the site s of p crashes and recovers after the invocation of $c1$ and before that of $c2$. Because of the crashcount mechanism, on the site of $p1$ and $p2$ no action of $p1$ can take place after $p2$ has started. Indeed if the request message that should give rise to $p1$ is received after $p2$ has started, it will be ignored because it carries an obsolete crashcount for s. If, on the other hand, the request message that initiates $p2$ is received while $p1$ is still in progress, the latter will be aborted because the message carries a higher crashcount for s than that registered by $p1$. Thus $a_1 \Rightarrow a_2$ for all $a_1 \in s\_actions[p1]$ and $a_2 \in s\_actions[p2]$, as required by POI2.

7.2 Extermination

Extermination is performed as part of crash recovery; before a computation is resumed after a crash, the rpc protocol will exterminate all the orphan computations left by pre-crash rpcs around the network. Extermination alone does not suffice to guarantee POI1 and POI2, for it is not effective against delayed request messages that were originated by pre-crash rpcs but reach the called site after extermination has completed. For this reason extermination is generally coupled with a crashcount-based mechanism (e.g. in [Nel]). Its advantage is that it minimizes the waste of resource caused by orphans.

7.3 Expiration

Expiration consists in assigning each (non-top) computation a *deadline* after which the computation will be aborted if still ongoing. Deadlines and rpc timeouts should be chosen in such a way that when an rpc returns abnormally any descendant rpc will have already returned abnormally and any descendant computation will have terminated. Thus, rpcs that return abnormally behave, with respect to interference, like lpcs (cf. NI1 and NI2, Section 4), and hence satisfy POI1 and POI2.

---

† Of course, if $p2$ existed before the crash, the recovery procedure should avoid restarting it

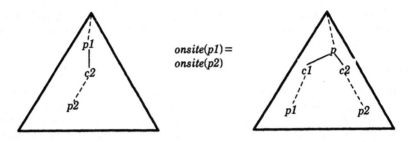

Fig. 7.1.a - *p1* and *p2* in **POI1**　　　　Fig. 7.1.b - *p1* and *p2* in **POI2**

8.　Concluding remarks

The independent failure modes introduced by distribution pose reliability problems not normally encountered in centralized systems. Thus the task of implementing the procedure call abstraction in a distributed environment is fraught with considerable difficulties. An important problem is that posed by interference between unwanted computations, the so-called orphans, and the intended one. We have made use of the occurrence graphs computational model to describe distributed programs containing remote procedure calls. Using this model, interference has been characterized rigorously, and a condition that ensures the interference-free execution of programs has been stated and proved. Another original contribution of this paper is the notion of monotonicity for occurrence graphs; we feel that, as in our case, it might often lead to simpler proofs.

Research in this area does not abound. A predecessor of this paper is [Shr], where interference was studied in an informal setting, and correctness criteria similar to our **POI1-POI3** were derived. Orphans and interference have been studied in [Nel], with an informal approach and a strong emphasis on implementation. Orphan detection techniques are presented in [Wal] and studied formally in [Gor]; their results are difficult to compare with ours because their objective is to provide at-most-once semantics.

If directly implemented, our correctness criteria might provide an interesting alternative to expiration.The latter is based on *prevention*: computations expire before they are made orphans by the abnormal return of the call they are serving. However, if time delays are difficult to estimate, it may be more convenient to resort to *repression*, i.e. to let orphan computations live until they would otherwise actually cause interference. Basically, this can be achieved (i) by incorporating into the rpc request message some encoding of the rpc's eact path, and (ii) by maintaining a database associating every ongoing computation with its eact path (inferred from the request message that originated the computation)†. Thus, the called site would be able to decide whether starting a computation in response to a request message might violate **POI1-POI3**, and, if so, whether **POI1-POI3** are to be enforced by ignoring the request or by suppressing some ongoing computation. Critical design issues are obviously who should make such decisions and manage the database at the called site, and how to avoid the database becoming a performance bottleneck. Further investigation is required, but a preliminary analysis seems to indicate that, given a

---

†　This notion of path extends that of [PS].

suitable target environment, this repression-based approach could compare favourably with expiration.

Acknowledgements

This work was supported partly by the RSRE of the UK Ministry of Defence. The authors would like to thank Luigi Mancini for many helpful discussions.

References

[ASU]   Aho A., Sethi R., Ullmann J., *Principles of Compiler Design*, Addison-Wesley, 1986.

[BR]   Best E. and Randell B., "A Formal Model of Atomicity in Asynchronous Systems", *Acta Informatica* 16 (1981), 93-124.

[Gor]   Goree J., "Internal Consistency of a Distributed Transaction System", M. Sc. Thesis, Tech. rep. LCS/TR-286, Massachussets Institute of Technology, 1983.

[LS]   Liskov B. and Scheifler R., "Guardians and Actions: Linguistic Support for Robust Distributed Programming", *ACM TOPLAS*, July 1983.

[LaB]   Lampson B., "Remote Procedure Calls", in *LNCS 105*, 246-265, Springer-Verlag, New York, 1981.

[LaL]   Lamport L., "Time, Clocks, and the Ordering of Events in Distributed Systems", *CACM* 21 (7), 558-565, July 1978.

[Nel]   Nelson B., "Remote Procedure Call", Ph. D. thesis, Tech. rep. CSL-79-3, Xerox Palo Alto Research Center, 1981.

[PS]   Panzieri F., Shrivastava S.K., "Rajdoot: a Remote Procedure Call Mechanism Supporting Orphan Detection and Killing", *IEEE Transactions on Software Engineering*, 14, 1, 30-37, Jan. 1988.

[Shr]   Shrivastava S., On the Treatment of Orphans in a Distributed System, in *Proc. of the 3rd Symposium on Reliability in Distributed Software and Database Systems*, 155-162, IEEE Computer Society, 1983.

[Wal]   Walker E., "Orphan Detection in the Argus System", M. Sc. Thesis, Tech. rep. LCS/TR-326, Massachussets Institute of Technology, 1984.

List of Authors and Addresses

R.L. Costello
Computer & Inf. Science Department
Ohio State University
Columbus OH43210
U.S.A.

M.J. Fischer
Department of Computer Science
Yale University
P.O. Box 2158 Yale Station
New Haven CT 06250
U.S.A.

E. Harel
Department of Applied Mathematics
Weizmann Institute
Rehovot   76100
Israel

J. Jaray
Centre de Recherche
en Informatique de Nancy
B.P. 239
F-54500 Vandoeuvre-les-Nancy
France

R. Kuiper
Vakgroep Theoretische Informatica
Technische Universiteit Eindhoven
P.O. Box 513
NL-5600 MB Eindhoven
The Netherlands

L.Y. Liu
333 Whitmore Laboratory
Department of Computer Science
Pennsylvania State University
University Park PA 16802
U.S.A.

L. Mancini
Computing Laboratory
University of Newcastle-upon-Tyne
Claremont Tower
Claremont Road
Newcastle-upon-Tyne NE1 7RU
U.K.

W.J. Cullyer
Computing Division
Royal Signals and Radar Estab.
St. Andrews Road South
Malvern, Worcs. WR14 3PS
U.K.

N. Halbwachs
Laboratoire de Génie Informatique
Institut IMAG
B.P. 53, 38041 Grenoble Cedex
France

M.P. Herlihy
Department of Computer Science
Carnegie-Mellon University
Pittsburgh PA 15213-3890
U.S.A.

R. Koymans
Vakgroep Theoretische Informatica
Technische Universiteit Eindhoven
P.O. Box 513
NL-5600 MB Eindhoven
The Netherlands

I. Lee
Department of Computer & Inf. Sc.
University of Pennsylvania
Philadelphia PA 19104
U.S.A.

G.H. MacEwen
Department of Computing & Inf. Sc.
Queen's University
Kingston Ontario K7L 3N6
Canada

J.A. McDermid
Department of Computer Science
University of York
York YO1 5DD
U.K.

G. Pappalardo
Computing Laboratory
University of Newcastle-upon-Tyne
Claremont Tower
Claremont Road
Newcastle-upon-Tyne NE1 7RU
U.K.

D. Pilaud
Laboratoire de Génie Informatique
Institut IMAG
B.P. 53
38041 Grenoble Cedex
France

A. Pnueli
Department of Applied Mathematics
Weizmann Institute
Rehovot 76100
Israel

S.K. Shrivastava
Computing Laboratory
University of Newcastle-upon-Tyne
Claremont Tower
Claremont Road
Newcastle-upon-Tyne NE1 7RU
U.K.

R.K. Shyamasundar
333 Whitmore Laboratory
Department of Computer Science
Pennsylvania State University
University Park PA 16802
U.S.A.

D.B. Skillicorn
Department of Computer & Inf. Sc.
Queen's University
Kingston Ontario K7L 3N6
U.K.

N. Soundararajan
Computing & Inf. Sc. Department
Ohio State University
Columbus OH 43210
U.S.A.

J. Vytopil
Computer Science &
Technical Applications
Catholic University Nijmegen
Toernooiveld
6525 ED Nijmegen
The Netherlands

H. Wupper
Computer Science &
Technical Applications
Catholic University Nijmegen
Toernooiveld
6525 ED Nijmegen
The Netherlands

E. Zijlstra
Foxboro Nederland NV
Koningsweg 30
NL-3762 EC Soest
The Netherlands

L.D. Zuck
Department of Computer Science
Yale University
P.O. Box 2158 Yale Station
New Haven CT 06250

A. Zwarico
Department of Computer Science
Johns Hopkins University
Baltimore MD 21218
U.S.A.

Vol. 296: R. Janßen (Ed.), Trends in Computer Algebra. Proceedings, 1987. V, 197 pages. 1988.

Vol. 297: E.N. Houstis, T.S. Papatheodorou, C.D. Polychronopoulos (Eds.), Supercomputing. Proceedings, 1987. X, 1093 pages. 1988.

Vol. 298: M. Main, A. Melton, M. Mislove, D. Schmidt (Eds.), Mathematical Foundations of Programming Language Semantics. Proceedings, 1987. VIII, 637 pages. 1988.

Vol. 299: M. Dauchet, M. Nivat (Eds.), CAAP '88. Proceedings, 1988. VI, 304 pages. 1988.

Vol. 300: H. Ganzinger (Ed.), ESOP '88. Proceedings, 1988. VI, 381 pages. 1988.

Vol. 301: J. Kittler (Ed.), Pattern Recognition. Proceedings, 1988. VII, 668 pages. 1988.

Vol. 302: D.M. Yellin, Attribute Grammar Inversion and Source-to-source Translation. VIII, 176 pages. 1988.

Vol. 303: J.W. Schmidt, S. Ceri, M. Missikoff (Eds.), Advances in Database Technology – EDBT '88. X, 620 pages. 1988.

Vol. 304: W.L. Price, D. Chaum (Eds.), Advances in Cryptology – EUROCRYPT '87. Proceedings, 1987. VII, 314 pages. 1988.

Vol. 305: J. Biskup, J. Demetrovics, J. Paredaens, B. Thalheim (Eds.), MFDBS 87. Proceedings, 1987. V, 247 pages. 1988.

Vol. 306: M. Boscarol, L. Carlucci Aiello, G. Levi (Eds.), Foundations of Logic and Functional Programming. Proceedings, 1986. V, 218 pages. 1988.

Vol. 307: Th. Beth, M. Clausen (Eds.), Applicable Algebra, Error-Correcting Codes, Combinatorics and Computer Algebra. Proceedings, 1986. VI, 215 pages. 1988.

Vol. 308: S. Kaplan, J.-P. Jouannaud (Eds.), Conditional Term Rewriting Systems. Proceedings, 1987. VI, 278 pages. 1988.

Vol. 309: J. Nehmer (Ed.), Experiences with Distributed Systems. Proceedings, 1987. VI, 292 pages. 1988.

Vol. 310: E. Lusk, R. Overbeek (Eds.), 9th International Conference on Automated Deduction. Proceedings, 1988. X, 775 pages. 1988.

Vol. 311: G. Cohen, P. Godlewski (Eds.), Coding Theory and Applications 1986. Proceedings, 1986. XIV, 196 pages. 1988.

Vol. 312: J. van Leeuwen (Ed.), Distributed Algorithms 1987. Proceedings, 1987. VII, 430 pages. 1988.

Vol. 313: B. Bouchon, L. Saitta, R.R. Yager (Eds.), Uncertainty and Intelligent Systems. IPMU '88. Proceedings, 1988. VIII, 408 pages. 1988.

Vol. 314: H. Göttler, H.J. Schneider (Eds.), Graph-Theoretic Concepts in Computer Science. Proceedings, 1987. VI, 254 pages. 1988.

Vol. 315: K. Furukawa, H. Tanaka, T. Fujisaki (Eds.), Logic Programming '87. Proceedings, 1987. VI, 327 pages. 1988.

Vol. 316: C. Choffrut (Ed.), Automata Networks. Proceedings, 1986. VII, 125 pages. 1988.

Vol. 317: T. Lepistö, A. Salomaa (Eds.), Automata, Languages and Programming. Proceedings, 1988. XI, 741 pages. 1988.

Vol. 318: R. Karlsson, A. Lingas (Eds.), SWAT 88. Proceedings, 1988. VI, 262 pages. 1988.

Vol. 319: J.H. Reif (Ed.), VLSI Algorithms and Architectures – AWOC 88. Proceedings, 1988. X, 476 pages. 1988.

Vol. 320: A. Blaser (Ed.), Natural Language at the Computer. Proceedings, 1988. III, 176 pages. 1988.

Vol. 322: S. Gjessing, K. Nygaard (Eds.), ECOOP '88. European Conference on Object-Oriented Programming. Proceedings, 1988. VI, 410 pages. 1988.

Vol. 323: P. Deransart, M. Jourdan, B. Lorho, Attribute Grammars. IX, 232 pages. 1988.

Vol. 324: M.P. Chytil, L. Janiga, V. Koubek (Eds.), Mathematical Foundations of Computer Science 1988. Proceedings. IX, 562 pages. 1988.

Vol. 325: G. Brassard, Modern Cryptology. VI, 107 pages. 1988.

Vol. 326: M. Gyssens, J. Paredaens, D. Van Gucht (Eds.), ICDT '88. 2nd International Conference on Database Theory. Proceedings, 1988. VI, 409 pages. 1988.

Vol. 327: G.A. Ford (Ed.), Software Engineering Education. Proceedings, 1988. V, 207 pages. 1988.

Vol. 328: R. Bloomfield, L. Marshall, R. Jones (Eds.), VDM '88. VDM – The Way Ahead. Proceedings, 1988. IX, 499 pages. 1988.

Vol. 329: E. Börger, H. Kleine Büning, M.M. Richter (Eds.), CSL '87. 1st Workshop on Computer Science Logic. Proceedings, 1987. VI, 346 pages. 1988.

Vol. 330: C.G. Günther (Ed.), Advances in Cryptology – EUROCRYPT '88. Proceedings, 1988. IX, 473 pages. 1988.

Vol. 331: M. Joseph (Ed.), Formal Techniques in Real-Time and Fault-Tolerant Systems. Proceedings, 1988. VI, 229 pages. 1988.